The international politics of Latin America

Latin America's challenging role in the international system is given an up-to-date assessment in this new textbook. From a neo-realist perspective it examines the interaction of states within the region, and their contribution to the development of international law and peacekeeping.

Peter Calvert begins by analysing the special characteristics of Latin America – its shared language and history, and its perceived status as part of the 'South' in economic terms. He then explores the factors which go into the making of Latin American foreign policies: the perceptions of actors such as states, political parties, social elites and armed forces; the distribution of natural resources; the linked economic demands of poverty at home and debts abroad; and the ideological framework of socialism, native American rights and international law. He examines the workings of the inter-American international system and the Organization of American States, which played a key role in the Falklands crisis. Finally he looks at the region's role in global politics, via the Non-Aligned Movement and the United Nations.

The international politics of Latin America

Peter Calvert

Manchester University Press

Manchester and New York

Distributed exclusively in the USA and Canada by St. Martin's Press

Published by Manchester University Press
Oxford Road, Manchester M13 9NR, UK
and Room 400, 175 Fifth Avenue, New York, NY 10010, USA

Distributed exclusively in the USA and Canada
by St. Martin's Press, Inc., 175 Fifth Avenue, New York,
NY 10010, USA

British Library Cataloguing-in-Publication Data
A catalogue record for this book is available from the British Library

Library of Congress Cataloging-in-Publication Data
Calvert, Peter.
    The international politics of Latin America / Peter Calvert
        p.   cm.
    Includes bibliographical references (p.   ) and index.
    ISBN 0–7190–3495–7 (hardback). —— ISBN 0–7190–3496–5 (paperback)
    1. Latin America——Foreign relations——1948— 2. Latin American
federation. I. Title.
JX1515.5.Z5 1994
327.8——dc20   93–50581

ISBN 0 7190 3495 7 *hardback*
     0 7190 3496 5 *paperback*

Photoset in Linotron Sabon
by Northern Phototypesetting Co. Ltd, Bolton

Printed in Great Britain
by Bell and Bain Ltd, Glasgow

Contents

Preface

Latin America today is attracting the interest not only of scholars, but of investors, traders and businessmen. Independent for more than a century and a half, with a shared tradition and culture, these developing states have their own very special interest to students of international relations.

The purpose of this study is to re-evaluate the relationship of the Latin American states to one another and to the outside world. Among its findings are that they have made a very important contribution to the development of international law and peacekeeping; played a key role in helping form today's international system; and shaped, for better or worse, the foreign policy of the United States. The Western hemisphere, as a result, has already become a test case for future relations between the developed North and the developing South. In the decades to come, it will be equally significant as a test case for the impact of national development on the global environment, and vice versa.

Thanks are due to my colleague, Caroline Thomas, and to others whose names I do not know, for their helpful comments on the draft typescript. I am most grateful but absolve them from all responsibility for what follows.

Peter Calvert
Southampton

Abbreviations

ABC powers	Argentina, Brazil, Chile
ACP	Africa, the Caribbean and the Pacific
AD	Acción Democrática
AIEC	Association of Iron Ore Exporting Countries
ALALC	Latin American Free Trade Area
CACM/CACOM	Central American Common Market
CAEM	Higher War College
CARICOM	Caribbean Community and Common Market
CARIFTA	Caribbean Free Trade Association
CGT	Confederacion General de Trabajadores
CIA	Central Intelligence Agency
COB	Central Obrero Boliviano
COMECON/CMEA	East European Economic System
CPIC	Intergovernmental Council of Copper Exporting Countries
CROM	Confederación Regional de Obreros Mexicanos
CZ	(Panama) Canal Zone
DOM	French Overseas Departments
EC	European Community
ECLA/CEPAL	UN Economic Commission for Latin America
ECOSOC	Economic and Social Council
ESG	Escola Superior de Guerra
FDN	Nicaraguan Democratic Force
FDP	Panamanian Armed Forces
FSLN	Sandinista National Liberation Front
FUNAI	Brazilian Indian Service

GATT	General Agreement on Tariffs and Trade
GEF	Global Environment Facility
GNP	Gross National Product
GPP	Guerra Popular Prolongada
IAEA	International Atomic Energy Agency
IAPF	Inter-American Peace Force
IBRD	International Bank for Reconstruction and Development
ICJ	International Court of Justice
IDB	Inter-American Development Bank
IMF	International Monetary Fund
IO	International Organisation
IRBMs	Intermediate Range Ballistic Missiles
ITA	International Tin Agreement
ITC	International Tin Council
IWW	International Workers of the World
LAFTA/ALALC	Latin American Free Trade Area
LAIA/ALADI	Latin American Integration Association
LDCs	Less-Developed Countries
Mercosur	South American Common Market
MFA	Minister of Foreign Affairs
MFO	Multi-National Force and Observers
MNC	Multi-National Corporation
NAFTA	North American Free Trade Area
NAM	Non-Aligned Movement
NATO	North Atlantic Treaty Organization
NGO	Non-Governmental Organisation
NIEO	New International Economic Order
NPT	Non-Proliferation Treaty
OAS/OEA	Organization of American States
OCT	British and Dutch Dependencies
ONUC	United Nations Organization in the Congo
OPEC	Organization of Petroleum Exporting Countries
PAU	Pan-American Union
PCC	Cuban Communist Party
PRG	Provisional Revolutionary Government
SELA	Latin American Economic System
SSA	Africa South of the Sahara

TIAR	Inter-American Treaty of Reciprocal Assistance
TNC	Trans-National Corporation
UFC	United Fruit Company
UNCED	United Nations Conference on Environment and Development
UNCTAD	United Nations Conference on Trade and Development
UNDOF	United Nations Observer Force
UNEF/UNEF I	United Nations Expeditionary Force
UNEF II	United Nations Emergency Force
UNFICYP	United Nations Forces in Cyprus
UNMOGIP	United Nations Military Observer Group in India and Pakistan
UP	Popular Unity
UPEB	Union of Banana Exporting Countries

Chapter One
The arena

Perspective

The approach used in this book can broadly be classified as neo-realist (Feinberg 1983; cf. Waltz 1959). For the realist, international relations is primarily about power politics (Morgenthau). The world is made up of states – generally referred to, rather misleadingly, as 'nation states', although there is no systematic correspondence between states and nations. These states act to defend their national interests within the international system, and they do so using all possible means, up to and including the use of armed force. In the age of the Cold War the imperatives of a bipolar world structured international power relations (Waltz 1959). Now that it is over the imperatives of power politics remain. Realism is the dominant perspective in the tradition – still strong in Latin America – of legalism. In a world where violence is commonplace, international law is seen as the only alternative to force, by which national interests can be defended.

Neo-realism sees states as remaining the principal actors in the world system but modifies the rather stark realist view by taking account of the way in which, despite the formal absence of authority in the world system, states in general behave in an orderly way which presupposes some notion of international order (Bull 1977). Neo-realism, as understood here, also incorporates functionalist, structuralist and pluralist perspectives. The basic assumption behind this modification is that for the past century or more we have been witnessing a process of *globalisation*, 'the process by which events, decisions, and activities in one part of the world can come to have significant consequences for individuals and communities in quite distant parts of the globe' (McGrew, Lewis *et al.* 1992, p. 23). Globalisation is the key characteristic of the modern economic system and even, it has been argued, of modernity itself (Giddens 1990).

From functionalism, we take the concept of *system*. By system we mean an enduring set of interactions between individuals, or, in this case, states. States are in themselves functional systems, and can be viewed either as such or as sub-systems within the larger international context. The concept of system, as will be seen later, is peculiarly appropriate to this area of the world. Not only is the Western hemisphere isolated by water from the main arena of world politics (Calvert 1988a), but it is even conceptualised by those who live there in system terms, and the notion of an 'inter-American system' has actually been embodied in regional international organisation (see Chapter Six).

From structuralism, Latin Americans and Latin Americanists have adopted the concept of *dependency*. By dependency, we mean that the political choices open to Latin American states (as with other countries in what latterly was called 'the Third World') are limited by their subordinate position in a global economy dominated by the advanced industrialised countries. The notion of dependency, in fact, originated in Latin America, and it remains the dominant strain in Latin American intellectual thought about international relations. It originated in neo-Marxism, though its proponents and opponents have by now all moved a substantial way from their respective points of departure. The dependency perspective is also shared by policymakers, despite the fact that they are still overwhelmingly trained in the tradition of legalism and usually have legal qualifications (see Chapter Five). However it remains very much a matter of debate what the causes and consequences of dependency actually are and, in particular, just how far, if at all, dependency limits the freedom of action of individual Latin American states.

From pluralism, we have learned (at least) to modify the more stark concepts of dependency to allow for a degree of *interdependence*. The world is a very complex place and with the speeding-up of communications during the present century we have all come to interact with one another, across national boundaries, to a much greater extent than ever before possible. Hence despite the formal absence of global political authority, states do act together co-operatively, with each other and with a whole variety of non-governmental organisations (NGOs) and international organisations (IOs) to make decisions that for the most part are effective.

Indeed, in some areas, such as TV broadcasting or air traffic control, they have no practical alternative. Though in some senses Latin American states are more acted upon than acting, a degree of reverse influence has always existed (see e.g. Vanucci 1986), and at times during the Cold War period was very evident, especially in relations between Cuba and the Soviet Union.

The systems approach

The concept of a system is now well established in international relations (Clarke and White 1989). However the way in which systems are defined is crucial, since systems are not 'real' entities.

Since the first encounter between Europe and the Americas in 1492 it has been customary to regard the world in maritime terms, as consisting of two separate hemispheres. Given the assumption of a separate Western hemisphere, the '*Western Hemisphere Idea*' (Whitaker 1954), it has been a natural step to try to embody it in an '*inter-American system*' (Connell-Smith 1966). However the formal structures established on this basis have, as we shall see later, excluded both Canada and the European colonies in the Caribbean. The advantage of the notion of a single inter-American system is that it rightly links the United States with the rest of the independent states of the region in a way that is politically realistic and likely to become more so. The disadvantages are firstly that changing modes of transport have made the idea of a separation of East and West obsolescent if not obsolete, and secondly that in this new global situation it can be argued that the Americas do not in fact form a system of their own, but only a regional sub-system of the world system.

The inter-American system does have, however, a legal identity of its own and on 1 January 1991, with the accession of Belize and Guyana, all the independent states in the region finally became members of it, though Cuba's membership has been suspended since 1962. However, as the exclusion of Cuba from its day-to-day operations continues to testify, the interaction at this level is too complicated for the system to act effectively and on most issues it has been the United States that has spoken in its name.

Obviously even with independence all links with Europe have not been severed. The term *the Atlantic triangle* has been used to describe the three-cornered relationship between Europe, Latin America and the United States (Whitaker 1951; Reidy 1964). A 'silent partnership' has indeed developed in recent years by which Latin American states have sought to counterbalance what they saw as the oppressive power of their northern neighbour (Grabendorff and Roett 1985). This is a logical equivalent of the strategy of Canada, for which Britain specifically undertook the balancing role.

Latin America is a term which suffers from fuzzy definition. There are many Europeans who tend to use it as if it designated a single country! The problem is that it is not in fact a geographical or political concept, but a cultural one. Historically it has been used to designate all the independent states south of the Rio Grande as it is known in the US, or the Rio Bravo, as the Mexicans call it. Eighteen of these states speak Spanish, one Portuguese and one French. They do, in fact, have other things in common. However the unity implied by the term is an unrealistic basis for analysis in political terms. Latin America (as distinct from the United States or the non-Spanish-speaking Caribbean states) is not, in fact, even a regional system within the global context (cf. Atkins 1977; see also Atkins 1989).

Hence we shall, in fact, find it more convenient in many cases to envisage the structure of relationships in the Western hemisphere in terms of not one, but two, distinct, though interlinked, regional systems (or sub-systems), which will here be termed *the Caribbean system* and *the South American system*. Common to both are the 'hinge states' of Venezuela and Colombia.

In turn the two American systems form part of the world political and economic system. Clearly, a distinctive feature of their position within the world system is their proximity to the world superpower, the United States. There is in fact no other single region of the world that has a similar unifying factor (Shearman and Williams 1988). However, although the United States has been a significant feature in the Caribbean since it became a Caribbean power with the Louisiana Purchase (1803), even in the twentieth century its interest in South America has been sporadic and inconsistent. In consequence South America has long had, and still continues to have, many of the characteristics of an independent continental system, characterised by constant and active interaction between the individual states which share its territory.

In both cases, however, the factor that created the system was sea power. In the case of the Caribbean the sea still exercises a dominant influence. Even in South America, which can in some respects be regarded as the Caribbean turned inside out, sea communications have played a much greater part in its development than is usually realised. It is only since the Second World War that air communication has opened up the interior and paved the way for new road systems which are already helping to create new relationships between old antagonists. A striking example is the growing penetration by Brazil of Guyana, as progress continues on the link road from Amazonia towards Georgetown.

History of the inter-American system

Prehistory

International relations in the Americas existed long before Columbus, even if the fact was not recognised at the time nor even conceived of as such. In North America, the Aztecs subdued most of the tribes in the Valley of Mexico and extended their rule over the remains of the Maya Empire, which had extended from what is now Honduras up into the Yucatán Peninsula. They established in addition trade relations with tribes as far south as modern Costa Rica, which appears to have been the source of the jade which they regarded as the most precious of all substances. Though the Maya had substantial rafts, capable of a voyage between the Caribbean islands, there is little evidence for any regular contact on this basis. However, South American food crops and methods of cultivation did spread as far as Santo Domingo.

In South America the Andean empire of Tahuantinsuyo was in turn displaced by the hegemony of the Incas, whose rule extended from its centre at Cuzco in modern Peru, north into Ecuador, and south into modern Bolivia, Chile and the north west of what is now Argentina. It was along the Inca trade routes, dotted along their length with storehouses for the local produce, that Pedro de Valdivía was to make his way southward along the chain of the high Andes before finally descending into the Copiapó valley.

Origins

Modern international relations in the Western hemisphere begin with the first voyage of Columbus in 1492. From his first landfall on 12 October in Watling Island (San Salvador) in the Bahamas, until the day of his death, Columbus himself insisted that the new lands that he had discovered lay off the coast of India – or possibly China. His mistress, the Queen of Castile, had more pressing problems, to ensure that the right of Spain to these new lands, evidently not part of the dominions of any other Christian monarch, was recognised by Spain's major maritime rival, Portugal.

Disputes between Spain and Portugal concerning the Atlantic islands had in the preceding century been ratified on more than one occasion by the Pope. The newly elected pope, Alexander VI, was of Spanish descent. The time was ripe for a new agreement. By the Treaty of Tordesillas (1494) the two powers finally agreed that the line of demarcation between their two hemispheres would be drawn along a north–south line 370 leagues to the west of the Cape Verde islands (approximately 49 degrees west of Greenwich). As a result, when Cabral came back in 1500 and reported that he had discovered Brazil, it turned out to lie on the Portuguese and not on the Spanish side of the line. Next to the Encounter itself, this was to be the most important fact determining the future shape of relations in South America.

Confined to a thin coastal strip by the mountains, Portuguese settlement in *Brazil* was initially sparse. With the failure of the succession to the Portuguese throne in 1580, Brazil, along with Portugal itself, became part of a single great empire ruled by Philip II of Spain from Seville. When Portugal rose in revolt in 1640 and asserted its independence, the first task of its rulers was to recover their former territory. It was not an easy one. The Dutch had in the meanwhile made significant inroads into the Caribbean and captured substantial parts of Brazil. It was by a series of accidents rather than by any carefully thought-out plan that in the end the Portuguese abandoned their chain of ports in India and Sri Lanka and were able at the same time to drive the Dutch out of Brazil, though they retained a foothold on the mainland of South America in the Guianas. From 1658 to 1822 Brazil was Portugal's most important overseas possession.

Since *Spanish America* was not accurately delimited, the Portuguese were able successfully to assert their control of the mouth of the Amazon in the eighteenth century, although in fact it lay on the Spanish side of the line of 1494. By the Treaty of Madrid of 1750 the

Portuguese even peacefully secured their claim to the mouth of the Amazon (which in fact lay on the Spanish side of the line of demarcation), and with it gained access to the Amazon basin. This was in time to give Brazil direct control of the greater part of the great 'inland sea' of the South American continent and indirect control of much of the rest.

Spanish policy focused on the vital importance of securing their sea communications with their vast empire. Columbus's initial settlements in Santo Domingo were soon abandoned in favour of Havana, which became the base for further Spanish exploration and conquest. In 1519–21 Cortez conquered Mexico and at last fulfilled the promise of unlimited wealth in the form of gold and silver bullion. In the next few years Central America was explored from both north and south, but proved to be devoid of interest; the northern desert of Mexico and much of the south of what is now the United States was equally unprofitable. In 1538–39 Pizarro conquered Peru and found in upper Peru (modern Bolivia) wealth to rival and even exceed that of Mexico. It was from this direction that Santiago del Estero, the first Spanish town in what is now Argentina, was founded. Meanwhile from the mines of Peru and upper Peru (now Bolivia), gold and silver bullion was shipped north from Callao to Panama. There it was transported across the isthmus on mules and reloaded, before the annual treasure fleet set sail for Havana, where it made rendezvous with the similar fleet from Vera Cruz in Mexico, and set sail again for Seville. Only twice in three hundred years did the fleet fail to arrive, though incidental losses were heavy, both to Caribbean storms and to pirates.

The closed sea

From the beginning the Spaniards treated the Caribbean as a 'closed sea', denying the right of other nations to sail its seas without their permission. This was in keeping with the principles of international law handed down from the Roman Empire. It was not, however, in accord with reality. For it was not gold and bullion that drew other nations like a magnet to the Caribbean islands. It was sugar.

Modern people can have little idea of the impact that sugar made on the sixteenth-century world. Previously the only practical sweetener known was honey. The supply was limited and bees have always shown a marked reluctance to part with it. As generations of wars in Europe began to erode Spanish power after 1600 other European powers successfully made their entrance into the Caribbean, beginning by establishing settlements on the smaller outer islands. Thus the English, who already held settlements in North America in Newfoundland, Virginia and Massachusetts, gained their first foothold in St Christopher (St Kitts) in 1628. Unsuccessful in trying to gain control of the Bay Islands off Honduras in the 1640s, the government of the Commonwealth won the major prize of Jamaica by treaty in 1655. By 1660 there was already a sharp difference between the Caribbean area, where a multi-polar system has effectively been established, and South America, which remained divided between only two non-contending powers. In 1763, at the Treaty of Paris, France swapped Guadeloupe and Martinique, which had been captured by Britain during the Seven Years War (US: King George's War), for the whole of Canada.

By 1800 the Spaniards had long had to share the Caribbean with Britain, Denmark, France, the Netherlands and Sweden, though they never did so with any enthusiasm. But their control of the mainland had never been successfully challenged, and the Spanish Empire stretched from Sacramento in California in what is now the United States to the Bío-Bío River to the south of Santiago in Chile. In 1780 Horatio Nelson almost lost his life in Nicaragua, trying to capture a Spanish fort on Lake Nicaragua in an attempt to gain for Britain control of one of the strategic routes across the Isthmus. In 1807, with Britain and Spain again at war, Sir Home Popham launched a daring attack on Buenos Aires. It was unsuccessful, but it did have the result of bringing nearer the disintegration of the Spanish Empire on the mainland from within.

Division and reunion

Independence came to the Americas as the result of Napoleon's invasion and conquest of Spain itself. This forced the local inhabitants to take measures for their own defence in the first instance, and later facilitated the emergence of independent governments. The Spanish Empire broke up in the inverse order to the way in which it had been created. First to go was inland Paraguay (1811), followed by Buenos Aires (1816) and Chile (1818), while in North America the United States seized Florida from Spain (1816) before Mexico proclaimed its independence (1821). Nor did this end the process of disintegration. Each of the four Viceroyalties broke up into at least three pieces, and that of New Spain most of all. Central America in turn seceded from Mexico (1824), and Guatemalan secession broke up Central America (1838–40) into the five Spanish-speaking states of today.

Brazil's independence was very different. In 1808 the Portuguese royal family had taken refuge on a British warship before Napoleon's troops reached Lisbon. They established their new capital in Rio de Janeiro. Not surprisingly, when the war was over the Crown Prince did not want to return to Europe. It was he who proclaimed Brazilian independence at Ypiranga in 1822 and Brazil remained united as an imperial monarchy until 1889. In 1993 there was serious talk of restoring the Empire as a solution to Brazil's persistent internal political divisions, but a major obstacle was that there was no one undisputed claimant to the throne.

An important problem for all the new states was the vagueness of the colonial boundaries. In each of the new capitals there were maps indicating that at some period they had had authority over areas now held by other would-be states. Spain did not recognise the legitimacy of any of the new states, so the first thirty years after independence saw a flurry of small boundary conflicts and the emergence of some more new states: Bolivia (1825), Uruguay (1828) and the five Central American states (1838–39). Eventually at the Congress of Lima (1849) the states gathered there agreed on what they termed the *uti possidetis juris*. This in effect stated that the boundaries between the states should be where they were on 1 January 1810. The only problem was, by that time very few of them were still in the same place.

Happily the huge distances involved and the weakness of the armed forces of the new states meant that most of the conflicts were local ones. In only two cases in the first century of independence did conflicts give rise to major wars.

The first began when the dictator-president of Paraguay, Francisco Solano López, declared war on Uruguay, and dispatched his troops through Argentine territory without first getting Argentine agreement. The result within weeks was war between his small country and Argentina, Uruguay and Brazil. Known in most other countries as the War of the Triple Alliance (1865–70), but in Paraguay itself as the National Epic, the conflict lasted for five years, at the end of which nine-tenths of the male population of Paraguay was dead and Solano López himself had been killed in battle. In the peace treaty that followed Brazil and Argentina annexed substantial portions of Paraguayan territory.

The second, the War of the Pacific (1879–83), broke out when Chile complained about the treatment of its nationals in the nitrate fields of Antofagasta, then the coastal province of Bolivia. Relying on their so-called 'Secret Treaty' with Peru, the Bolivians rejected the Chilean demands. The result was a ferocious war in which the technologically superior Chileans destroyed the Peruvian fleet, occupied not only Antofagasta but also the Peruvian provinces of Tacna, Arica and Tarapacá, and in a surprise attack on Callao captured Lima, where they dictated peace.

Relations with Britain and France

The independence of Latin America was made possible by the great European conflict of the Napoleonic Wars. Having initially supported it in order to weaken a possible continental coalition, in the 1820s Britain continued to take a keen interest in the region for reasons of trade. A chance conjuncture of circumstances caused its interest to focus in the first instance on the Río de la Plata.

Britain's involvement with what was to become Argentina began as early as 1806, when Commodore Sir Home Popham, who had been sent to the Cape of Good Hope to secure it from the Dutch, saw a chance to stir the South American colonies into action against Spain. On his own initiative he set sail across the South Atlantic for Buenos Aires taking with him the 71st Highland Regiment of Foot (later to be called the Highland Light Infantry) under the command of Brig.-Gen. William Carr Beresford. The attack caught the Spanish authorities completely by surprise and Buenos Aires was captured. However before the news reached London, the local inhabitants had risen in revolt and defeated Beresford's forces, and some months later under the command of Santiago de Liniers they were also to achieve the even greater feat of defeating a relief force of some 10,000 men under the command of Lt.-Gen. John Whitelocke. These two actions, known in Argentina as 'the English invasions' or as the reconquest (la Reconquista) and the defence (la Defensa) respectively, did however succeed in their original intention.

After the citizens of Buenos Aires deposed the Spanish Viceroy on 25 May 1810 his successor was able to maintain a base across the river in Montevideo. However this was disputed territory, and not long afterwards Brazil took advantage of the unrest to conquer Uruguay (the Cisplatine Province) and so push its frontiers down to the banks of the Rio de la Plata. This was deeply unpopular both with Buenos Aires and with the Uruguayans themselves. Thirty-three of the latter rose in revolt under their leader José Artigas, and fought a vigorous war against both Brazil and Buenos Aires. After peace had been signed in 1815 both France and Britain had an interest in restoring peace in the region and eventually in 1828 together they mediated the conflict and enabled Uruguay to emerge as a buffer state; in those days the smallest on mainland South America.

The rise of Juan Manuel de Rosas as Governor of Buenos Aires and Dictator of the Argentine Confederation, however, was to lead both countries to continue to intervene in the struggles of the dissident provinces. In his attempts to recover Uruguay he imposed a nine-year blockade on Montevideo, and in return the European powers boycotted Buenos Aires. Eventually in 1852 a coalition of his enemies from the inland provinces, supported by Britain and France, successfully defeated his forces at the Battle of Monte Caseros. The fallen dictator took refuge on a British warship, whose captain, Capt. R. W. Day came from Southampton, and it was there that General Rosas spent the last twenty-five years of his life before he died peacefully in his bed in March 1877.

By then British financial interests in Argentina and Uruguay had begun to increase substantially. The spread of railways and the development of the refrigerated ship enabled Britain's rapidly growing urban population to be fed at low cost on the produce of the Argentine pampa.

But the interest of outside powers had another side, and there was a price to pay for the fact that the Royal Navy effectively protected the Latin American states from reconquest by Spain. Britain needed a naval base in the region from which it could guard the passage round Cape Horn, which was becoming increasingly important to trade. In the Falkland Islands, whose sovereignty it had since 1767 disputed with Spain, the Admiralty took steps to establish its control, and the British flag was raised there in 1833. However apart from an eccentric bid by a German naval captain to establish a German protectorate in Brazil in 1911 – an action subsequently disowned in Berlin – there was no other attempt by any European power to establish formal control in the area.

In the Caribbean area the pattern was very different. Most obviously, Spain continued to retain control of Cuba and Puerto Rico and so continued to pose a threat to the mainland states. It was not however able to protect the Spanish colonists of Santo Domingo against conquest by neighbouring Haiti, which had gained its independence from France as early as 1804, and in 1844 they asserted their own right to independence rather than risk a return to Haitian rule.

After 1815 France made no attempt to recover its former territories in the Caribbean, though it retained its smaller island possessions and its foothold on the mainland in Guyane (Cayenne), site of the notorious Devil's Island convict settlement to which, at the end of the century, the young Captain Dreyfus was sent to serve his unjust sentence. However irritation with the unstable Mexican government of Santa Anna led the French government unwisely to try to punish it by sending an expeditionary force to seize the harbour of Vera Cruz in 1838. The Mexican Army surprised the force so completely that its commander found the cakes still hot that had been cooked for it and ate them, giving this incident its name of the Pastry War (Guerra de los Pasteles).

French interests continued to accumulate debts in Mexico and in 1863 this fact formed the pretext for a fresh intervention. This time there was an ulterior motive, the desire of Napoleon III to win glory in the New World by establishing a client Mexican Empire with a scion of the Habsburgs, the Archduke Maximilian of Austria, as Emperor. Once the French forces had established control, a rigged plebiscite signalled the desire of the Mexican people to invite Maximilian to assume the cactus throne, which he did in 1864. However with the end of the American Civil War and the war of 1866 between Austria and Prussia, the French prudently decided to withdraw. Maximilian refused to accompany them, and the conservatives who had backed him melted away as the Republican forces recaptured their lost territory. Finally Maximilian himself was captured and executed at Querétaro in 1867.

The coming of the French Third Republic did not end all French interest in the region. The architect of the Suez Canal, Ferdinand de Lesseps, took up the challenge of trying to build an inter-oceanic canal between the Atlantic and the Pacific through the Colombian province of Panama in the 1880s. Eventually, bankrupt and with his men dying in droves from tropical diseases, he had to admit defeat and died in poverty if not obscurity.

Britain, on the other hand, had at the Treaty of Vienna increased its already substantial possessions in the area and confirmed its rights to what it held. Britain had had certain rights in Belize (British Honduras) since Scottish pirates had taken refuge there in the seventeenth century but had always recognised Spanish sovereignty; most recently in 1786. Following the independence of Central America British Honduras was given its own government and became a British colony. In what was to become Nicaragua Britain established a protectorate over Mosquitia, and took control of the Bay Islands off Honduras.

Britain's ability to act in the Caribbean region stemmed from the fact that for fifty years after 1815 the Royal Navy had almost unquestioned command of the seas. Even the United States had to recognise its interest in the passage across the Isthmus as late as 1849, when the two states signed the Webster-Ashburton Treaty establishing that neither party could construct an isthmian canal without the permission of the other. However awareness of the rising power of the United States led Britain to withdraw from Mosquitia and the Bay Islands in 1860.

Rise of the United States

It is easy now to overestimate the importance of the US in the nineteenth century. The United States served as a beacon to the precursors of Latin American independence, and continued to be seen as a model and an inspiration down to 1898. At the same time, the United States as a country pursued its own objectives, first and foremost among which was to secure a safe frontier to the south. Its inability to do this, because of the continuing survival and indeed expansion of European empires in the Caribbean, was to shape the whole future nature of relations between the US and the emerging Latin American states.

The roots of the future US foreign policy were laid by the first president, George Washington. Like other makers of American independence he believed that the Western hemisphere was uniquely favoured by its separation by distance from the corruption of Europe. The United States should, he believed, hold aloof from European conflicts and eschew all 'entangling alliances'. 'It is our true policy to steer clear of permanent alliances with any portion of the foreign world,' he wrote.

When the opportunity came to exclude France from the Western hemisphere, it was Thomas Jefferson who overrode his doubts about the constitutionality of his actions and brought the US down to the shores of the Caribbean by the Louisiana Purchase (1803). He was keen to buy Cuba from Spain, but the Spaniards, for whom it was the key to the Caribbean, refused to sell.

Once the Napoleonic Wars had come to an end, and the United States was safe for the time being from European intervention, two important steps followed. Two brief military campaigns secured Florida from Spain (1816, 1819) and rounded off the southern coastline of the US itself. Then in 1823, when invited by the British Foreign Secretary, George Canning, to join in a declaration supporting Latin American independence, Secretary of State John Quincy Adams advised President Monroe to act unilaterally. His declaration, subsequently to be known as the *Monroe Doctrine (1823)*, stated clearly the view that, though the United States would not interfere with existing European colonies in the Americas (the non-intervention principle), it regarded the Americas as inappropriate for any further colonisation (the no-colonisation principle) and would resist strongly any move to transfer territory from one European country to another (the no-transfer principle) (Perkins 1960). However neither Madison nor Monroe offered the struggling governments anything but sympathy, and it was left to Haiti (independent in 1804), to give financial support to Bolívar and so set him on the road to the liberation of South America (Gleijeses 1992).

The Monroe Doctrine

- *Non-intervention*: With the existing colonies or dependencies of any European power we have not interfered and shall not interfere
- *No colonisation*: The American continents, by the free and independent condition which they have assumed and maintain, are henceforth not to be considered as subjects for future colonisation by any European powers
- *No transfer*: We could not view any interposition for the purpose of oppressing them, or controlling in any other manner their destiny, by any other European power in any other light than as

the manifestation of an unfriendly disposition towards the United States.

It was several decades before the Monroe Doctrine came to be regarded as such, and then only because it was increasingly associated in the public mind with the notion of Manifest Destiny. This was the view that the United States was destined ultimately to fill the whole of North America from the Atlantic to the Pacific, and from the Arctic to the Isthmus of Panama. It emerged from a belief in its physical and moral superiority to take political shape in the 1840s. In the meanwhile US settlers who had moved into the north of Mexico in the 1820s had become so numerous that in 1836 they successfully seceded and formed the independent Republic of Texas (1836–45). In 1845 the Texans were granted membership of the American Union, and in the war that followed, which lasted from 1846 to 1848, and is known in the United States as the Mexican War and in Mexico as the War of 1847, the United States seized half of Mexico's national territory and secured its agreement to its conquest by the Treaty of Guadalupe Hidalgo in 1849.

By a cruel irony within a few days gold was discovered in California, and the Californian gold rush followed. Although the 'Bear Flag' state was hastily admitted to the Union, it remained isolated by more than 2,000 kilometres of desert and mountain from the rest of the United States. This led to a brief but significant interlude of interest in Central America, where Commodore Vanderbilt established a shipping line to take would-be prospectors from New York to San Francisco by way of the San Juan River and Lake Nicaragua. Shortly afterwards William Walker, the 'gray-eyed man of destiny', tried with the aid of southern 'filibusters' (soldiers of fortune) to turn Nicaragua into an American protectorate, with himself – briefly – as President.

Though the Civil War put a stop to further involvement in the isthmus for a generation, enough interest remained for the Grant administration (1869–77) to commission feasibility studies of possible routes for an inter-oceanic canal, and to negotiate with its government the possible annexation of the Dominican Republic.

Four years later, James G. Blaine, Secretary of State in the short-lived Garfield administration (1881), invited the other independent American states to join in an international conference to discuss trade problems. In 1889–90, when he was again Secretary of State under Benjamin Harrison (1889–93), the first pan-American conference took place. This initiative was to lead ultimately to regular conferences of the American states in early twentieth century and ultimately to the formation of the Pan-American Union. One of the consequences was certain other American states, notably Mexico and Brazil, came to be recognised as full members of the world community, and were represented at the First Hague Conference. In the early years of the new century Brazil consolidated its boundaries by a series of negotiations with its neighbours initiated by its most famous Foreign Minister, the Baron of Rio-Branco, and seemed well on the way to becoming the great power of South America.

The US as a Caribbean power

The rapid economic growth of the United States in the last three decades of the century was accompanied by a revival of belief in Manifest Destiny. While the new lands acquired in 1849 were being settled and incorporated in the Union, US influence spread out into the Pacific, marked by the opening up of trade with Japan, missionary activity and settlement in Hawaii and a growing interest in China. In 1895 Secretary of State Olney was to claim, vaingloriously, that the United States was 'practically supreme' on the American continent. In fact, however, the years from 1865 to 1895 saw relatively little US activity in Latin America, with the exception of northern Mexico, which, though politically independent, was linked into the US economy by the cattle trade and the construction of three major railroad links.

In 1898, by the *Spanish–American War*, the US signalled its arrival as a world power, as Japan was to do by its defeat of Russia in 1905. The immediate occasion of the war was an explosion which destroyed the battleship USS *Maine* while at anchor at Havana. For the three years since the poet José Martí, armed with two pistols and carrying a pocket edition of Cicero, had landed in Cuba and proclaimed its independence, the Cubans had been waging a bitter guerrilla war against the Spaniards, who had responded by herding the local population into concentration camps (*campos de reconcentración*). They had called for American help, but so far it had not been forthcoming. Now led by William Randolph Hearst, the explosion was ascribed to the Spaniards and the 'yellow press' bayed for blood.

In the declaration of war that followed, Senator Teller from the mountain state of Colorado inserted a clause saying that the United States sought no territorial gain in Cuba and promised to give it its independence. This was eventually done in 1902, though on terms (the so-called Platt Amendment) which gave the United States effective control over Cuban government finances and reserved the right to intervene in the island in order to protect democracy. The United States had also captured Puerto Rico. It had not promised to give it its independence, and in due course it was formally annexed. So, too, were the Philippines, far away across the Pacific. In the course of one brief campaign the United States had acquired a small but significant overseas empire. It had also gained three other things: responsibility for a substantial indigenous population in its conquered territories, a new belief in its moral superiority over its neighbours and the need to extend its system of defence to cope with the new demands that might be made upon it in a multi-polar world of competing great powers.

It was the need to maintain a two-ocean navy, specifically, that triggered the next development: the decision to go ahead with the construction of an inter-oceanic canal. De Lesseps's rights in Panama had passed to a French consortium that was anxious to do business with the United States. Ultimately they were successful in persuading the US Senate to accept their proposed route and to reject the rival possibility of a canal through Nicaragua. The Colombian government, however, held out for more money. They were rudely surprised when a 'revolt' for 'independence' broke out in Panama (3 November 1903). While US warships stood off the coast to prevent Colombian reinforcements reaching Panama, the US government recognised the new government, and, within days, had signed a treaty with it by which the infant government of Panama signed away sovereign rights in perpetuity over a ten-mile wide strip of territory on either side of the proposed canal route, and granted the US government the right to build, operate, fortify, collect tolls and generally do anything necessary to the operation of a canal.

With the independence of Panama in 1903 the break-up of the Spanish empire in the Americas was at last complete, some ninety-six years since it had first begun. It was a great irony, therefore, that it was followed, not by a new wave of independence, but by the establishment of US hegemony in the Caribbean, which has lasted ever since.

There have been three phases in this relationship so far:

1   *1898–1933*: Overt intervention
2   *1933–53*: The 'Good Neighbor' policy
3   *1953–89*: Covert intervention

Since 1989 we have clearly moved into a new age. It has a name, 'the New World Order', given to it by President Bush. What 'the New World Order' amounts to in practice, however, is still far from clear (see Chapter Eight).

US policy towards Latin America

Overt intervention   Key to the emergence of American hegemony in the Caribbean was the Panama Canal. Its construction began in 1904 and the canal was opened in 1914, three days after the outbreak of the First World War (McCullough 1977). The completion of the canal created an unusual situation, an emerging great power that was dependent for its military security on an internal route that lay outside its boundaries. Hence by the establishment of the Panama Canal Zone (CZ), as US sovereign territory, the attempt was made to internalise it as far as possible. There were two further consequences.

Firstly, with the acquisition of both the CZ and Puerto Rico, with garrisons in both places and a naval base at Guantánamo Bay in Cuba, the Roosevelt administration (1901–9) had in effect created an 'iron triangle' of power within the Caribbean basin. Not only did this enable the US to deploy forces with great rapidity to any part of the region, it actually gave it a strong incentive to do just that, in order to protect its newly acquired strategic interests. At the same time, the continuing presence of European colonies within the region, and suspicions about the intentions of both imperial Germany and newly emergent Japan, led to a re-evaluation of the USS diplomatic position.

The result was what became known as the *Roosevelt Corollary* (to the Monroe Doctrine). Broadly speaking, the theme of the president's statement (1904) was that, since the United States could not permit outside powers to intervene in its hemisphere, it would have to do so for them.

> Chronic wrongdoing . . . may in America, as elsewhere, ultimately require intervention by some civilized nation, and in the Western

Hemisphere the adherence of the United States to the Monroe Doctrine may force the United States, however reluctantly, in flagrant cases of such wrongdoing or impotence, to the exercise of an international police power.

The main occasion for European intervention, of course, was the failure of states to pay their debts. Changes of political power, generally brought about by violence, were almost invariably followed by default. In 1905 the President of the Dominican Republic effectively agreed to his country being placed in 'receivership', so that (as in Cuba and Panama) this contingency could not arise (Rippy 1937). The following year the President of Cuba, whose bid for re-election was being strongly contested, appealed for US aid under the terms of the Platt Amendment. The result of the second intervention in Cuba was in effect a brief return to colonial rule under a US military government (1906–9) (Millet 1968). In the same year when war broke out between El Salvador and Honduras Roosevelt dispatched the USS *Marblehead* to El Salvador and brought about a ceasefire (Munro 1964).

Under Roosevelt's successor, William Howard Taft (1909–13), civil war in Nicaragua led to the landing of US marines in 1912. With the onset of the First World War there was even stronger pressure on the next administration to intervene. The new Democratic President, Woodrow Wilson (1913–21) was chiefly concerned with domestic policy. Events were to conspire to frustrate this intention. Mexico was already in the first throes of what was to prove to be the Mexican Revolution and a few days before Wilson took office, power had been seized by a military dictator, Victoriano Huerta. After a long period of growing hostility, US forces captured the Customs House at Vera Cruz in 1914 to prevent a shipment of arms being landed to reinforce Huerta's troops (Quirk 1964). Further intervention followed in the Dominican Republic (1914) and Haiti (1915). In 1916–17 American forces were again sent into Mexico, following a border incident attributed to the revolutionary 'Pancho' Villa. In 1917 the US bought the Danish Virgin Islands from Denmark to prevent them being occupied by Germany, and initiated pressure on the dictatorial president of Costa Rica which was eventually to lead to his resignation two years later.

By 1920, in any case, the United States was already the dominant economic power in the region. Two things symbolised its growing ascendancy. The first was the success of Edward L. Doheny in establishing the Sinclair Oil Company in Mexico, against stiff competition from the British interests of Weetman Pearson (later Lord Cowdray), sold to Shell at the end of the First World War. The second was the creation in 1922 by Samuel Zemurray of the giant United Fruit Company of Boston, which was for several decades to dominate Central American government and politics through its control of the banana trade. Between 1921 and 1933 the United States was closely involved in the politics of the Caribbean region, where it maintained in effect a substantial 'informal empire' (Munro 1974).

The Good Neighbor policy   A reappraisal of American interventionism in the light of changing world conditions was triggered as early as 1928 by the preparation of the so-called *Clark Memorandum*. In this, the solicitor to the State Department, J. Reuben Clark, demonstrated clearly (1) that the Monroe Doctrine was merely a unilateral statement of US policy and had no validity in international law; and that (2) in consequence the Roosevelt Corollary could no longer be sustained. No new intervention took place under Herbert Hoover (1929–33). However it was Franklin D. Roosevelt, with his ear for a dramatic phrase, who used the term 'the Good Neighbor policy' to describe what he hoped would be a new era in US–Latin American relations.

The withdrawal of US forces from Central America took place speedily under the new administration, and by 1934 was complete. The US retained its base in Cuba and its substantial presence in the Canal Zone. But at successive Inter-American Conferences it sought in effect to internationalise the Monroe Doctrine, by gaining the assent of the other states to a form of collective security. In 1936 a new Treaty with Panama gave the Panamanian government a sharply increased share of the revenue for the canal, though this did not still nationalist opposition.

But if intervention had been unpopular, ceasing to intervene also proved to have some very awkward consequences. With US forces out of the way, state after state in the Caribbean region succumbed to dictatorship. This was part of a general trend: throughout South America, too, 1930 had seen the beginning of a wave of military coups, and authoritarian governments were the norm. It was these governments, with their very dubious credentials, who now insisted that the United States promise not to intervene again – and one can readily see why. In 1936 the new Roosevelt administration formally agreed at the Buenos Aires Conference of the Pan-American Union to the Declaration of Principles of Inter-American Solidarity and Co-operation, which included the principle (3b): 'Intervention by one state in the internal or external affairs of another states is condemned' (Connell-Smith 1966, p. 99), a statement which was widely hailed in Latin America as marking the formal end of the Monroe Doctrine.

The United States, however, did not share this interpretation. Rather, its leaders believed that what they had done was persuade the Latin American states to take part in enforcing it, and this view was reinforced by the Declaration of Lima in 1938. Furthermore, on the outbreak of war in Europe in September 1939 the United States unilaterally proclaimed what became known as the 'hemispheric safety belt'. Within a 200-mile-wide strip of water, stretching right round the two continents south of Canada, the United States, Roosevelt declared, would treat any attack on an American state as an attack on itself. In 1940, in a deal with Britain, the United States rounded off its defences round the perimeter of the Caribbean by acquiring bases in British colonies, in return for letting Britain have fifty 'over-age' destroyers. Few expected Britain to survive long anyway, and Guatemala, under Jorge Ubico, asked at the Inter-American Conference of 1940 to be given Belize in the event of a British defeat. It was politely but firmly asked to wait. However when in December 1941 the United States was attacked at Pearl Harbor its new friends leapt to its defence. The first nine countries to declare war on Japan in its support were Costa Rica, Cuba, the Dominican Republic, El Salvador, Guatemala, Haiti, Honduras and Nicaragua. It was a considerable irony that taking part in a war fought for the *Atlantic Charter* and Roosevelt's 'Four Freedoms' subtly and effectively undermined many of the dictators who had led their countries into battle. The huge piles of arms sent to Central America, too, were first put to use a generation or more later – against a new wave of dictators.

The Second World War, which saw the United States emerge as a world superpower, also saw it come into regular contact for the first time with the states of South as well as Central America. Again the purpose was military. The United States needed to be able to get troops quickly to the war in North Africa. Given the poor strategic situation and the limitations of air transport at the time, this meant that the US had to be able to use air bases in Brazil. As part of the price, Brazil insisted in taking an active role in the war. Mexico was the only other American state to do so, sending an air squadron to the Pacific in the last days of the war against Japan. Otherwise the US discouraged the other South American states from an active role, hoping instead to draw heavily on them as sources of essential raw materials for the conflict. Only in the last months of the conflict were they all, even Argentina, persuaded to break off diplomatic relations with Germany and Japan so that they could become members of the newly-established United Nations.

In the new post-war world, which was to be founded on collective security, the Latin American states constituted 20 of the first 51 members of UN. In 1947 they joined with the United States in signing the Inter-American Treaty of Reciprocal Assistance, known in English for short generally as the *Rio Pact*. At Bogotá in 1948 they signed the Charter of the new regional organisation, the *Organization of American States*, which was to replace the old Pan-American Union. Democratic revolutions in Guatemala and El Salvador (1944), Costa Rica (1948) and Bolivia (1952) were supported by the US. Later, as the Cold War deepened and the paranoid fear of communism came to the fore in US politics came the first stages of a new wave of intervention (Parkinson 1974a; Martz and Schoultz 1980; Martz 1988).

Covert intervention   The Soviet Union was a latecomer to the politics of Latin America. It was not until the Second World War, when it was, after all, one of the Allies, that diplomatic relations, which had previously been few and erratic, were extended to it by most of the major Latin American states (Clissold 1970).

No sooner had a Republican President, Dwight D. Eisenhower, taken office in 1953 than anti-communism became the first objective of US policy. Eisenhower was determined that no further ground would be lost on 'his watch' (Rabe 1988). Plans were laid for clandestine intervention in Guatemala. Neither President Jacobo Arbenz (1950–54) nor his government were in any sense 'communist', but his land reform programme involved the expropriation (with compensation) of some of the unused lands of the United Fruit Company (UFCo.). In what later was to become known as a 'two-track' policy, a diplomatic offensive was unleashed against the

Guatemalan government. Under cover of this, a force of 'exiles' was trained, which eventually launched an 'attack' in Guatemala from Honduras in 1954. Though the force was too small to form a real military threat, it did spur the Guatemalan Army to act. It deposed Arbenz, and US diplomatic pressure ensured that his ultimate successor was the hand-picked leader of the 'exiles', Colonel Castillo Armas (Immerman 1982; Schlesinger and Kinzer 1982).

The success of this clandestine intervention was such that, after becomingly disenchanted with the Cuban Revolution of 1959, and increasingly suspicious of the new Government's attempts to open up links with Moscow, Eisenhower gave orders for plans to be prepared for a similar operation. Launched instead by the Kennedy administration in 1961, the landing at the Bay of Pigs was, however, a complete fiasco, and was followed by Castro's formal declaration in December 1961 that he was a 'Marxist-Leninist'.

After the Bay of Pigs President Kennedy warned that in the eyes of the United States, the Monroe Doctrine was still very much a reality:

> Any unilateral American intervention, in the absence of an external attack upon ourselves or an ally, would have been contrary to our traditions and to our international obligations. But let the record show that our restraint is not inexhaustible. Should it ever appear that the inter-American doctrine of noninterference merely conceals or excuses a policy of non-action – if the nations of this hemisphere should fail to meet their commitments against Communist penetration – then I want it clearly understood that this Government will not hesitate in meeting its primary obligations, which are to the security of our Nation. (quoted in Connell-Smith 1966, p. 24)

The decision of the Soviet Government to place nuclear missiles in Cuba the following year, therefore, enabled the United States to regain much of the lost ground. Though as the price of a negotiated withdrawal it had to agree to continue to tolerate a communist government in Cuba itself, the missiles were withdrawn. Nevertheless as a result of the experience many of the other states of the region were willing voluntarily to join in excluding Cuba from the inter-American system, and by 1964 this had effectively been achieved. In 1965, fearing that the Dominican Republic would go the way of Cuba, President Lyndon Johnson ordered US marines to intervene in a civil conflict there (Black 1986).

Though zeal for active intervention was dampened by the experience of the Vietnam War, and for a time detente lessened the pressures of the Cold War on the freedom of Latin American states (Parkinson 1974b), the idea of intervention regained a degree of respectability under Jimmy Carter (1977–81), provided that it was used to promote human rights. Under the Reagan/Bush administrations (1981–93), a further period of active intervention followed, both clandestine (Nicaragua, El Salvador initially) and overt (El Salvador subsequently, Grenada, Panama). During this period, as a result, the Caribbean emerged much more clearly as a distinct region with common concerns (Barry, Wood and Preusch 1984; Thompson 1987; Ferguson 1990a; Sutton 1991). With the collapse of the Soviet Union in 1991, however, the Bush policy towards Latin America tailed off into uncertainty. Though it is not yet clear whether we have entered a new stage, the present interlude looks set to continue.

Regional organisations

The one organisation linking all the countries of the hemisphere on a regional basis is the Organization of American States. Canada has long held aloof from this body because of the influence on it of the United States, but acceded in 1991, and since then both Belize and Guyana have been admitted, despite long opposition to their membership from Guatemala and Venezuela respectively.

The OAS has a permanent Secretariat in Washington, DC, headed by the Secretary General, currently João Baena Soares of Brazil. Its main organ is an annual meeting held each year at a different time in a different capital. In case of emergency, Foreign Ministers of member states can and do hold special meetings of consultation in Washington.

Led by the Presidents of Mexico and Venezuela, an organisation was established in 1975 to promote economic co-operation between regional states. Its membership (currently twenty-eight) was planned specifically to exclude the United States and to include Cuba. It is called the Latin American Economic System (SELA), and has its headquarters in Caracas.

The idea of economic collaboration in the region, however, is far from new. A Latin American Free Trade Area (LAFTA/ALALC) was established in 1961, consisting of the South American states and Mexico, with its secretariat in Montevideo, Uruguay. Central America was covered by a separate organisation, the Central

American Common Market (CACM), founded in 1960, with its permanent secretariat in Guatemala City. This however disintegrated following war between El Salvador and Honduras in 1969, which took eleven years of negotiation finally to end. In the meanwhile LAFTA had proved to be effectively unworkable, and in 1980 it was reconstituted on a three-tier basis, according to the level of economic development of the countries concerned. It is now known as the Latin American Integration Association (LAIA/ALADI). Decisions are made by the Committee of Representatives of member states, subject to the direction of the Council of Ministers.

There are a number of sub-regional organisations devoted to economic co-operation, other than CACM. The oldest and most successful to date has been the Andean Pact (Acuerdo de Cartagena), which covers Venezuela, Colombia, Ecuador, Peru and Bolivia. An Amazonian Pact has been agreed, but has failed to take effect. Much more recently the governments of Argentina, Brazil, Bolivia and Paraguay have signed an agreement to create a South American Common Market (Mercosur). Under this agreement complete abolition of tariff barriers is to take place in a very short timescale, by the end of 1994.

Detailed consideration of the structure and function of the modern inter-American system will be given in Chapter Six.

Methodology and problems of study

The study of international relations in the Americas suffers from a number of difficulties. Obviously, the immediate task is to understand current situations. However:

1 Because of persistent military intervention and the suspension of constitutional government from time to time, a free press, radio and television cannot by any means be taken for granted. Even the public record of recent decisions, may, therefore, be difficult to decipher. The investigator can of course utilise various interviewing techniques in conjunction with newspaper and magazine reports. Fortunately inter-service rivalry and faction struggles within individual services mean that information is sometimes deliberately disclosed about such matters that might not otherwise have seen the light of day.

2 As elsewhere, all decisions involving current politicians are
   sensitive, and diplomatic decisions doubly so, because of the
   possible charges of treason or incompetence that may follow
   from unpopular ones.

A further set of problems confront those who wish to examine the
diplomatic record.

3 Latin American politicians live in a stormy environment. Trains
   to and from Bolivia can be expected to be full of politicians either
   going into exile or returning from it. Hence they keep interesting
   papers to themselves, and, like politicians of the United States,
   tend to take them with them when they leave office. As a result,
   given the accidented history of the region, historical source
   material has in the past survived as much by good luck as by good
   judgment.
4 National archives are not always much help. In some important
   countries, e.g. Colombia, access to the national archives is barred
   to outsiders. In others, important material has been lost, in Peru
   because of the War of the Pacific, and in Belize and other
   Caribbean countries because of hurricane, flood and termites.
   Researchers tend, therefore, to work in countries where good
   archival material is available and is also well organised, which is
   not always the same thing. Inevitably this influences our overall
   perception of events.
5 Even within well established archives, the influence of the armed
   forces, the history of dictatorial rule and uncertainties about the
   future of democracy can lead to an over-zealous application of
   the idea of national security.

There is in addition an awkward problem which is quite specific to
the region, and to which no exact parallel exists elsewhere.

Because of the historical dominance of the region by the United
States, access to the foreign relations of other states in the area is
often in the first instance through the diplomatic history and the
extensive archival holdings of the United States. Naturally this
carries with it the danger that the perspective adopted will be unduly
influenced by American policy considerations. Multi-archival
research – checking information in a number of sources – is of course
a well established way of countering such influences.

However the problem goes much deeper, to the root of the

relationship between Latin America and the global superpower with which they have to share the Western hemisphere. There has long been concern among Latin American policymakers about US dominance of the news media. This is of such long standing and structurally so entrenched that even the views of opponents of US policy reach the outside world, if at all, through the major news agencies, the most important of which are US owned and controlled. The power that control of news gathering can confer was recognised as long ago as the last century when the British government took shares in Reuters, and both Cuba on its own account and other Latin American states collectively have in recent years sponsored similar ventures to try to offset the US perspective on their affairs.

Recent writers in the United States clearly recognise that the 'reality' of Latin America presented by the US media is a social construct. For decades North Americans and Latin Americans have maintained carefully cherished stereotypes of one another, which from time to time have actively impinged on world politics. In a recent study, Pike (1992) explores these stereotypes and convincingly argues that these stereotypes are in essence as old as European settlement in North America. They derive, it is argued, from divergent views about the relationship of civilisation to nature; for the Hispanic settlers nature was a work of God to be accepted for what it was, while for the North Europeans it was something to be conquered and dominated. North Americans, therefore, came to identify their own culture with 'civilisation', while regarding Latin Americans as hopelessly trapped in the primitive.

The North American stereotype, Pike further argues, did not originate in 'Latin America' at all, but in settlers' views of the North American Native Americans they termed Indians. It was transferred in turn first to African Americans and then in the nineteenth century to the rapidly expanding tide of immigrants from southern and eastern Europe. In this process Latin America was incorporated into the American psyche as a sort of 'deepest South', its resistance to actual physical incorporation being seen as just one more sign of residual barbarism. Such stereotyping was the easier to accept, facilitated as it was by a combination of invincible ignorance, Manifest Destiny (in which the Mexicans played the role of victim, and hence acted as surrogate for the rest of the hemisphere), and the 'boosterism' of a people proud to the point of hubris with a technological age that had given them railways, steam shovels, barbed wire and the Remington repeater.

However, at the same time North Americans often felt the need to refresh their masculinity (and later femininity too) at the well-spring of the primitive. Some, like Theodore Roosevelt, who did much to improve the North American view of Brazil, did so to ensure that the urge to conquer and dominate was still in working order. Others, however, brought Indo-American elements into an emerging counter-culture. This counter-culture, in turn, was to be ferociously attacked as potentially, if not actually Communist, and so subversive to everything for which the United States stood. Hence the Good Neighbor policy, which did so much to improve the Latin American image of the United States, paradoxically stoked North American hostility towards Latin America.

Latin American stereotyping of the United States is of much more recent origin. The term 'gringo' itself, originally Mexican but by now widely used throughout Latin America as a contemptuous term for North Americans, dates only from the war of 1847, and the perception of the United States as a continent plunged in materialism from the emergence of *arielismo* (see Chapter Five) in the last years of the nineteenth century. Those who know little of the United States and like what they see even less, could easily assume that the stereotype of 'the avaricious gringo with money-stuffed pockets' (Pike 1992) must be 'right'; the more so since, as a picture of modern, urbanised Latin America, the US view of a Latin American as a cute figure in a picturesque floppy hat sleeping in the shade of a cactus is clearly 'wrong'.

But they could hardly overlook similar stereotypes within Latin America. Argentines, seeing themselves as an extension of Europe beyond the Atlantic, felt destined to settle accounts with the 'paper empire' of Brazil, and despised Brazilians both for their racial miscagenation and their tropical indolence. Towards Uruguay, which is only the size of a single Argentine province, their attitude is proprietorial. Other Latin Americans historically have disliked Argentines for their wealth, their brashness and their aggressive masculinity: 'the ego', one witticism has it, 'is the little Argentine we all carry around inside us'. Argentines see Chileans as aloof and rather serious; their fear of Chilean immigration into Patagonia stems at least in part from the belief that they present serious competition. Chileans see Peruvians as unreliable, hostile and probably dirty. In short, wherever one turns, perceptions of 'otherness' mark off one Latin American state from another.

Special characteristics of the region

To sum up, therefore, what are the special characteristics of the region?

1   The states of the region have mostly been independent for more than 150 years – much longer than Ireland, India or Israel, for example.

2   Eighteen of the states share a common language. Since Spanish and Portuguese speakers can understand one another, even if each talks in his/her own language, it is hardly surprising that most (if not all) of the Spanish-speaking states feel that they have much in common with Brazil also.

3   It often seems curious to an outsider that so much emphasis is laid on nationalism in a region whose states have so much in common. Here nationalism is not based on religion or ethnic identity, but on something much more intangible, a sense of shared historical experiences.

4   Until the emergence of the Arabic-speaking countries, the Latin American states were by far the largest group speaking the same language. Inevitably this distinctive bond has facilitated the emergence between them of the rationalist model of international relations, based on a common set of legal ideas. Hence, as we shall see later, Latin Americans have been active pioneers in the development of public international law. The Americas were the scene of the first regional organisation for political co-operation (1889) and the first international court (1907). They formed the only major non-European bloc in the founding and early development both of the League of Nations and of the United Nations and its associated agencies.

5   Friendship, or, if that is too strong a term, a tendency towards collaboration between states has been helped, in modern times at least, by their relatively limited capacity to harm one another. Armies, navies and air forces exist, and have to be taken seriously, but their prime purpose had not been the pursuit of diplomacy by other means.

6   The majority of the Latin American states feel themselves in

economic terms to be part of the 'South' or the 'Third World'. Economic development is a prime, if not overriding part of their external policy, though it is not always fully integrated with the military-diplomatic aspects. A further factor for unity is a common perception of being dependent on the United States, whose rise to superpower status has at every stage been accompanied by immediate implications for the independent Latin American states.

Chapter Two
The actors

The states

States are, it is now generally accepted, not the only actors in international politics. However since the whole world is now parcelled out among them, and all other forms of organisation – bigger or smaller – have to depend on them ultimately for home and sustenance, they come first and foremost in our analysis.

The traditional twenty Latin American states vary in almost all respects that can be measured. However they do have two very important things in common:

1   They have all in the past experienced colonial rule.
2   They were all at one time subject to the sovereignty of the King of Spain – though in Brazil's case only for the period of the 'Babylonian captivity', 1582–1640.

Economically, they are almost all middle-income countries, as defined by the World Bank. Three, Venezuela, Argentina and Uruguay, rank as 'upper-middle-income' countries, with per capita GNP figures of $3,250, $2,520 and $2,470 respectively. Sixteen, led by Brazil, with a per capita GNP of 2,160, are classified as 'lower-middle-income'. The poorest of these, Bolivia, with a per capital GNP of $570, is not much better off than, Haiti, which is classified as 'low-income', with a per capita GNP of only $370 (World Bank 1990). None, not even Haiti, ranks as low as China, India, Nigeria or Ghana. On the other hand, even the wealthiest, Venezuela, is less well off than the poorest country in Western Europe, Portugal and more sophisticated measures, such as quality of life indicators, confirm these disparities.

As we shall see later, part (though not necessarily all) of the problem is that these states are disproportionately dependent on the export of primary products: either mineral, as in the case of Chile's copper, or vegetable, as in the case of Argentina's grain or Colombia's coffee. These economic facts place limits on the capacity of states to make independent decisions, though the precise nature of these limits may vary considerably. Hence economic growth remains a most desirable objective.

Most of the newly independent Caribbean states share the language of the high-income United States, but they share the level of economic development of their Latin American neighbours, and increasingly they are coming to act in the same way. Statistics are hard to come by except for the bigger economies. However Trinidad & Tobago, with its oil wealth, is closely comparable to Venezuela, and has a slightly higher GNP per capita figure of $3,350, while Jamaica ($1,070), heavily dependent on agriculture and bauxite, is comparable to Ecuador ($1,120). This has facilitated the integration of the Caribbean countries into the inter-American system, where they have been able to some extent to perform a bridging role between the United States and the established Latin American states. However there are also very significant political differences between them. The Caribbean is much less integrated as a region than is South America. There is no overall organisation, political or economic, which gives it sub-regional coherence, and the legacy of past colonial ties leaves it wide open to the influence of the United States.

Role of the state

The Latin American states are the inheritors of the tradition of Spain and Portugal. The dominant economic orthodoxy of the period was mercantilism. In keeping with mercantilist ideology, these empires were as far as possible organised to be completely integrated economically, with the view to maximising the amount of gold and silver bullion, then regarded as the sole form of wealth, that flowed into the treasury of the colonial power. Politically, they placed all power in the hands of a colonial bureaucracy, though one that was highly structured and subject to considerable restraints. It is hardly surprising, therefore, to find that Latin American political parties of all persuasions have traditionally been *statist*. In other words, the state has been seen as the ultimate beneficial owner and hence as the prime motor of economic development. Nor was there any effective difference between left and right on this question; their differences were, rather, about whose interests should be served.

It is not easy to disentangle fact from fiction in the rival view from the United States that the role of the state should be minimised as far as possible. The rapid economic growth of the United States in its early years is undoubtedly impressive. But the United States had advantages of climate and soil which most of Latin America did not. Even more importantly, it had a government that used military force to seize very large tracts of land and then sold it to would-be freeholders at the knock-down price of $1.25 an acre ($3.08 a hectare). Its terrain was eminently suitable for building railways – a technology it inherited and/or borrowed from the former colonial power, Britain. In addition, its government gave the railway companies rights over the surrounding land as part of the incentive to build. With the dawning of the twentieth century the US increasingly used, as we have seen, both its military and its economic power overseas, in the service of its national interest.

Hence when today the US urges neo-liberal free market solutions on developing countries, it is hard to say whether it is a case of 'do as I say, don't do as I do', or whether they genuinely have forgotten or misunderstood the lessons of their own history. The American neo-liberal philosopher, Ayn Rand, for one, was not fooled by businessmen who used the rhetoric of free enterprise. She could see how American capitalists of her day made use of the state in their own interests, and she criticised them strongly. They were, she believed, doing the very opposite of what they professed to be doing and slowly destroying the very benefits she believed the free market could bring.

However, whatever they may do to the United States (and the 1980s has seen a massive deterioration in US terms of trade and a huge increase in the national debt), in Latin America free-market solutions have one great disadvantage. They take no account of the social realities of the countries concerned. As a Mexican Finance Minister said not very many years ago: 'The problem with asking Mexicans to tighten their belts is that many of them have no belts to tighten.'

The theory behind neo-liberal strategies is that by opening up the country concerned to international competition, its industry will become more 'efficient'; that is to say, it will shed jobs. It will then, again in theory, be able to compete more effectively in the marketplace. State enterprises are particularly disliked by such theorists, since they are seen as being overstaffed and inefficient. Since 1983 there has therefore additionally been strong emphasis on the privatisation of state-owned enterprises as part of an overall strategy.

Privatisation as a strategy for bankrupt governments has much to commend it. If one is not too concerned whether the activity will be kept going or not, it has two obvious virtues: it offloads the responsibility for providing the service on someone else, and it brings in a 'one-off' return for the sale which can be used to pay off the national debt. However the problem is finding buyers for loss-making activities, as, for example, in Mexico, where government figures for the reduction of state economic activity include mergers and bankruptcies of state firms such as Aeroméxico, and Argentina, where the first companies to be sold off (ENTel, Aerolíneas Argentinas) were sold at bargain prices, and little or no attempt has been made as yet to avoid turning public monopolies into private ones.

Political organisation

The political organisation of the Latin American states dates from the early nineteenth century. It was not, it should be said, in general, modelled directly on that of the United States. Rather the framers of early Latin American constitutions adapted their own past, and reproduced in a republican form the structure of the Spanish monarchy, tempered by Enlightenment ideas about the separation of powers and the primacy of the people.

Primacy in the system, therefore, went to an elected President, with formidable powers which were easily extended by war or coup d'état. Three battles which in the case of the United States had been resolved before independence, remained to be settled in Latin America by civil war. They were: the struggle between centre and periphery; the struggle between Church and State; and the struggle between executive and legislature. The far-seeing Simón Bolívar, the Liberator, foresaw that in the absence of a moderating power (*poder moderador*), such as he recommended in his model Constitution for Bolivia (1825), these struggles would be endless. And so indeed it turned out.

Within these presidential systems the President is ultimately responsible for the conduct of foreign policy. It is the president who formally accredits ambassadors and it is to that official that ambassadors from other countries present their credentials – sometimes with rather surprising results, as when a British Ambassador to Uruguay proudly announced her joy at being in Bolivia. Presidents have generally more freedom to make appointments than is allowed under the American system, and the historical subservience of Congresses has meant that they have seldom questioned foreign policy decisions on a routine level. But presidents are not just chief executives and heads of civilian political parties, even in Mexico (1992). They are also commanders-in-chief of the armed forces, and so, as we shall see later, have a very close relationship to the armed forces which differs substantially from the pattern that prevails in Europe, even if it resembles in some respects that of the United States. Hence not only have governments tended to be in practice very fragile, but their fragility stems from the dominance of the armed forces, and particularly the army, as an institution.

That said, today, with the retreat of the armed forces in the 1980s, most presidents are civilians. Typically they will be from middle-class origins, educated and trained in the law, and active in political life from their student days onwards. Foreign policy is seldom a vote-winner in Latin America, so their main preoccupations will be with domestic issues. However in view of the international context of economic decisions and the need to service sizeable national debts, good relations with other countries are in fact a necessity if domestic problems are to receive any kind of effective treatment. Relations between presidents and congresses are, moreover, to a considerable extent governed by the nature of the party system. Mexico is in a unique position: within a virtual one-party context presidents have historically been able to take the concurrence of Congress for granted, not least since with the principle of no re-election to any elective post, deputies and even senators rely on presidential favour for their next steps on the political ladder.

There is, as has already been noted in Chapter One, a strong tradition in Latin America of legalism. However this does not mean that judges are independent of political pressures, nor that they play, as such, a prominent role in politics. The combined inheritance of Roman Law, the Spanish colonial tradition embodied in the *Recopilación de las Leyes de los Reynos de Indias* and the influence of the Code Napoléon ensures that they have very little room for discretion. Even in Mexico, where the Constitution allows the Supreme Court some latitude in establishing legal precedents, the few judgments that have done so have been made at a time and in a way which enabled the executive to avoid embarrassment. On the other hand, in Argentina, Chile and in many other states, the judges have connived at subverting the Constitition by accepting the decisions of de facto military governments as valid.

The conquest of Latin America was as much the work of Church as of State. The Church established a parallel hierarchy of power, established social norms, determined legal disputes relating to the family, was by far the biggest landowner after the Crown, acted as a development bank and had an effective monopoly of the means of education, through which it preached obedience to the constituted authorities. Though in the nineteenth century a series of conflicts between Church and State were resolved in the main in favour of the latter, the Catholic faith remains a significant unifying factor within the region. On more than one occasion in recent years ecclesiastical mediation has been successful in bringing about a peaceful settlement of intractable secular disputes. The most recent example (1993) is the mediation of Cardinal Miguel Obando y Bravo in the conflict between the so-called 're-contras' (former contras who have again taken up arms) and 're-compas', former Sandinistas who still conditionally support the Chamorro government of Nicaragua.

Role of the elite

At the formal level, foreign policy is invariably the special concern of an elite. In the case of Latin American states, however, historically it has been an elite within an elite, for until very recently political decision making was the jealously guarded prerogative of a small, educated group principally of European descent. In the early, heady days of independence, universal male suffrage was adopted in many states, according to the best liberal principles of the day. But by the end of the nineteenth century illiterates were debarred from voting, and remained excluded from the formal political process in Peru, for example, until 1980.

Within this intimate setting, politics was both patriarchal and patrimonial. It was – and to a large extent still is – dominated by small, cohesive extended family groups. These family groups were in turn characterised by sense of mutual obligation to the family. The characteristic form of indigenous economic development was the family conglomerate, combining with its key institution, the large rural estate or *hacienda*, a variety of mills, mines, smelters, fish processing plants and an import/export business, with newspapers, television stations and a bank. Alliances between such family groups were a major factor in the creation and dissolution of political coalitions. In Brazil they account for both the rise and fall of President Collor, and their destruction was a major objective of the military government of Peru under General Velasco Alvarado (1968–75).

In Central America, though Guatemala and Costa Rica represent two extremes of the social scale, in both cases a significant fraction of nineteenth- and twentieth-century power-holders are descended from the first conquerors. The natures of the ruling elites, Stone (1992) suggests, vary according to the size of the indigenous population: the smaller the fraction of the total population, the greater the tendency towards endogamy. In one family in El Salvador there have been marriages between first cousins in each of five generations, despite the fact that each required a specific Papal dispensation. However everywhere the traditional elite seems in time to have incorporated or accommodated all political persuasions.

All the presidents of Costa Rica except one (38 – discounting some uncertainty about the legality of interim officeholders) have been descended from one man, Cristóbal de Alfaro. Over half of them (24) were or are also descended from Juan Vázquez de Coronado Anaya, *alcalde mayor* and *adelantado* of Honduras, Nicaragua and Costa Rica, who was, not coincidentally, the brother of Francisco ('Coronado'), conquistador of New Mexico. One of the nineteenth-century presidents, Vicente Herrera Zeledón, is today probably almost unknown outside his native country. Some four hundred of his descendants, however, still meet annually to commemorate their relationship to him and to one another.

The descendants of Vázquez spread throughout the isthmus: eleven Presidents of Nicaragua could also trace their descent from him. There were close family ties between the Somozas (and their henchmen), the Sandinistas, and other actors in the drama of the Nicaraguan Revolution, notably Rodrigo Carazo Odio, the Costa Rican President whose support was decisive in the Sandinista victory, though it does not follow from this that this relationship was a conscious factor in events. Neither the elder Somoza nor the Ortegas were directly descended from the conquerors. However Anastasio Somoza García could trace his descent in the direct line from Francisco Somoza y Gámez Ballesteros, who settled in the New World in the late seventeenth century, and was of the 'new' nobility. Through his wife, Salvadora Debayle Sacasa, their sons, Luis and Anastasio, could trace theirs to Juan Vázquez de Coronado Anaya. The Ortegas, too, are of the 'new' aristocracy, and they, like many of the 'Contras', grew up, were educated and worked alongside other members of the elite. Conversely, Violeta Barrios de Chamorro is by marriage, through her late husband Pedro Joaquín Chamorro, whose assassination on Somoza's orders in 1978 triggered the Sandinista Revolution, third cousin to the Cardenal brothers (Stone 1992).

Role of the armed forces

The armed forces are an integral part of the government of most Latin American states (see *inter alia* Lieuwen 1961a; Johnson 1964; Finer 1975; Loveman and Davies 1978; Clapham and Philip 1985; Philip 1985; Calvert and Milbank 1987). Cuba under Castro is no exception, but states that are exceptions are Costa Rica, where the army was abolished in 1948, and Mexico, where civilian pre-eminence is well established, and military expenditure has since the 1930s been redirected into far-reaching programmes of social reform, which had, however, run their course by the mid-1970s. Elsewhere for a combination of reasons the armed forces are able successfully to assert their traditional role of defenders of the Constitution. This enables them directly to intervene in political decisions on various levels, depending on the urgency or salience of the issue concerned.

Since foreign policy decisions often have defence implications, they have a special interest in these, and in many cases it has historically been difficult to separate foreign policy from defence policy. At times, with military leaders in power and military personnel executing their orders, they were often effectively the same thing.

The power of the armed forces stems from their institutional strength. Not only are they an integral part of the governmental system and publicly funded, but the nature of the presidential system gives the army three routes by which direct influence can be exerted on the presidency.

1 As *head of state*, the President is surrounded by military aides, who sit in his antechamber and observe who comes and who goes and what their business is.
2 As *chief of the armed forces*, the President is directly accessible to the chiefs of staff, who have by tradition almost complete autonomy from civilian influences and form a virtual 'military cabinet' parallel to the civilian one.
3 As *head of government*, the President usually finds it prudent to appoint a senior military officer as Minister of Defence. The result is that, instead of a civilian overseeing the army, a soldier oversees the Cabinet.

The relationship of the armed forces – and specifically of the army, the prime military actor in politics – to the civilian policy-making elite has often been misinterpreted. Armies have very special structural characteristics:

1 They are constituted in strict hierarchies within which the power of command, indeed the power of life and death, rests with a very small group, the *officer corps*, representing roughly one-tenth of the total. Given the small size of most Latin American armies, this is a very small number indeed and hence in all but the biggest armies the officer corps exhibits a high degree of institutional coherence. Those members of the officer corps who seek to pass their time in conspiracy have ample opportunity to do so.
2 Members of officer corps are typically drawn from provincial middle-class families with political influence that will secure their sons a nomination. Recruits for the officer corps are drawn from all over the country and not disproportionately from one province or department. Only in Ecuador do a disproportionate number tend to come from one province, although in both Brazil (Stepan 1971, 1988) and Venezuela, for historical reasons, rather more senior officers than might otherwise have been expected, come from Rio Grande do Sul and Táchira respectively. The most important thing they have in common, therefore, is their common membership of the military institution.
3 They are recruited during their most formative years and trained

together in military academies where a strong emphasis is placed on two bonds: loyalty to one's year group (*tanda*), and loyalty to the senior cadet (*centenario*) who acts as your guardian in the first year of service. They are united further by their institutional training and membership, and the personal and social factors which motivate them have to be seen within the institutional context of regular assessment and promotion in which they operate. They acquire a national rather than a provincial view of their own country.

4   At or before graduation they form alliances with the daughters of other military families or with the civilian elite of the capital, and relationships of blood, marriage and *compadrazgo* bind them together.

5   Their institutional membership of the armed forces is the key to all these relationships: it is central to their social position and their future economic wealth. Take it away and they are of no importance. Some neo-Marxist writers have even been prepared to accept that, in Marxist terms, they form 'a class in itself'.

6   Military security gives them the freedom to conspire with impunity. Their arms give them the power to intervene to modify, displace or, in extreme cases, supplant civilian government entirely. The typical Latin American military coup is so well planned that in more than 70 per cent of all cases in the twentieth century no one at all has been killed.

7   The military see themselves as trained professionals. They share with the civilian technocrats whom they typically bring with them into government a belief in the primacy of elite professionals and an active dislike of politics and especially those politicians whom they believe have sold out the nation to foreign interests.

8   Their greatest fear is of successful revolt from below. After 1959 no Latin American military officer could or would forget for a moment that Batista's officers had been first against the wall when the Cuban Revolution came. The 'national security ideology' which came to govern much of military policy was not an alien import from the United States. Though it was undoubtedly reinforced by the anti-communist propaganda of US military instructors, and was to give rise to a paranoid fear of 'subversion' which led to the torture and death of thousands, it

had its roots in a clear perception of institutional and personal self-interest.

These distinctive characteristics ensure that armed forces are not the military wing of the capitalist class. Rather the political elite forms the civilian wing of the armed forces; or at least there is a close symbiotic relationship between the military and the civilians. The relationship is most elaborate in Brazil, where an aspiring politician will have military support as well as the support of a political party, financial interests and a section of the media. Politicians who lack all military support are not likely to get very far, at least not in national politics. In Guatemala in 1970 all three major political parties chose military candidates so that, whoever won, the armed forces would respect the result.

No aspect of the military role is more misunderstood than their propensity to *intervene* in politics (Needler 1966, 1975; Finer 1975). In all countries where armies exist, they form at the least a high spending department of government, constantly lobbying for increased funds. However, given the special characteristics of Latin American states, there they are prepared to intervene, not just as a lobby, but to ask for the appointment and/or dismissal of individual members of the government, and if they fail to get that, to displace governments or even to supplant governments altogether and to impose military rule.

The fact that a country is led by a military leader does not necessarily mean that it has a military government. Nor does it follow that a military government will be more likely than a civilian government to wage war upon its neighbours. When the Chaco War, the only major way this century to disturb the peace of South America, broke out in 1932, both Bolivia, which fomented the conflict, and Paraguay, whose forces fired the first shot, were led by elected civilian presidents.

Moreover, military influence and the disposition to intervene varies quite a lot even within each of the two sub-regions of Latin America. In South America, in Paraguay, the army has dominated politics for more than 150 years. At the other end of the scale, Colombia has enjoyed almost uninterrupted civilian leadership for all but six years of its independent history. However in recent years the failure of formal agreements to end guerrilla warfare, and the alliance of the guerrillas with the growing power of the drug barons of the Medellín and Cali cartels, has brought the army back into the political arena. In Central America, similarly, Guatemala offers one of the clearest examples of a state under subjection to its own armed forces. On the other hand, following the revolution of 1948, the interim government of José Figueres dissolved the armed forces of Costa Rica and handed the main military barracks over to the Department of Education to use as a museum.

Military rule is usually brief, and, while it lasts, exercised either through the Chief of the Armed Forces (or Chief of Staff), or by a committee or junta of the heads of the armed services, who on what is called the 'fourth man' principle, appoint a fourth officer as de facto President, while they themselves act as a kind of legislature authenticating decree laws and other government actions. A good example is Argentina from 1976 to 1981, under Generals Jorge Videla (1976–81) and Roberto Viola (1981). In December 1981, however, General Galtieri, the army member of the Junta, deposed Viola and then persuaded his two colleagues to choose him as President while allowing him to remain a member of the Junta. Another example is Chile, where General Pinochet in 1974 persuaded his three colleagues (in Chile the police or *carabineros* are one of the four services) to do the same, and today, after the restoration of democracy under President Aylwin, he is still commander-in-chief of the armed services.

In Brazil, where the army became the dominant factor in politics as a result of the Paraguayan War (1865–70), their ambitions led them to depose the Emperor and to proclaim a Republic (1889), which they then dominated in various guises down to 1930. Professionalised by the experience of the Expeditionary Force in Italy during the Second World War, the army stepped into the power vacuum left by the suicide of Vargas in 1954, intervened again at the resignation of Quadros (1961) to limit the power of Goulart, and in 1964 finally assumed power with the intention of holding it for as long as was required to modernise Brazil and turn it into a power capable of holding its own against all comers.

In the past, when Latin American armies intervened in politics, they did so for negative reasons, to stop developments they did not like. Once their intervention had succeeded, they allowed the political process to take its course and withdrew from power – until the next time. The wave of military coups that began in 1961 initially formed a limited response to the Cuban Revolution and to local circumstances (Lieuwen 1964).

The *military developmentalism* of the 1960s – the doctrine that the military should stay in power for long enough to create a strong army in a strong country with a strong economy – started in 1964 with Brazil, but was soon followed by intervention in Argentina in 1966, in Peru in 1968, in Chile and Uruguay in 1973, and in Argentina again in 1976 (Philip 1984; cf. O'Brien and Cammack 1985). Something of the same trends, though in lesser degree, can be seen in Guatemala and Honduras in Central America.

In Brazil, where a series of 'prestige' projects such as Brazil's first nuclear power station near Angra dos Reis (Angra I), the Trans-Amazon Highway, and the vast dam at Itaipú with its sixteen turbines were conceived of as part of an overall strategy of development, the full powers of the state were used in each case, regardless of cost, confident that the return would more than justify the investment, which had to be met by borrowing from overseas. The institutional structure of the regime was correspondingly complex, leading in stages to the creation of a quasi-constitutional regime in which two officially approved parties went through the ritual of contesting elections (Stepan 1973). In Argentina the dictatorship of General Onganía simply sought to put politics into cold storage while it attacked inflation and tried to restore growth by encouraging foreign confidence and hence investment. But in practice the regime never got beyond this first stage, and the problem of political institutions was in the end solved by handing the responsibility back to the civilians.

The military developmentalist strategies were derailed by the first 'oil shock' of 1973, and its consequences, the second oil shock of 1979 and the steep rise in interest rates in the United States. Throughout the region, beginning in Ecuador, civilians began to return to power as the military, more or less reluctantly, withdrew from power. It was the civilians who were left to pick up the pieces: a combination of inflation, debt and unemployment. With minor exceptions, however, it did seem as if the lesson had been learnt. The armed forces currently seem notably reluctant to intervene openly, though in Chile General Pinochet remains commander of the armed forces and there is no doubt that in Brazil, Chile and Peru, in different degrees, they retain much influence behind the scenes. Argentina stands out as an exception: there the fall from power was unexpected and was in fact precipitated by the failure of the military to perform properly in their specialist role, fighting wars.

Since that time the military hold on politics has eroded where civilians have been able to solve old problems successfully without their help, as, for example, in the long-running dispute between Argentina and Chile over the delimitation of their common frontier. Where possible conflict has been replaced by positive co-operation, there have been signs that those who believe that peace is a positive concept and not simply the absence of war have been proved right. In the Southern Cone the inception of Mercosur, the economic pact between the River Plate countries (Argentina, Brazil, Paraguay, Uruguay), has already been mentioned as an example of regional collaboration.

At the same time there are signs that in times of crisis the old habit has not been lost of the civilians turning to the military and the military being only too willing to respond. Two attempted military coups in Venezuela, the coup d'état (*autogolpe*) of President Fujimori in Peru, and the saturation of down-town Rio de Janeiro with troops at the time of the Earth Summit of 1992 – each, in their way, is a sign of the continuing importance of the armed forces in political calculations.

The making of foreign policy

As in other countries, responsibility for the day-to-day conduct of foreign policy in Latin American states rests with the Minister of Foreign Affairs (MFA). In all Latin American states the MFA is the senior member of the Cabinet, and may indeed be in formal line of succession to the presidency in that capacity. However in presidential states all ministers are expendable. As President Carlos Menem put it in 1992: 'Ministers are like fuses – they are changed when they are worn out.' And though foreign ministers are both relatively senior and less likely than most to form a useful sacrifice for the president, presidents who are in political difficulties may, and frequently do, require their whole Cabinet to resign so that they can carry out a cosmetic reshuffle. Hence if a foreign minister is to have the opportunity to plan and execute a systematic foreign policy strategy, they have to have several years to do it and the backing of the president for the time being.

Ministers are usually members of political parties, and parties, inevitably, tend to be strongly personalist. They are subject to repeated splits and re-organisation as rivals contest for political power. In this struggle local and regional power-bases are of great significance. Such localist influences can and do have an important consequential influence on foreign policy priorities.

There are various other restraints on foreign ministers' freedom of action. First of all, senior ambassadorships are often given as a reward for various forms of political services, and such individuals may well enjoy alternative lines of communication to the president, which it would be surprising if they did not use. Secondly, the quality of the permanent employees of foreign ministries varies greatly, and the lack of a serious programme of work results in defective reporting, poor record-keeping and erratic decision making (Calvert 1986). Thirdly, foreign ministries form only one organisation within the constellation of organisations that make foreign policy, and each contributes to the overall process of decision making in terms of its major objectives: the defence of its personnel and its budget against all comers (Allison 1971). Fourthly, the fluidity of governmental structures means that the constant process of appeal to the President against the decisions of rival agencies results in sudden and unpredictable reversals of position.

Unfortunately for a variety of reasons information on the actual working of foreign ministries is very uneven. There is general agreement, however, that in South America the Brazilian Foreign Ministry – generally known as the Itamaraty, from the name of the palace it used to occupy in Rio de Janeiro – is by far the best organised and the most professional. The Itamaraty was the creation of the Empire in the nineteenth century, but gained its present prestige from the tenure of the Baron of Rio-Branco, who held office for ten years from 1902 to 1912 (Burns 1966). The prestige it established then and has maintained since even protected the members of the career foreign service from interference in the days of the military governments after 1964. Indeed, it was used by that government as a source of trained personnel to staff other ministries (Barros 1984). Consequently Brazilian diplomats are well trained and can draw on the resources of an extensive archive. They arrive at meetings well briefed and fully informed about what they are supposed to achieve. They are, therefore, highly effective.

The foreign services of both Chile and Mexico, similarly, are seen as having a high level of professionalism. In Mexico the stable succession of governments in the hands of a single official party since

1929 has been paralleled by the development of strong traditions and a businesslike foreign policy (Camp 1984). However the geographical position of Mexico imposed severe constraints on its ability to pursue an independent foreign policy, and it gained the ability to project power outside its boundaries only in the 1950–70 period (Domínguez and Lindau 1984).

In the case of Chile, despite the violent events of 1973 there is very marked continuity in foreign policy between pre- and post-1973 governments. Though Allende's MFA, Clodomiro Almeyda, saw his job as being ' "to create external conditions in order to make feasible the development (of the) project of socialist transformations" and "to contribute to strengthening in the international political arena those agents that struggle convergently for the transformation of a capitalist society into a socialist one at world level" ' (Wilhelmy 1984, p. 51), in practice foreign policy reflected the internal divisions of the Popular Unity (UP) government. The foreign service was not restructured, as had previously been promised, and survived essentially intact into the Pinochet years, to serve a very different, but no less ideological regime.

The foreign service of Argentina, on the other hand, is generally agreed to have suffered seriously from political intervention at the hands of successive governments. Since the Second World War it has been 'purged' by both the Perón (Conil Paz and Ferrari 1966) and the Perón-Perón governments (1973–76) and, more recently, by the military government of General Videla in 1976, when two army captains, a naval captain and two air force captains were appointed to 'assist' the foreign minister to re-evaluate foreign policy, though at the same time some personnel were drawn off to work in other departments (Milenky 1978). In 1983 the new civilian President, Raúl Alfonsín, appointed a close personal friend, Dante Caputo, to the job of Foreign Minister, and, despite his evident limitations, continued to give him maximum personal support throughout the five and a half years he was in power. When Caputo's travelling expenses were the subject of criticism by Congress in what were to prove to the the last months of the Alfonsín government, an anonymous artist scrawled across the door of a garage in downtown Buenos Aires the comment: 'The trouble with Caputo is not that he travelled, but that he came back.'

As a result Caputo's control of the Palacio San Martín was questioned and there was criticism of some of the more political appointments. Fortunately the same mistakes were not repeated when the Peronists succeeded the Radicals in 1989. Though senior political appointees abroad were of course replaced by those more in tune with the new government, able career diplomats have been promoted and the quality of foreign policy advice has improved steadily since 1983.

In Peru what appeared to be a radical change in foreign policy following the military assumption of power in 1968, was in fact a conscious and systematic policy of actually implementing policies which Peruvian ministers and diplomats had been maintaining for many years (see e.g. Einaudi 1972, pp. 28–32). The strategy of the government was outlined in Plan Inca, which though not made public until 1974, actually embodied the programme drawn up in the Higher War College (Centro de Estudios Altos Militares or CAEM). It included a section on international relations, criticising the country's excessive dependence on the United States, its weakness in defending its interests in the face of US pressure, its poor standing internationally, its absence of links to the Third World and its lack of a coherent strategy to protect its frontier areas. But organisationally

> the only change made within the Foreign Office was the replacement of the minister, the new minister bringing with him a military adviser to guarantee the link with the armed forces. The rest of the organizational structure remained unchanged. The first thing the new foreign minister did was to ask that the different departments bring him all previously established plans of action so that they could be studied in terms of their feasibility in the new situation. This strategy contributed to the adoption, within a few months, of a series of very concrete lines of action. (Jaworski 1984, p. 204)

Cuba

Cuba presents special problems of analysis. Since the Revolution, in pursuit of its tricontinental strategy of fomenting revolution simultaneously in Africa, Asia and Latin America, Cuba has been accustomed to maintaining a very large and expensive foreign establishment, which served the triple purpose of acting as a voice abroad, averting diplomatic isolation at the hands of the United States and forming cover for its intelligence service, the G2, and its related services in the Soviet Union and East Germany (Shearman 1987).

The emerging economic crisis at home and failing Soviet support in the later 1980s led to a steep run-down in its establishment and the closing down of embassies in smaller states such as Sierra Leone.

Policymaking has during the same period gone through a number of phases. In the first phase, from 1959 to 1961, the provisional government operated without constitutional structure, largely but not exclusively according to the views of Fidel Castro as leader of the Revolution, who preached a new austerity in order to build up the economic power of the Cuban state (Balfour 1990, p. 80). It was he who in response to external US pressure and the abortive Bay of Pigs expedition, moved both foreign and domestic policy to the left and who, in December 1961, linked Cuba to the Soviet Union by proclaiming it a socialist state. There was no formal representative assembly, despite the claim that it was something called the National General Assembly of the People of Cuba, which approved the First Declaration of Havana on 2 September 1960 and the Second on 4 February 1962 (Government of Cuba 1962).

In the second phase, from 1961 to 1975, Cuban foreign policy was characterised by the development of the tricontinental strategy of fomenting revolution throughout the world. During this period Cuba's substantial foreign policy establishment was built up, especially in the Third World. At the same time as with other socialist states a parallel network of party to party relationships was developed, a substantial propaganda organisation was developed and a variety of friendship organisations and other bodies were developed to promote cultural ties. The government remained without formal constitutional structure and there were no representative bodies to which it had to report, even in theory. Both in 1965, with the collapse of the industrial strategy, when he started to criticise the Soviet Union as publicly as he had previously criticised the United States, and after 1970, with the failure of the 'Harvest of the Ten Millions', when he devoted increased emphasis to his role as a world leader, Castro adjusted course sharply, successfully outflanking any possible political rivals and reconsolidating his personal leadership.

In the third phase, 1975–89, in response to Soviet pressure, government was placed on a constitutional basis and a Soviet-style constitution adopted (1975), affirming the 'leading role' of the Cuban Communist Party (PCC). Under it a pyramid of People's Power assemblies was created, the lower ones directly and the national one indirectly elected in competitive though one-party elections. Castro, previously formally only Prime Minister, was elected executive President, reporting annually to the National Assembly of People's Power. However, though Castro's leadership was not contested, it was no longer exercised with the unfettered freedom of the 1960s, while until the late 1970s there was a considerable degree of stability in the composition of the Politburo and a slow but definite militarisation of the regime. The principal cause of the latter was the launching of *Operación Carlota*, which was to involve Cuba directly in a military operation overseas in support of the Marxist government of Angola. The evidence is that the decision to launch this dramatic foray was very much the personal responsibility of Castro himself, his brother Raúl, as Minister of the Revolutionary Armed Forces and a small group of largely military advisers. For obvious reasons, no public announcement was made until a substantial number of Cuban troops had already reached Luanda. Within a few months Cuban troops had also been sent to Ethiopia, where they served as part of a Soviet formation and played a key role in the campaign to drive the Somalis out of the disputed Ogaden region (Patman 1990, p. 232–3).

The result at home in Havana was a substantial boost to the power of the armed forces and their representation among the policymaking elite. However, dissatisfaction at the military call-up was one of the contributory causes to the storming of the Peruvian Embassy compound by more than 10,000 would-be exiles, who were permitted by Castro, in a moment of impatience, to leave the island for the United States in an organised boat-lift from the port of Mariel. The Cubans took advantage even of this moment of apparent concession to empty their prisons and mental hospitals, to the great indignation of the United States (Domínguez 1982).

In 1986 Castro launched the Rectification Campaign, dedicated to rooting out corruption and inefficiency. Unlike *perestroika* in the Soviet Union, the campaign was limited in duration and directed primarily at specified targets. Within a few months it was abruptly ended. It was, ironically, just at this moment, when the fear was growing in Havana that in the new climate of detente Cuba would be abandoned by the USSR, that Cuban and Angolan troops won the decisive battle of Cuito Cuanavale (May 1988), that forced South Africa to withdraw from Angola and to recognise the independence of Namibia (Balfour 1990, p. 158; Stubbs 1989, pp. 101–4).

Security and strategy

We have already noted that an over-zealous application of the idea of security may act as a serious handicap to the researcher. The problem is twofold. Firstly, the definition of security is usually narrowly military. Secondly, it is often carried to ridiculous extremes. For example, notices all round the docks at Valparaiso warn visitors not to photograph warships, and a startling number of armed guards seem quite ready to enforce the prohibition. Since the warships concerned are all 'off the peg' purchases from Europe or the United States, mostly second-hand, in fact any information a hostile power could possibly want could easily be obtained elsewhere, if not from the suppliers probably in the excellent and informative pages of *Jane's Fighting Ships*.

Security, however, is an ill-defined concept and it is by no means clear that it can and should be limited to purely military concerns. The security of the region, of the state and of the individual citizen are each involved. Each interacts with the others. What constitutes security depends on the nature and the salience of the threat in each case (Calvert and Forbes 1988).

What then is the threat that security in the Latin American context seeks to guard against? Again we find that security is normally perceived from the US point of view. Latin America is seen as a place in which US interests are threatened, in different historical periods by different factors. Thus before 1914 US fear was of European colonial expansion or conflict. In the inter-war period (1919–41) their fear was of the infiltration of the alien creeds of nazism and communism. In the Cold War era, with nazism defeated, international communism was seen as the sole enemy, though the nature of the threat took many forms: military adventurism by the USSR itself, the spreading of revolutionary propaganda by its surrogate Cuba, internal subversion by communist agents in other Latin American states, etc.

As Lars Schoultz has pointed out, lacking as it did a clear definition of what security might mean in the Latin American context, the United States settled instead for stability (Schoultz 1987, pp. 34ff.) From the Latin American point of view the picture was, however, much more complex, not least because of a very different perception of the role of the United States.

For Latin Americans the main threats to the existing order came from:

1 *The United States.* The United States combines almost all the aspects which make it a security problem to the lesser states of the region. It is a state with a long history of armed intervention in their internal affairs. It operates as an ideological opponent of many of the beliefs on which they were founded. Its business interests dominate their relatively fragile economies, and its government has in the past acted, as far as they can see, as much for economic as well as military considerations. Lastly, as a world superpower, it has established and seeks to maintain *hegemony*, thus limiting the freedom of their peoples to make their own decisions.

2 *Their neighbours.* The bigger states of the regions share the unendearing characteristics of bigger states everywhere. They all too readily assume that their national interests are paramount and that their smaller neighbours are a proper object of their attentions. The smaller states, as smaller states will, make alliances with more powerful ones, or with one another. All seek to maintain or to alter the *balance of power*. Whatever the state of the debate between 'realist' and 'liberal-pluralist' writers in Europe, most of the rather erratic Latin American literature on foreign policy operates within a 'realist' perspective dominated by a balance of power framework. Though emphasised more by military writers and strategists, civilians too exhibit a strong influence from *geopolitics* (see Chapter Five).

3 *Cuba.* Only in 1962 when the Soviet Government actually emplaced intermediate range ballistic missiles (IRBMs) in Cuba, did the other American states begin to see Cuba as a threat to their own security, and join with the United States in a series of counter moves, including ultimately the formal exclusion of Cuba from the Inter-American System. (This action had relatively little impact, Fidel Castro describing the Organization of American States graphically if not entirely elegantly, as a 'pile of dung', and subsequently rejecting all well-meaning attempts by self-appointed mediators to bring Cuba back into the organisation.)

From the course of events we can recognise action on each of Waltz's (Waltz 1959) three levels of analysis:

1 *Territorial defence strategies, which ensure participation in*

national security at the level of the individual or locality. Most major states have compulsory military service for adult males. Where states have been threatened by insurgency, regular armed forces have been freed for combat duty by the creation of local militia forces, which, as in Guatemala and El Salvador, additionally function as an effective vehicle of social control, thus reinforcing the stability of the existing, authoritarian state.

2 *National security policy based on self-help solutions to conspicuous weaknesses in the social, political or military order.* Use of 'civic action' programmes in the 1960s had some beneficial results, if only, as in Peru, in bringing the armed forces face to face with reality of life in the poverty-stricken countryside.

3 *Alliances among groups of states.* Since 1948, however, all such alliances within the region have been subsumed to the overarching Rio Pact and the Organization of American States.

It may be assumed that the Chiefs of Staff of each Latin American state have plans for all recognised military emergencies. Certainly, if they have not, they are not doing their duty. The nature of such plans is, of course, one of the most closely guarded of military secrets, and even the Defence Ministries of neighbouring states can only infer, from their knowledge of the assumptions on which they are based and the capabilities of their arms inventories, what might be in them. However, the fiasco of the South Atlantic War (Guerra de las Malvinas) has revealed something about the planning process in Argentina.

The first surprise is that Argentina did not, apparently, have a contingency plan for occupying the islands, or, if it did, it needed extensive updating to make it effective. The second is that, on assuming power, the naval member of the military Junta, Admiral Anaya, ordered a new plan to be prepared in the greatest secrecy (Cardoso, Kirschbaum and van der Kooy 1983, p. 17); secrecy which was in fact so great that the plan was very nearly compromised by the separate decision to land Argentine naval personnel, thinly disguised as salvage workers, on South Georgia. The collapse of the plan to seize the islands was only averted by the failure of the British Government to respond to the provocation, which led the Junta to conclude, in a moment of over-confidence, that there would be no response to the occupation of the Falklands themselves and when it came to a confrontation the United States would in any case be on the

Argentine side. This view was reinforced by the self-flagellation of the British press and eagerly supported by the Anglophile (*sic*), Minister of Foreign Affairs, Dr Costa Méndez (Cardoso, Kirschbaum and van der Kooy 1983, pp. 57–61, 75).

The desire to capture the islands overrode any genuine attempt to evaluate Argentina's real security interests – if Argentina had been spared involvement in war for so long, the presence of a British garrison of eighty-two men in the Falklands was a small price to pay for the protection of Argentina by the Royal Navy over three generations. Links between security and strategy can be very tenuous, and lives sacrificed in pursuit of objectives which are deeply harmful to the real interests of the nation.

In fact, of course, war is in practice a very unlikely contingency for most of the armies of the region. In 1982 the Argentine Army had not been engaged in a real war since 1870. In the entire region only the Brazilians had any real understanding of the nature and implications of modern warfare gained at high cost around Monte Cassino by the Expeditionary Force in the Second World War. For a combination of military and political reasons, in fact, military preparations in Latin America are characterised by three very clear tendencies:

1 To spend too heavily on arms.
2 To build up useless inventories, often because of inter-service rivalry.
3 To spend on 'prestige' projects rather than useful ones.

Between 1945 and 1969 the United States was the sole supplier of modern armaments to most of the Latin American states. As a result, it succeeded in a policy of maintaining an embargo on the supply of high-performance jet aircraft to any government. No doubt this served the strategic interests of the defence of the United States. But it brought no benefit to US arms dealers and it saved a great deal of money for the struggling economies of the region. The embargo was broken when the Swedes succeeded in opening up the market to European competition, the US government procrastinated over the sale of Northrup Aviation F-5 jets to Peru and in retaliation the military high command forced Belaúnde's government to clinch a deal in 1967 for far superior, but very much more expensive Mirage jet interceptors (Einaudi 1972, p. 43). An arms race ensued, as a result of the bilateral competition between Peru, Chile, Argentina etc., which was to be very expensive to all concerned.

Arms salesmen continue to this day to be significant actors in the strategic context. The significance of external suppliers lies both in the arms they sell directly to Latin American states and in their use of Latin American destinations as recognised switching points for more sensitive targets such as the Middle East, and the supply in this context of false 'end-user' certificates. In addition, several Latin American states, notably Brazil and Argentina, have built up a very substantial indigenous arms industry. In Argentina by 1982 Fabricaciones Militares was by far the largest native company and had extended its operations far beyond its original purposes, to the extent that it commanded access to key raw materials of strategic importance. Since 1989 its privatisation has emerged as a significant issue for the Menem administration. In an interesting reversal of past practice, which has important implications for both sides, Brazil, which lent transport aircraft to Argentina during the Falklands War, has since supplied Embraer jet trainers to the Royal Air Force.

The making of economic policy

It is a conspicuous fact that even under military governments there is one post in the government that is given to a civilian. The capacity of any government to act, in the last analysis, depends on the economic resources available to it. The military developmentalist regimes of the 1960s and 1970s were particularly sensitive to the need to build a strong economy if they were to achieve their primary objective of a strong army in a strong country. However they themselves lacked specialist training in economics and so each regime tended to co-opt a leading specialist in financial matters to manage the economy for them. The fact that those they selected actually believed in a free-market system was to create serious tensions and in each case, after a longer or shorter period of boom, to lead to economic crisis.

In Brazil the military regime that took power in 1964 immediately embarked on a period of economic stabilisation, reining in inflation and seeking to restore business confidence. By the use of indexation President Castello Branco's Minister of the Economy, Roberto Campos de Oliveira, minimised protests at the regressive effects of his policies, and what unrest there was was firmly repressed. Campos, formerly head of the National Bank for Economic

Development, had been a lecturer at the Escola Superior de Guerra (ESG) for the previous ten years, and the promoters of the 1964 'revolution' had adopted his ideas as their own and presented them in a package to the public (Stepan 1971, p. 218).

Campos himself was eased out at the transition to the Costa e Silva government in 1967. The new Minister of Finance, Antonio Delfim Neto, who was to hold office until 1974, now brought the Ministry of the Economy under his control and assumed full responsibility for economic matters. Little by little much of the original complex ten-year plan was abandoned, but the basic strategy of promoting economic growth by channeling both public and private funds into the south east continued. In December 1968 the Fifth Institutional Act put an end to the majority possible overt opposition and ushered in the most repressive phase of the regime. When between 1968 and 1973 there followed a period of spectacular economic growth, in which per capita GNP increased at an average of 7 per cent per annum, this was widely hailed as evidence of the success of conservative economic ideas and a victory for the free market. In fact, as Wynia points out, the military government inherited a developed economy with a well-established foreign and state-financed industrial base. Most significantly, some 60 per cent of the investment in the economy during these years came from the state and not from private enterprise, domestic or foreign (Wynia 1978, p. 234).

By the time Delfim was succeeded by his protegé Mário Hénrique Simonsen in 1974, the fateful decision had already been taken to respond to the oil crisis by accelerating public borrowing, while the new president, Ernesto Geisel, sought to allow a gradual relaxation of military control (*distensao*) which would lead in time to the opening up (*abertura*) of the political system. By 1976 Brazil had the largest public debt of any Third World country, $29 billion, but in a world awash with 'petrodollars' to be 'recycled', bankers fell over one another to invest yet more. By 1982, when the debt crisis finally became insupportable, Brazil's foreign debt was over $100 billion.

In Argentina between 1946 and 1983 44 people under nine different titles held the reins of economic policy. In *Argentina 1946–83; the economic ministers speak* (di Tella and Rodríguez Braun 1990), a representative selection of them described their periods of office in their own words and their own way. The contributions themselves almost without exception explain how the authors assumed office in dire economic circumstances, took resolute action, and had just succeeded in bringing matters under control and pointing Argentina towards the road to economic prosperity when their term of office came to an untimely end. Not surprisingly, the editors warn that 'the explicit requirement of some of the authors, and our own feelings, compel us to state clearly that their presence in this book indicates no more than that they succeeded one another in office' (p. vii). In other words, former Argentine economy ministers tend not to be on speaking terms with one another.

Two periods in particular stand out. The dictatorship of General Onganía (1966–70) gave exceptional powers to the 'civilian technocrat', Adalbert Krieger Vasena, Minister of the Economy and Labour 1966–69. His chief 'remedy' for the country's ills was the systematic destruction of trade union power. Allowing entrepreneurs free rein in a 'government-manipulated market economy' (Wynia 1978, p. 224) brought a brief period of forced development led by the large multinational corporations, but foundered in working-class riots as early as 1969.

After increasing political chaos, the multinationals welcomed the return of the military in 1976. The 'process of national reorganisation' under General Videla (1976–81), however, was primarily concerned with stamping out subversion, by the arrest, detention, torture and 'disappearance' of individuals suspected of being 'subversives'. Meanwhile as Minister of Economy 1976–81, José Martínez de Hoz, a scion of an old Argentine family, presided over another short-lived economic boom, fuelled by an overvalued currency which at its height in 1979–80 drew in vast amounts of consumer goods and made it worthwhile for the wealthy to shop in Miami rather than Buenos Aires. With the economy overheating, Martínez de Hoz was replaced at the change of military government in March 1981. He himself, however, has been at pains to point out that the policy he executed was not his own, but that of the armed forces:

> When I was in office, I was considered to the the 'tsar' of the economy. I was often called that, as maybe Alvaro Alsogaray had been in his time, but both of us know that this is nonsense. No Economic Minister is a tsar in Argentina. In the first place there are many important spheres beyond his power, such as the Welfare Ministry, Fabricaciones Militares (Military Manufactures) and the like. I have been asked how much of a hindrance the Armed Forces were. I would say

that the whole of the public administration, both civilian and military, showed a remarkable inertia and rigidity after so many years of interventionism. The Argentine military man is a representative of our population at large, with the same virtues and defects. (Martínez de Hoz in di Tella and Rodríguez Braun 1990, pp. 166–7)

In countries where ambitions are not so great or the number of civilian economists is relatively limited, we often find that the person selected is a banker rather than an economist; often the President of the Central Bank. However the training of a banker is of a largely technical nature and such a post holder has generally acted as a stopgap before the appointment of a new minister, rather than acted to set policy in his own right.

Conclusion

Military strength and civilian weakness are two sides of the same coin. Brazil, Panama and Central America all illustrate different aspects of that dominant role of the military which undercuts civilian institutions. In Brazil, President Collor had been elected as a media personality. As a political outsider from the state of Alagoas, he lacked the support of any of the major political parties and had to deal from the outset with a hostile Congress. In Panama in the Reagan years the United States had connived at the emergence of overt military rule by the leader of the Panamanian Defence Forces, General Noriega. Armed intervention by President Bush, nominally to topple a dictator, removed one embarrassment and replaced it by another: an unpopular civilian government clearly seen as weak, ineffective and wholly subservient to the United States. In Honduras the US built up a formidable military presence for the first time during the same period, in order to facilitate military pressure against Nicaragua. They established in the process a client-state and created a permanent problem for the future. Even in Costa Rica there has been strong, and partially successful, pressure for the militarisation of the police forces.

In the Caribbean, with the conspicuous exception of Suriname, militarism is not yet a problem. However again after its well planned intervention in Grenada in 1983 the US has exercised strong pressure for a military build-up in the island states of the Eastern Caribbean, for whom military forces represent an expensive and wholly useless indulgence with no conceivable value in terms of external defence (Sutton 1988). Throughout the region much of the limited amount of *foreign aid* available has gone to strengthen the military, while the positive effects of the limited amount of civilian aid available have been undercut by repatriation of capital.

The dominant role of the armed forces in policymaking is reflected in a realist perception of foreign policy as a process dedicated to maximising power and security regardless of cost. On the other hand, economic realities and the dependence since 1945 on the United States as the major source of arms, military training, military aid and alliance support have combined to emphasise the importance to a strong military of a strong economy. Military or civilian, changes of government or personnel make relatively little difference to the objectives of foreign policy. What changes is the priority placed on different foreign policy objectives and the seriousness with which they are pursued. Rarely do other actors acquire international significance for more than a brief period. However, certain individuals, such as the rubber tappers' leader, Chico Mendes, in Brazil, or the Nobel prizewinner, Rigoberta Menchú, in Guatemala, do acquire symbolic significance, and, with it, the power to influence the behaviour of major actors.

Chapter Three
The physical environment

General geographical characteristics

Inevitably the physical characteristics of a region act to structure the possibilities for relations between the states of which it is composed.

The ocean isolated the Americas from Europe and Africa, but it also became the route by which the first Europeans arrived. Distances on the curved surface of a globe can be deceptive. The distance by sea from Southampton to Buenos Aires is in fact slightly less than the distance from Buenos Aires to New York. Until the Second World War the dominant feature of the region remained the relative ease of sea transport compared with any other means. Even today, if you can wait long enough, it is cheaper to send goods from New York to San Francisco by sea through the Panama Canal than to deliver them overland. Columbus was the first European successfully to discover the Americas because he started in the most favourable latitude and enjoyed the benefit of the trade winds. Command of the seas gave Britain a virtual monopoly of sea-borne transport with the Americas in the nineteenth century.

European access to the interior of North America was facilitated by the existence of two great river systems: the Saint Lawrence/Great Lakes system in the north and the Mississippi/Missouri/Red River system in the south. In South America only one major river system gave access to areas of potential settlement: the Paraguay/Paraná/ Uruguay system, whose estuary is known as the Río de la Plata. The river basins of these and other rivers, such as the Magdalena in Colombia or the Orinoco in Venezuela, have helped determine the shape of modern states. Rivers mean ports, and Mexico's lack of good ports has not only hampered her commerce but has resulted in the almost complete disappearance of the Spanish maritime tradition.

The hard crisp lines delimiting international boundaries on modern maps create an illusion of order which is nowhere more deceptive than in South America. Modern international boundaries are where they are usually because the states concerned lacked the determination or power to extend them further. The boundary between Argentina and Chile was confirmed as the watershed of the Andes by the Boundary Treaty of 1881. Yet this was done only two years after Bolivia had made an unsuccessful attempt to draw Argentina into the War of the Pacific by offering to cede the strip of land between 24° and 27° south, adjoining its pre-war frontier with Chile, and Argentina, taking an idealist rather than a realist position, had failed to act on the offer (Etchepareborda 1978, p. 160–1). The boundary between Brazil and Paraguay follows for the most part the line of the river. But some, such as the rectilinear frontier between Mexico and Guatemala, simply reflect the relative strength of one and the relative weakness of the other.

Special geographical characteristics

Geological and climatic instability

Geographically the Americas are the product of their tectonic structure. The American Plate, on which they ride, is in collision both with the Pacific Plate, which carries the coastal strip of California and Lower California, and with the Cocos–Nazca Plate, which is responsible for the growth of the Andes. At the same time, the Pacific Plate and the Cocos–Nazca Plate are moving sideways relative to one another, creating the chain of volcanic mountains which is Central America, and squeezing the Caribbean zone.

As a result much of the area is geologically extremely active. The Andes are the most recent range of high mountains in world. Their growth, it is now believed, played a significant part in ending the earth's long summer and inaugurating the ice ages. Today the main significance is that Latin American states generally enjoy horizontal rather than vertical divisions of climate. The majority can be divided into a hot coastal and/or rain forest zone, a temperate zone of hills and river valleys where the bulk of the population lives, and a high cold upland. Even in Colombia, some seven degrees north of the equator, the snow covered mountains of the Sierra Nevada de Cocuy pierce the clouds. Most significantly, the mountainous structure of the region means that a surprising portion of it is arid or semi-arid, with the ever-present risk of drought.

Though the Caribbean forms a zone of relative stability from the point of view of earthquakes, its climatic properties are another matter. The power of the tropical sunshine, which makes it so attractive to the tourist, is also the source of its agricultural wealth, whether it be sugar in Jamaica, nutmeg in Grenada or bananas in St Vincent. However the energy involved is so great that towards the end of each summer season huge tropical disturbances begin to form out at sea. As long as their path takes them over the open sea, or over the lesser islands, which have little or no appreciable effect on their progress, they can and do build up into hurricanes with wind speeds well in excess of 100 mph (180 kmh). Happily today they can be and are tracked by weather satellites, so they result in relatively little loss of life, but the destruction of homes and crops represents in itself a major catastrophe for the relatively weak economies of much of the region – in Honduras in 1974 over 90 per cent of the banana crop was destroyed and tens of thousands made homeless. Given the huge quantities of rain that fall during such storms, it comes as a surprise to many people to be told that on many of the smaller islands water shortages are a major problem, and in extreme cases (as in the Bahamas) water has to be imported, at huge cost, from the mainland.

In political terms this had two consequences which affect relations between states. Firstly, they are for the most part separated by formidable barriers of mountain, river and swamp, though this has not by any means eliminated competition for territory where such barriers were wanting. Secondly, they all face recurrent natural crises, either in the form of volcanic eruption, earthquake and land-slip, or within the Caribbean from hurricanes, and in some cases from both. In almost all cases the question of whether or not these become disasters is a political one, a key determinant being the relationship of the country concerned to the international community. In 1973 after the Managua earthquake, Nicaragua received massive aid from the United States on account of the client relationship of the Somozas with that country; most of this aid was subsequently embezzled. In 1974 the Hondurans got virtually nothing, since the US Ambassador felt they did not need it.

Uneven distribution of resources

The legend of the Americas as Eldorado dies hard. 'El Dorado (the golden one)' did indeed exist: in what is now Colombia a local chief used to be coated with gold dust before bathing in the waters of a lake in a ritual ceremony, and the remains of the gold artefacts of this relatively undeveloped civilisation are so striking that what has been lost is almost beyond imagination. However, of the immense wealth in bullion torn from Mexico and Peru over five centuries (Galeano 1973), almost all has long since been dissipated in European wars. The last great wars to be paid for in this way were the Napoleonic Wars, when, after the fall of Spain itself to Napoleon's armies, the Royal Navy was able to ensure that the last drops of the wealth of the Indies were drained instead into the vaults of the Bank of England. The majority of the present-day inhabitants of these once profitable regions are in fact 'beggars on golden stools'.

Water and soil were the real resources on which the Spanish Empire rested, and it is the distribution of these that determine the present-day structure of the region. Exploitation of the subsoil, however, remains very significant to individual countries. Silver in Mexico, copper in Chile and Peru, tin in Bolivia, iron ore in Venezuela and petroleum in all these countries, plus Colombia, Ecuador and Guatemala, have all shaped the international economic relations within which each has to subsist. Their exploitation, too, has major consequences for the environment, with increasingly important implications for the relations between Latin America and the outside world (Goodman and Redclift 1991; Thomas 1992).

Water Water, as noted above, is very unevenly distributed in the Americas. Though some areas enjoy heavy rainfall and others suffer from periodic flooding, much of the region is arid. A large part of the western coast of South America consists of desert punctuated by occasional river valleys. The Atacama Desert in Chile is the driest place on earth. In this arid climate were formed over thousands of years the great nitrate fields which were seized by Chile in the War of the Pacific and became the foundation of its wealth and power until 1920. But over on the other side of the Andes, beyond where the rain falls, the north-eastern provinces of Argentina are also short of water and environmental degradation has become a significant problem in recent years.

Lack of safe and reliable drinking water supplies is the prime cause of the transmission of infectious diseases, in particular gastroenteritis, a major killer in Central America. Such diseases are no respecters of national frontiers. Indeed national rivalries act powerfully to help them spread. The 1991 cholera epidemic – the first in the region since the 1880s – began in Chimbote, Peru. Before the Peruvians were prepared to admit it, the disease had already spread along the coast down into Chile and up into Ecuador and Colombia. Within weeks of taking hold in Peru's coastal cities it had crossed the watershed into the Brazilian Amazon and reached Manaus, while a conference of Latin American health ministers were vainly trying to agree a concerted policy for combating the epidemic. Later it leapt from Colombia to Mexico, probably carried by a light aircraft engaged in drug smuggling (see also Chapter Eight).

Soil Soil, unlike pure water, is a complex concept and generalisations are more difficult to make. In colonial times there seemed to be no problem. There was an abundance of virgin forest to be cleared. The continent was seen as a 'desert' or a 'wilderness' to be mastered and made fertile.

Unfortunately today less than 2 per cent of the Brazilian coastal forest (the *Mata Atlántica*) remains, and it has been realised, often too late, that many of the soils of the Amazon region are excessively fragile. Both the rain forest of Brazil and Paraguay, and the marshy plains of the altiplano of Ecuador, Peru, Bolivia and Chile, are the product of very long periods of evolution, in which the competition between species is so intense that all the goodness of the soil is locked up in the delicate and irreplaceable plant life.

In the case of the rain forest, faced with the pressure of their growing urban populations, particularly in the north-eastern coastal cities, the military government of Brazil actively encouraged settlement in the Amazon region by offering land free of charge to anyone who would clear it. To facilitate access they drove great roads across the countryside, beginning with the vast Transamazonica. The scale of this highway, and the ecological catastrophe it represents for the local wild-life, can be judged from the fact that it is only the second artificial construction on the face of the Earth to be visible with the naked eye from the moon. Once opened up, settlers moved in. They cut down a few trees to provide kindling, then set fire to the rest. Within days they had created a cleared area many times larger than they could use, and at first from the stored riches of the ashes their crops were very successful.

But within two or three years the pattern changed. Its goodness exhausted, the red laterite soil was baked hard forming an impervious, waterproof surface. The rains ran straight off into the rivers, carrying with them the ten centimetres or so of topsoil and the result was a sterile desert. Finally the settlers left, as they had intended to do in the first place, for the slums of Rio de Janeiro or São Paulo.

In established rural areas the problem is not necessarily the quality of the alluvial soil, much of which has been cultivated for many centuries and still shows a high degree of fertility. Rather it is the quantity of soil and its location. The problem is twofold. First of all, the conquerors took the best lands, and drove the indigenous inhabitants (where they survived in significant numbers) up into the mountains. Secondly, even before it was subdivided, the mountainous terrain is broken up into so many small valleys that the communities that are dependent upon it easily outgrow its capacity to support them. In Central America, this has occurred to an extreme degree in the region surrounding Lake Aititlán in Guatemala. In pre-Conquest times the Incas of Peru and Bolivia developed complex irrigation systems to extend cultivation up the hillsides, carrying water many kilometres in the process. However these systems have been disrupted by natural damage from earth movement and landslip, which in the colonial period, given the steep decline in the local population, was not repaired. There are important political implications that have to be borne in mind.

Firstly, despite the official professions of unity, for many Latin Americans the first point of reference has often been not the nation state but the local community (*patria chica*). Federalism and regional autonomy each offered possible alternatives to secession for nineteenth century regional ambitions, but for a variety of reasons a durable compromise was seldom achieved. One of the consequences, discussed further below, is that territory itself has been disputable and a legacy of boundary and other disputes over territorial control have been bequeathed to the states of today.

Secondly, the fact that the conquest was followed by the formal allocation of the best lands to the conquerors has meant that in some countries, Guatemala being one of the best examples, the bulk of the indigenous population was forced up on to the marginal lands of the uplands and highlands of El Quiché and Alta Verapaz, where today they face the consequences. The most important of these is that when today's rapidly growing populations try to share out their traditional lands, the resulting plots are too small to support life, driving the peasant cultivators into dependence on migratory labour on the big coffee, banana or cotton plantations of the lowlands. In 1978 the Panzós massacre inaugurated a race war in Guatemala in which the military-backed landowners attempted to extirpate the threat from the Indian majority to their continued domination of the economy (Plant 1978; *Observer*, 3 April 1983; *International Herald Tribune*, 9 May 1983; *Guardian*, 28 October 1983; Painter 1987).

It is through foreign control of major sectors of plantation agriculture that external interests gain their powerful grip on the local economy, such that they can and do dictate terms to the governments within the Caribbean system. Cuba before the Revolution, and Honduras today are both examples. This patron–client relationship is replicated in the political linkages between the smaller states of the region and the powers of Europe and North America.

In the high Andes, on the other hand, aridity and cold combine to limit the possibilities for agriculture beyond the subsistence level. Only one valuable crop seems to exist which can replace dependence on dwindling mineral resources and that is coca, the greater part of the market for which is illegal.

Subsoil   Below the soil lies the subsoil, whose rich mineral resources originally attracted the Spaniards, and today still attract modern multi-national corporations (MNCs). Gold continues to have a real role in the modern world, both as a transportable form of wealth and as a hedge against endemic inflation. Certainly the lure of gold continues to cast its baneful influence over the Amazon region of Brazil, where the *garimpieros* (prospectors) are prepared to risk death by asphyxiation or assassination to wrest a bare living out of a muddy hole, and the movement of disaffected and unsuccessful prospectors down into Guyana threatens new international tensions. But though Mexico is still a major producer of silver, its gold mines now contribute an insignificant amount to its modern, diversified economy.

The minerals that modern companies seek are much less romantic but much more useful. Chief among them is copper, mainstay of the economies of Chile and Peru. Tin was for decades the chief export earner of Bolivia. The exhaustion of the mines was already straining the capacity of deep mining to compete in the world market before the collapse of the World Tin Agreement in 1985 sent the price of tin on the world market into free fall. In the ensuing economic crisis, inflation rose to over 16,000 per cent per year and the 'corrective' measures that followed left 40 per cent of Bolivians out of work (Crabtree 1987). Among the results was the spectacular increase of illegal cocaine production, swamping markets in the United States and to a lesser degree in Western Europe.

Rapidly growing population   No subject is more controversial than that of population. Latin American rates of population increase are among the highest in the world. In some places, certainly, such as the uplands of Guatemala, this increase is putting a severe strain on the available land resources. However, availability is not determined simply by nature, but also by political power. The bulk of the native population was long ago deprived of access to the best lands by the Spanish conquerors, and it is for this reason that now, after many generations, plots have been so subdivided that they are no longer able to sustain the families that depend on them.

In Guatemala this pressure has sustained some forty years of guerrilla warfare against a heavily militarised state. However like most other countries in the area it remains underpopulated compared with Europe or India; the only major exception being El Salvador, the smallest of the Spanish-speaking Central American states. Immigration into El Salvador from its sparsely populated neighbour, Honduras, led to nationalist tensions on both sides. Sparked by a disputed decision in the third qualifying round of the World Cup, riots led to a short-lived international conflict (Cable 1969). The curious origins of the so-called 'Football War', however, have inevitably tended to draw attention away from the deep seated and long established ecological causes of the conflict (Durham 1979).

Happily the existence of a common culture, even one from which certain sectors of the population are in fact excluded, has spared Latin America this far the ethnic conflicts that have stained the recent history of Europe or the Middle East. In addition to the inter-mingling of European and indio, a major factor has been the influence of the slave trade. A country like Colombia exhibits a striking range of 'racial' types within one nation. An important unifying factor, as noted above, is the Catholic religion, which prohibits the use of artificial methods of birth control. In practice this is of relatively little significance, since it is clear that those members of the middle classes who can afford contraception, disregard the ban, and those of the poorer classes who cannot afford to provide properly for children, cannot afford to avoid having them anyway.

In the run-up to the Earth Summit at Rio in 1992, there was fresh evidence of the very strong feeling in Latin American countries that their problem is not overpopulation, but lack of economic development. This feeling is coupled with the view, exploited by some unscrupulous politicians, that the 'real' agenda of the developed countries is to limit the population of less developed ones, in order to protect their own standards of living. There is just enough truth in this accusation to make it very difficult to refute the argument that the Latin American countries are underpopulated: it is for the rich industrialised countries, that are overpopulated, to take measures not only to limit, but to reduce their excess populations. Besides the family is still the main agency of social security and welfare for many people in the region, while to the politicians population is in fact the only 'resource' they control that is increasing, and in fact likes to do so.

Filling the national territory

From the conquest onwards, a major objective of government in the Americas had always been to fill the national territory. The legal position of Spain and Portugal however differed significantly. The claims of Spain had always rested on two things: the right of first discovery and the formal legal basis of the papal award of 1493 and the line of demarcation established by the Treaty of Tordesillas. It took them two-and-a-half centuries to occupy even the greater part of the vast tracts they then claimed, and even then much remained effectively outside colonial control. After 1640 the Portuguese, on the other hand, inclined increasingly towards the more modern view that what mattered was effective occupation. This was hardly surprising, seeing that their settlement had by then spread well to the south of the line of demarcation.

With independence the rules of the game changed. The first problem now was to define just what was the national territory. A glance at the map of South America in 1830 will show a very different picture from that which exists today.

Brazil was unique in obtaining the formal recognition of its new status from the former ruling power, Portugal. In the case of the Spanish speaking states the picture was very different. They themselves regarded themselves as the heirs of Spain. However Spain did not. Far from welcoming the new states to the international community of nations, Spain bitterly resented and resisted their independence. Mexico was not recognised until 1839, Argentina not until 1859 and Honduras not until 1894, seventy-three years after Central American independence in 1821. There was therefore no formal, legal act of cession which transferred a defined territory to the new authorities. Hence in the international law of the day the new states had at best a *conditional* legitimacy. They would have to make good their claims to rule before their right to do so would be generally accepted.

But Spain in particular had taken a rather casual attitude to what were for it merely internal boundaries between its colonies. Both under the Habsburgs and under the Bourbons there had been a series of revisions. Large tracts of land had been moved from one jurisdiction to another for the convenience of the colonial authorities. In each of the new capitals there were whole sets of old maps showing how far their territorial jurisdiction had extended at various times. But map making had been very difficult, given the great geographical obstacles, and with the loss of the Netherlands Spain had in any case lost its best map makers. So both the definition and the application of the old colonial boundaries were disputable.

Had Bolívar's abortive Congress of Panama (1826) actually taken place, the Latin American states might have agreed to respect the colonial boundaries. They eventually did reach such an agreement at the First Congress of Lima in 1849, when they agreed to accept the colonial boundaries as they had been on 1 January 1810. Unfortunately by that time few of those boundaries still had any meaning. (The African states agreed reluctantly to respect existing colonial boundaries in 1962, and as a result both internal and international war have been effectively restrained. The European states failed to understand the dangers they were facing after 1989, and the civil wars now raging throughout the former Yugoslavia and in parts of the former USSR show clearly what a better knowledge of Latin America could have saved them.)

The result was that, in the drive to fill the national territory, war was inevitable. In some states this took the form of continuing the colonial pattern of conquest. The 'Conquest of the Desert' in Argentina (1879) and the subjugation by Chile of Araucania, the region south of the Bío-Bío, brought under the control of nineteenth-century republics indigenous peoples who the Spaniards had never been able to subdue. Within a generation the Yagan of Tierra del Fuego were extinct. In Mexico, under the rule of Porfirio Díaz, a pure-blood Zapotec, the Yaqui of Sonora were subjected first to a series of punitive expeditions and later to mass deportation to the *henequén* (sisal) plantations of Yucatán. They were saved from extermination by the outbreak of the Mexican Revolution, though at the price of assimilation.

In the reverse case, states proved incapable of holding on to the territory they had inherited, either because of secessionism or because of the presence of powerful neighbours. Mexico, as we have seen, lost over half its national territory to the United States. But the only thing that was unusual about this was that the territory was acquired by a non-Spanish speaking country. Peru lost half its territory by the secession of Bolivia. Paraguay lost half its territory to Argentina and Brazil, then regained some from Bolivia. Ecuador lost much more than half its territory. Some of it went peacefully enough to Colombia and Brazil. The greater part was seized by Peru. Of the provinces that proclaimed their independence at Tucumán in modern Argentina several became part of modern Bolivia, while much of what is now Argentina remained completely unexplored for more than a generation afterwards.

The secession of both Ecuador and Venezuela from Gran Colombia reflected long-standing regional rivalries. However Chile was able to exploit secessionist feeling in the Peru-Bolivian Confederation formed in 1835 to bring about its disruption in 1839 and so consolidate its dominance on the Pacific coast. Similarly in 1903 the US exploited long-standing resentment in Panama at rule from Bogotá by offering it the means to fulfil its aims, i.e. military support and the prospect of a guaranteed source of income for the future. Not surprisingly, therefore, some governments have been prepared to go to great lengths to encourage immigration to fill up their territory. Both after 1945 and again since 1989 Argentina has actively encouraged the settlement of refugees from Europe, as did Mexico under Porfirio Díaz in the late nineteenth century or Bolivia in the 1970s.

Brazil had the particular problem that its settlement had spread well to the west and south of the line of demarcation, and possession of the mouth of the Amazon had been asserted in feigned ignorance of its true position (Poppino 1968, p. 69). Alone of the South American states, therefore, it adopted the new doctrine that effective occupation was the only true title to the possession of territory. Furthermore, at this time it had not yet been agreed that military conquest alone did not give a valid title in international law; this position was adopted only in 1945 (Jennings 1962, p. 53). Hence there was a strong incentive for states to establish a military presence on their frontiers, so that in future negotiations it could be used as evidence of effective occupation. This was what Spain itself had done in the Bourbon period by setting up military frontier commands in much of what is now the United States. The Brazilians used the same technique to annex the Acre region, with its substantial rubber production, partly from Bolivia in 1899 and partly from Peru in 1929 (Poppino 1968, p. 142–3). In 1962 the Brazilian government pre-empted discussion about its right to build the Itaipú Dam by sending troops in to occupy the Salto de Guairá (Sete Quedas) (Nickson 1982, p. 1).

Geopolitics

In Britain and the United States there has been relatively little interest in the theories of *geopolitics* in the twentieth century. Indeed its association with the concept of *lebensraum*, which is inevitably associated primarily with the Nazis, even though it originated in the work of Karl Haushofer, has done much to discredit it in the Anglo-Saxon world. However, geopolitics is very much of interest to the military and naval academies of Latin America (Child 1985), and in the hands of prominent military politicians, notably General Golbery do Couto e Silva of Brazil and his followers at the Escola Superior de Guerra, known popularly as the 'Sorbonne', had a massive impact on Brazilian government policy, not least during his tenure of the key post of Head of the Military Household to General Geisel (President 1974–79).

Golbery not only wrote his own textbook, *Geopolítica do Brasil* (1947), but translated into Portuguese the works of the Germans

Haushofer and Kjellen, the US writers Mahan and Spykman and the British geographer Mackinder. In Chile Gen. Augusto Pinochet both translated Golbery into Spanish and wrote his own work, *Geopolítica* (1968), in which he argued, like the Brazilians, for an integration of capitalist forces under the leadership of the United States. After the overthrow of the Allende government in 1973 he was to seek to put his theories into practice (Schilling 1978, p. 258).

Among the works that have had most impact on Latin American theorists are those of the British geographer Sir Halford Mackinder. Mackinder believed that the control of any block of land surrounded by sea would be contested between those who held the land and those who commanded the sea. The key advantage in this conflict, however, would go to the land power who controlled what he termed the 'heartland'. Mackinder himself was of course primarily interested in the struggle for control of what he termed the 'world island' of Europe, Asia and Africa, whose heartland he saw as located in the region of the Caucasus mountains.

The South American system

Latin American theorists in the 1960s developed their own geopolitical doctrines on the assumption that they would also be applicable to the 'island' of South America. Both in Brazil and in Argentina they identified the 'heartland' of the continent as roughly conterminous with the colonial presidency of Charcas, now part of modern Bolivia (Bailey 1966). Bolivia adjoins no less than five other Latin America states and as we have seen in the nineteenth century was unable to find a strategy to protect it from the rapacity of its neighbours. In the new age of the Cold War Argentina, Brazil and Peru all found themselves again in competition for control of the Bolivian government, this time by affording support for factions within the Bolivian armed forces. Following the sudden death of René Barrientos in an air accident in 1969, these factions fought each other openly for the succession, the victory going in August 1971 to Hugo Banzer, who was supported by Brazil. In return, Banzer supported Brazilian financial interests, opening up eastern access to his country and signing a contract for Brazil to exploit the iron ore of Mutun close to its frontier (Dunkerley 1980, pp. 38–9). Meanwhile by the Act of Iguazú (1966) and the Treaty of Itaipú (1973), the Brazilian government had effectively displaced Argentina as the dominant influence in Paraguay, and since that time, as a result of the construction of the dam, there has been a very large influx of Portuguese-speaking settlers into the eastern part of that country. In the latter year, 1973, the Brazilian government also sponsored the 'soft coup' that gave the armed forces of Uruguay control of that country.

After some eight years in office – the longest period of any Bolivian president – Banzer was in turn toppled in 1978 by his protegé General Juan Pereda. A further military coup in 1980, led by General García Meza with the help of special forces lent by the Argentine military government, pre-empted a possible return to democracy at that time (Dunkerley 1980, pp. 80–2). With the fall of military government in Argentina, and its discrediting in South America in general, the return to democracy did eventually take place, but only after the Bolivian economy had been destroyed and many Bolivians reduced to poverty.

Geopolitics is not concerned purely with land power, and army officers such as Argentina's Divisional General Juan E. Guglialmelli have played an important role in expanding Argentina's ambitions in the South Atlantic and Antarctica. For Argentina geopoliticians, behind the main threat to Argentina becoming a major power in the South, namely the British presence in the Falkland Islands, South Georgia and the South Sandwich Islands, lies the Chilean navy. What seemed to outsiders to be over-reaction to the award in 1977 of the Beagle Channel islands to Chile stemmed from the belief (soon proved to be correct by the inept words of Chile's leader, General Pinochet), that Chile would use its undisputed possession of the islands to claim a seaward zone off the Atlantic coast (Rojas and Medrano 1978, fig. 3). If this were not resisted, even in the event of the 'recovery' of the Falklands, Argentina would find Chile established with legal rights within what Argentine theorists termed 'the arc of the Southern Antilles', and in a position in due course if not to cut off at least to threaten Argentina's rights of access to Antarctica (Guglialmelli 1980; cf. Alvarez Natale 1984).

At the same time there seems to have been a real fear in Buenos Aires that Brazil, utilising the doctrine of 'continental projection' might also claim a sector of Antarctica, which would have a similar effect on Argentine ambitions (Schilling 1978). When the first Brazilian expedition returned from the Antarctic it was challenged by an Argentine warship, but refused to heave to as requested and proceeded on its way.

The Caribbean system

Application of geopolitical theories to the Caribbean basin system has centred on Cuba. Obviously a maritime basin cannot have a 'heartland' in Mackinder's sense, though the 'heartland' for North America is, of course, to be found in the United States and the United States has dominated the rest of the Caribbean since 1898.

However for the Spaniards, with their maritime perspective and doctrine of the 'closed sea', Cuba, the 'ever-loyal island (*la isla siempre leal*)' was the key to the Caribbean. So it was still for Cuban writers of the early 1960s, by which time a combination of circumstances had conspired to move the island state out of the sphere of influence of the United States and into a new dependent relationship with a European power, the Soviet Union. The emplacement of nuclear missiles in Cuba in October 1962 would have made it a major strategic threat not only to the United States, but to all the states within the Caribbean basin. Not surprisingly, therefore, it was these states that actively supported the United States in its attempts to remove the missiles and to isolate Cuba, while resistance to the US position was consistently felt most strongly from the major South American states who lay outside the optimum range of the missiles.

Using an island as what geopoliticians call a 'platform of manoeuvre' presents certain problems, however. For it to be effective, command of the sea is essential. Throughout the period since 1969, however, command of the sea in the Caribbean basin has rested continuously with the United States (Ronfeldt 1983), which not only dominates the heartland of the North American Continent, but has been able to use listening devices, sonar and radar to monitor all movement across and under the sea (Sutton 1988).

During the initial period of the Cold War Cuba's strategy to foment revolution in the hemisphere had two facets: a local strategy for the Caribbean and a wider one for South America. Fidel Castro himself had taken part in an early student expedition to overthrow dictatorship in the neighbouring Dominican Republic. With the assassination of Trujillo in 1961, every encouragement was given to left-wing forces to follow Cuba's example, but US intervention in 1965 precluded further moves in that direction. Less well known, outside the US, was the considerable propaganda effort that went into promoting the idea of independence for Puerto Rico. This effort proved however to be in vain, since the Puerto Ricans themselves, offered the chance to do so, failed to vote for the independence option.

Che Guevara's expedition to Bolivia in 1966–67 was an even bolder move, to realise the hope of Castro 'to make the Andes the Sierra Maestra of South America'. With its failure, Cuban interest shifted outside the hemisphere to a global strategy in which Africa took first place during the 1970s.

This successful phase came to an abrupt end when, following the Soviet invasion of Afghanistan, Castro tried to rally support for the Soviet Union. In 1979 two new left-wing states had emerged in the Caribbean: Nicaragua and the island state of Grenada. However as US hostility to Nicaragua became more and more apparent, the Cubans came to realise that there was no room for two Cubas in the hemisphere, and self-interest dictated that the one that remained should be Cuba. They warned the Nicaraguans that they would have to live with the United States and advised a conciliatory position. Fortunately for them, the Reagan administration's obsession with seeing the Soviet Union behind everything that Cuba did was tempered with a considerable degree of caution, and the Iran–Contra scandal brought a marked relaxation of US pressure on Nicaragua.

With the disintegration of Eastern Europe in 1989 Cuba ceased even in a political sense to be a platform for Soviet influence in the Caribbean. The collapse of the Soviet Union itself in 1991 merely confirmed this – in 1990 it had already become clear that the large subsidies the Cuban government had enjoyed for so many years were, in the new era of world market prices, a luxury the Soviet Union could no longer afford.

Boundary disputes

Wherever a boundary has not formally been agreed, a dispute can always arise at some period in the future (see also Calvert 1983). Agreement may not be reached for reason of traditional hostility or ideology even where the boundary follows some well marked geographical feature such as a river or estuary. Even when agreement has formally been reached, and a treaty signed, a real or imaginary change either in a geographical feature or in understanding of it, may lead to the dispute being reopened. Thus in the case of Mexico and the United States the Chamizal dispute, settled in 1962, arose from a change of course by the Rio Bravo/Rio Grande.

In the case of Argentina and Chile the 1881 Boundary Treaty was so vaguely worded that on no less than four occasions fresh disputes have arisen over its precise interpretation. Article 1 of the Treaty establishes the greater part of the land frontier thus:

> The boundary between the Argentine Republic and Chile is, from North to South as far as the fifty-second parallel of latitude, the mountain range of the Andes. The frontier line will run in this section along the highest peaks of the said mountain-ranges that divide the waters and will pass along the watersheds that divide one side from another. Difficulties which may arise as a result of the existence of certain valleys formed by the bifurcation of the range, where the line of the watershed may not be clear, shall be resolved in a friendly fashion by two experts one nominated by each side.

> El límite entre la República Argentina y Chile es, de Norte a Sur hasta el paralelo cincuenta y dos de latitud, la cordillera de los Andes. La línea fronteriza correrá en esa extension por las cumbres más elevadas de dichas Cordilleras que dividan las aguas y pasará por entre las vertientes que se desprenden a un lado y otro. Las dificultades que pudieran suscitarse por las existencias de cierto valles formados por la bifurcación de la Cordillera y en que no sea clara la línea divisoria de las aguas serán resueltas amistosamente por dos peritos nombrados uno de cada parte. (Alvarez Natale 1984, p. 171, my translation)

However, clear as this seems, it left the way open for two quite different interpretations of what it meant, since the watershed (*divortium aquarum*) was in many places a long way from the highest peaks. Argentina held that the line should follow the highest peaks; Chile that it should follow the watershed. Had the Argentine position been sustained, Argentina would have obtained an outlet to the Pacific. This danger was averted when in 1893 an additional protocol to the treaty of 1881 confirmed that Argentina should not have an outlet to the Pacific, nor Chile to the Atlantic. Then in 1899 a new cause for dispute arose as the result of the cession by Bolivia to Argentina of the Puna de Atacama, as part of a comprehensive boundary settlement between the two countries. Since President Roca took the view that the cession was non-negotiable, and Chile in practice already occupied part of the disputed area, this raised the spectre of an arms race and possible war between the two states. However this catastrophe was in the event averted by the Arbitration Treaty of 28 May 1902 (the Pactos de Mayo). The arbitration of

King Edward VII (the King's Award) later the same year awarded 39,915km² to Argentina and 54,225km² to Chile and was immediately accepted by both sides (Etchepareborda 1978, pp. 164–8). Despite this further disputes about the interpretation of the Treaty have arisen. One such dispute was successfully resolved by judicial means in 1971 (Jennings 1972) and another is still current.

In the dispute over the Beagle Channel Islands the relevant passage in Article 3 reads:

> As regards the Islands, there belong to the Argentine Republic the Isla de los Estados (Staten Island), the islets immediately adjacent to it and the remaining islands which there are on the Atlantic, to the east of Tierra del Fuego and the eastern coast of Patagonia; and there belong to Chile all the islands to the south of the Beagle Channel as far as Cape Horn and those which are on the west of Tierra del Fuego.

> En cuanto a las islas pertinecerán a la Repúblic Argentina la isla de los Estados, los islotes próximamente inmediatos a ésta y las demás islas que haya sobre el Atlántico al oriente de la Tierra del Fuego y costas orientales de la Patagonia; y pertinecerán a Chile todas las islas as Sur del canal 'Beagle' hasta el Cabo de Hornos y las que haya al occidente de la Tierra del Fuego. (Alvarez Natale 1984, p. 172, cf. Lanús 1984, p. 531, my translation).

It seems clear however that there was agreement in 1881 that in what has since become standard practice the boundary followed the deep-water channel, and a series of Argentine maps dating from the late nineteenth century show that at that stage the Argentine government agreed that the channel ran east–west and hence to the north of the islands of Picton and Nueva. As late as the 1960s the island of Lennox, immediately to the east of Navarino Island, was accepted to be Chilean. Later the Argentine government changed its mind (if an entity such as a government can be said to have a mind) and claimed that the true deep-water channel skirted the coast of Navarino Island, leaving not only Picton and Nueva, but Lennox also, on the Argentine side of the line. What had changed, of course, was the assumptions about the coastal zones to which possession of a sea coast gave access.

The causes of boundary disputes can be broadly classified as symbolic, strategic, economic and ethnic/linguistic (Calvert 1983). Fortunately the last category, so significant in Europe, has been unknown in Latin America, at least in the twentieth century.

All disputes, large and small, have a *symbolic* meaning. Defence of the national territory brings political rewards; its alienation can speedily result in the collapse of governments or even in military intervention. The loss of Acre to Brazil was a contributory factor in the fall of Augusto Leguía to a military coup in Peru in 1930. However the Acre region also had potential economic value. Rarely is it the case that a disputed territory has only a symbolic value. Guatemala's claim to Belize came to assume overwhelming symbolic importance in the minds of Guatemala's rulers. It was enshrined in the 1945 Constitution and supported by a law that made it a capital offence (sic) to question the validity of Guatemala's claim. However to Guatemala Belize would not only have had a substantial economic value, by increasing substantially its national territory, but it also would open up a new and easier access route to the sea from its northern province of El Petén (which accounts for almost one-third of its present area).

Strategic considerations weigh strongly with the armed forces. Fear that Bolivia would pursue its extreme claim by occupying the Chaco Boreal and establishing garrisons on the west bank of the Paraguay River made resistance to Bolivian pretensions a matter of national survival and hence was a significant factor in the lead-up to the Chaco War (1932–37). However such concerns can also be rather unrealistic. In one sense, it is of course true that Britain's possession of the Falkland Islands poses a threat to Argentine territory – but only if you regard the islands as themselves being Argentine territory under occupation, which Britain does not.

Economic factors are of two kinds: direct and indirect. The former is the desire to obtain directly access to or control of an important natural resource. Chile's frontier dispute with Bolivia which led to the War of the Pacific enabled Chile to obtain control of the world's richest supply of natural nitrate. Later, however, it was also dis-covered that the area contained valuable deposits of copper (Dennis 1967, pp. 75–7). An important factor in the struggle for the Chaco was the belief that under it would lie an extension of the southern Bolivian oil field. So far this has not turned out to be the case.

The latter usually takes the form of seeking access to the outside world through a specific trade route. The case of Belize has already been noted. Two cases in South America this century have led to armed conflicts, both involving disputes over access to the Amazon. The first, the Leticia dispute, arose from Colombia's desire to maintain a deep-water port on the Amazon. In negotiations with Peru leading up to a treaty in 1922, the Colombian government obtained confirmation of its possession of Leticia. But by agreeing to cede to Peru an area south of the Putumayo which had been ceded by Ecuador to Colombia in 1916, the boundary was drawn in such a way as to place it in an untidy salient (the 'Leticia trapezium') which it would be difficult to defend militarily. In 1932 a small Peruvian force occupied the city, but was persuaded by the League of Nations to withdraw following the assassination of the Peruvian president, Col. Luis M. Sánchez Cerro (Wood 1966, p. 245).

The second, the Marañon dispute, led to full-scale fighting between Ecuador and Peru in July 1941, as a result of which the Peruvian army advanced far into Ecuador. The dispute arose from Ecuador's progressive exclusion from the Amazon basin by a series of treaties between its neighbours, of which the 1922 treaty between Colombia and Peru was the most recent. Subsequently Peruvian settlers had continued to move into the disputed area adjacent to the Marañon River. In the aftermath of Pearl Harbor, Ecuador was forced to accept the terms dictated by Peru, as a gesture towards inter-American solidarity in a time of grave international crisis. However Ecuador bitterly resented the terms of the Protocol of Rio de Janeiro of January 1942, which meant as far as it was concerned giving up some $310,000km^2$ of territory in the Amazon region, losing its access to the Marañon and retaining only a very limited right of navigation through Peru on the River Putumayo (Wood 1966, p. 318–19). Its governments have consistently refused to implement the protocol by defining the boundary wherever the terms were so imprecise that they could be disputed, though an attempt in 1960 to declare the protocol void on grounds of unfair pressure was rejected by the four guarantor powers (Argentina, Brazil, Chile and the United States) (Connell-Smith 1966, p. 239).

In February 1981, shortly after Peru's return to civilian government, fighting broke out in one of these unmarked areas, the Corderillera del Condor, but was terminated after a few days by the joint action of the guarantor powers, who established a cease-fire zone with provision for monitoring from the air (*The Times*, 30, 31 January; 2, 3, 5, 21, 23, 24 February; 4 April 1981). The causes of this outbreak have still not been established, so it is not known whether it had official sanction or was simply the result of excess of zeal on the part of a local military commander. The odd thing about the dispute is that Peru, which has direct access to the Amazon at the deep-water port of Iquitos, has no real economic need for the additional territory it now controls, while any strategic value it might have is wholly negated by the vulnerability of Ecuador to a direct attack from Peru along the coast.

The use of force to settle such disputes is of course contrary to the Charter of the United Nations, to say nothing of the Charter of the Organization of American States. In practice, however, internal political considerations have presented significant obstacles to the solution of disputes by such techniques as arbitration or mediation. In the Peru–Ecuador dispute both countries agreed to submit the issue to arbitration in 1887, but in 1910 the arbitrator, the King of Spain, withdrew, because the Ecuadorean government had indicated that it would not accept the proposed solution. Between 1936 and 1938, when Ecuador's ambitions had already been sharply curtailed, mediation was unsuccessful, owing to Ecuadorean suspicions that any mediator was likely to favour Peru – suspicions which in Ecuadorean eyes were proved entirely correct by the events of 1941–42.

The one apparent exception, the settlement of the Chaco War, is instructive. In this case a bilateral agreement between the two states was disguised for the purposes of public relations as an arbitral award (Wood 1966). The 'award' confirmed Paraguayan possession of the Chaco, leaving Bolivia with a frontier less favourable than any that had been proposed since 1879. In return it was guaranteed rights of navigation on the Río Paraguay, thus ensuring its access to the Atlantic by that route.

Other South American disputes

One of the most intractable of all South American disputes is that between Chile and Bolivia about the latter's access to the sea, a dispute which for historical reasons also involves Peru.

Chile has frontiers only with Argentina, Bolivia and Peru. Until 1903 it was the only South American state not to have a common frontier with Brazil (there are now two more, Panama and Ecuador). In the early nineteenth century the northern frontier of Chile was defined by the Río Salado, north of the modern Chilean province of Atacama. Soon afterwards Chile's intervention was decisive in preventing the reunification of Peru and Bolivia. In return Bolivia, in 1866, agreed to cede to Chile the land north of the Río Salado to the

24th parallel, and this became the new frontier in 1874, when Chile also obtained special rights to work nitrate deposits in the Bolivian coastal province of Antofagasta. It was not long, however, before problems arose about the conditions of Chilean workers in Antofagasta, and when the Chilean Nitrate Company refused to pay the export taxes imposed on its product in 1878, its rights were withdrawn by Bolivia.

On 14 February 1879 Chilean troops occupied Antofagasta. The Bolivian government, counting on the support of Peru under a 'secret' treaty of 1873, declared war. Having captured Antofagasta and sunk the entire Peruvian navy, the Chilean forces now captured in turn Tarapacá, Arica and Tacna from Peru, and finally, in a daring sortie, occupied Lima itself.

Peacemaking proved an arduous business. In 1883 Chile and Peru negotiated the first Treaty of Ancón. Peru recognised Chilean sovereignty over Tarapacá, while Chile was to retain Tacna and Arica for a period of ten years, after which a plebiscite would be held to determine their fate. The following year (1884) hostilities between Chile and Bolivia were ended by the Treaty of Valparaiso, under which Chile retained possession of Antofagasta pending a definitive peace settlement. Twenty more years had to pass before a further treaty ending the war and recognising Chilean sovereignty over Antofagasta, in return for an agreement that Chile would build a railway from the port of Arica to La Paz, capital of Bolivia. Meanwhile the promised plebiscite had not been held, and the Peruvian government, strongly resenting what it saw as an attempt to deny it its rights, strongly protested about Chile's failure to implement the treaty of 1883, and in 1910 severed diplomatic relations. Direct negotiations were not resumed until the 1920s and then only under pressure from the United States (Dennis 1967).

The result was the second Treaty of Ancón of 1929. By this, Tacna was returned to Peru while Chile retained Arica, but agreed to accord Peru port facilities at the terminus of the Arica–Tacna railway. Both sides agreed that no territory covered by the treaty could be alienated to a third party, i.e. Bolivia, except with the consent of the other party. This treaty effectively checkmated Bolivian hopes of regaining direct access to the sea. The result has been that access to the sea has become a major issue in Bolivian politics, and as the centenary of the conflict approached passions rose which the fragmented and unstable Bolivian political system was not able to manage.

The crisis came when President Hugo Banzer seized power in Bolivia in 1971 with the support of the military government of Brazil, which had obtained in return a promise to upgrade rail links into eastern Bolivia and to develop the iron ore resources of that area. At this point the dictator of Chile, General Pinochet made what appeared at first sign to be a generous proposal. Chile would indeed cede a land corridor to Arica (*Keesing's Archives* 1974 26688A; see also *The Times*, 9 April 1974, for Peru's attitude).

However as negotiations proceeded it became public knowledge that there were three conditions. Firstly, Chile would have to be compensated by an equal area of land. Secondly, Chile wanted to be able to choose which area of Bolivia it should receive, and proposed the Los Lipez region, which although at a great height above sea level and today almost deserted, was a rich mining area in colonial times. Thirdly, the area of land ceded would have to be equal not only to the area of the land corridor but also to that of the 200-mile maritime zone to which a coastal strip would entitle Bolivia (*Prensa Latina* Bulletin 674, 1976). Within a few months, Banzer had been deposed in a military coup (1978) and subsequently, 1979, denominated the Year of the Sea in Bolivia, passed without any further move towards a settlement.

Civilian government was restored in Bolivia in 1982 and in Chile in 1989, and since that time negotiations have been reopened. Arica remains the main outlet for 90 per cent of Bolivia's legal exports and the road from Arica through the National Park of Lauca to Tambo Quemado on the Bolivian frontier carries a constant stream of Bolivian trucks on their way to the sea. In addition, on 1 July 1993 President Jaime Paz Zamora stepped into the Pacific at Ilo to commemorate the lease by Peru to Bolivia of a 162-hectare freeport zone.

Peru's disputes with Colombia and Ecuador have already been discussed in the previous section. In fact, Colombia has land frontiers with five countries: Ecuador, Peru, Brazil, Panama and Venezuela, and a sea frontier with a sixth, Nicaragua (see below). Its boundary with Ecuador was settled as early as 1832, only two years after Ecuador's secession from Gran Colombia. The frontier with Peru was finally settled after the Leticia dispute and is no longer contested by either side. Agreement on the frontier with Brazil was reached in 1907, when Colombia surrendered territory on the Caquetá and Río Negro (Lins 1965, p. 371–2). The boundary between Colombia and its former province of Panama, which seceded in 1903, was agreed by the Thompson-Urrutia Treaty of 1921. Colombia's land frontier with Venezuela has long been fixed. But, though it ceded the uninhabited islets of Los Monjes as recently as 1952, no decision has as yet been reached on the boundaries of the respective maritime zones, though after a brief show of strength by Venezuela both sides are committed to resolving this and all other outstanding questions by peaceful means.

On the other hand the Venezuela–Guyana boundary dispute originates in a dispute which was settled by arbitration in 1899. The roots of the dispute lie far back in the colonial period, but were complicated by the fact that from 1648 to 1814 the territory later to become British Guiana was Dutch. The arbitrators found largely in favour of Britain, ruling that the Essequibo valley was British, but that the territory to the West, including the mouth of the Orinoco, which Britain had claimed, was Venezuelan (Lieuwen 1961b).

No problem arose from this award for many years. Then Venezuelan writers began to claim that Britain had been a great power at the time of the award and that this was in itself unfair. There were allegations, made by a Venezuelan diplomat long after the occasion and shortly before his death, that the arbitrators had been bribed. No supporting evidence for this allegation has yet been produced.

When Guyana became independent in 1966, Venezuela claimed the entire county of the Essequibo (*The Times*, 19 September 1966). Although relatively small by Venezuelan standards, the area claimed amounted to some two-thirds of Guyana's territory. Venezuela may have hoped to obtain support for its claim from the US, but if so it was disappointed. On 18 June 1970, by the Protocol of Port-of-Spain, Venezuela agreed to 'freeze' its claim for a period of twelve years. Before this period expired, following a change of government, Venezuela gave notice that the protocol would not be renewed (*The Times*, 4 April 1981). This notice actually took effect during the South Atlantic War, in which Venezuela took a view strongly supportive of the Argentine military government. However before any serious crisis could arise, it was announced in September 1982, on the occasion of an official visit to Brasília by Mr Forbes Burnham, the Prime Minister of Guyana, that Brazil had agreed to construct a road through the Essequibo to link Brazil to Georgetown. The declaration was greeted in Caracas by a storm of protest, but it effectively checkmated Venezuelan pretensions (*The Times*, 15 May 1981;

27 October 1982). At the time of writing the road has been partially completed, though it has still some distance to go before it reaches the capital. An unwanted consequence has been a substantial influx since 1982 of Brazilian *garimpieros* to join the many Guyanese who are seeking a sudden fortune panning for gold.

It is hard to see why Venezuela has been so intransigent about this issue. The Essequibo is rich in hydro-electric resources and apart from gold, is well stocked with mineral deposits. Venezuela, however, is already rich in both respects, and about half of its existing territory, including most of Venezuelan Amazonia, is still unexplored and unexploited. On the other hand, possession of the Essequibo would be a strategic liability rather than an asset, since it would draw Venezuelan forces further to the east, away from Caracas and the oil fields, while Commonwealth neighbours are hardly likely to fail to support Guyana in the event of attack. It seems that, as with other boundary disputes, the matter has in the course of time assumed a symbolic significance out of all proportion to its economic or strategic value.

Central America

There is one factor which above all others makes boundary disputes in Central America different in kind from those in South America. This is the fact the the five countries at one time formed one state, and continue to believe that unity is a natural situation.

Mexico's frontiers with Guatemala was settled by treaty in 1882, though not before Mexico had managed to annex not only Chiapas and Soconuzco, but also a large part of what is now the Mexican State of Tabasco (the well-known sauce, incidentally, comes from New Orleans). In 1933 Guatemala settled its boundary dispute with Honduras by arbitration, surrendering a significant sector of land close to its only major port on the Caribbean, Puerto Barrios. The Salvadoran frontier was agreed in 1936. Despite his willingness to compromise these boundary disputes, it was President Jorge Ubico who activated Guatemala's most serious frontier dispute, its claim to the whole of the territory of British Honduras, now the independent state of Belize. But this is only one example of the way in which the dream of a united Central America lives on, despite the vested interests which over a century and a half of independence the separate and now quite varied national elites have learned to enjoy.

A long-running dispute between El Salvador and Honduras has yet to be settled, though the omens are currently good. Agreements in 1895 and 1918 were not implemented. After the fall of Maximiliano Hernández Martínez in 1944, Salvador's growing population began to flood across the border in search of work on the plantations of sparsely populated Honduras. The resulting tensions led to rioting in the aftermath of a disputed decision in the third qualifying round of the World Cup in 1969, and, as a result, to the outbreak of the 'Football War'. Though the war only lasted for thirteen days before a cease-fire was brokered by the OAS, some two thousand people were killed during the fighting and El Salvador's main oil refinery was put out of action by Honduran air attack. Subsequently it took thirteen years to bring about a formal treaty of peace between the two neighbouring states, during which time the refusal of Honduras to take part effectively put an end to the work of the Central American Common Market (CACM). Under this treaty, the contentious issue of some thirteen small pockets of disputed ground along the common frontier are to be resolved by negotiation, but the existence of a state of civil war in El Salvador since 1980, and the consequent desire of Honduras to keep the frontier closed, have not facilitated agreement.

War was only narrowly averted in 1957 in the case of a major boundary dispute between Honduras and its southern neighbour, Nicaragua. The conflict originated from a dispute about the partitioning of the territory that before 1859 had constituted the British protectorate of the Mosquito Coast (Mosquitia). Many years passed before Nicaragua effectively annexed the region in 1895. The following year Nicaragua and Honduras agreed a boundary treaty and commissioners were appointed to survey and delimit the frontier. However they were only able to agree on approximately a third of it. The area that remained in dispute covered a substantial area to the south of the Coco River on the Caribbean coast.

Under the 1896 treaty the matter was therefore referred to the arbitration of King Alfonso XIII of Spain. In 1906 the arbitrator awarded the area south of the Coco River to Nicaragua, and established the river itself as the southern boundary of Honduras. This award was accepted by both countries. However in 1912, after a new government had come to power in Nicaragua with the backing of the United States (Munro 1964), it took advantage of a technical error in procedure to denounce the award, and while retaining its control of the area covered by the award, additionally advanced a new claim to a large area to the north of the Coco River as far as the Patuca River and Cape Camarón.

No further progress on the question was made until after the death of Anastasio Somoza García and it was not until 1957 that Honduras took steps to reclaim the tract of land awarded to it in 1906, by formally constituting it as a new Department of Gracias a Dios. Both countries then mobilised their forces and on 1 May 1957 Honduras, claiming that Nicaragua had invaded its territory by placing military forces to the south of the 1906 line, invoked the Rio Pact. An investigating committee of the Organization of American States (OAS) then persuaded both sides to accept a cease-fire, and further international pressure was exerted to get them to refer the matter to the International Court of Justice (ICJ). In 1960 the court held that the 1906 award was valid and that Nicaragua was obliged to give effect to it, which by 1962 it had done (Connell-Smith 1966, pp. 239–40).

Honduras regards the Swan Islands as falling within the scope of the 1906 award. However they are, and have been since 1863, claimed by the United States, which made use of them in 1961 to launch the disastrous Bay of Pigs expedition against Cuba (Parker 1964, pp. 198–9).

Since independence, Colombia has owned two groups of islands in the Caribbean, far from its own shores and relatively close to those of Nicaragua. These groups consist of two principal islands, San Andrés and Providencia, and a number of smaller cays. The rival claims of Colombia and Nicaragua to the islands were decided in favour of Colombia by the United States as arbitrator in 1929. San Andrés became a free port in 1953 (Fluharty 1957, p. 243) and 'the Colombian Caribbean' makes a small but significant contribution to Colombia's tourist trade.

On the fall of Anastasio Somoza Debayle in 1979, the provisional government of Nicaragua denounced the 1929 settlement, and renewed its claim to the islands. Its foreign minister, Fr Miguel d'Escoto, justified his country's position on the grounds that in 1929 Nicaragua was occupied by the United States, which had therefore taken unfair advantage of its position. This charge was ignored by the United States. The response of President Turbay Ayala of Colombia was secretly to reinforce the garrison of the islands and subsequently to reveal the fact in order to deter possible Nicaraguan aggression (*Latin American World Report*, 4 January 1980). Though the renewed dispute has not been resolved, it seems by now to have been tacitly dropped, but not before in 1982 it had led Sandinista Nicaragua to support the claim of the right-wing military government of Argentina to the Falkland Islands.

Nicaragua has also a long history of frontier disputes with its southern neighbour, Costa Rica. These go back to 1825, during the brief period of a united Central America, when the province of Guanacaste was transferred from Nicaragua to Costa Rica. After the break-up of the union in 1838–40 disagreement on the boundary was inevitable, and was only temporarily resolved in 1858 by an agreement establishing what has been the de facto boundary ever since. This agreement, like others before it, remained unratified, but despite conflicts between the two countries in 1949 and 1955 the boundary was unaffected. Since 1978 decisive Costa Rican support for the Sandinistas in their war against the Somozas has improved relations between the two countries to the point at which any challenge to the status quo seems most unlikely.

Conclusion

The physical structure of Latin America has facilitated internal war and secession but has moderated international conflicts. The vertical division of climate has conditioned the range of economic possibilities and the division of land at the conquest has prolonged and extended colonial dependence on the export of a few primary products. A number of boundary disputes have survived into modern times, in both South and Central America. A variety of crisis management techniques have been devised empirically to deal with these but the tendency in recent years for the United States to act unilaterally has, as we shall see later, prevented the regional structures of the Organization of American States and the Inter-American Treaty of Reciprocal Assistance from establishing themselves as an effective crisis prevention regime.

Though the force capabilities involved are much less, there have been proportionately far more disputes in Central rather than in South America in recent years. This seems to reflect three principal factors: the tradition of Central American unity, the nature of the terrain and the fact that such conflicts take place in an area of international concern and so involve the potential or actual intervention of third parties. Hence though the area, logically, forms an exceptionally favourable milieu for the rationalist construction of a crisis prevention regime, rivalries both within and between the Central American states have prevented this, and here as elsewhere the most effective co-operation has been in the economic field.

Chapter Four

The economic environment

The economic environment

There is a widespread view that the insertion of Latin America into the world economy is responsible for much, if not all, of its current economic problems. The first problem comes with determining just at what point Latin American economies can be said to have become part of the world economy. The second is to say just what significance should be attached to it, so long after the event.

In a sense, of course, the process everywhere began with Columbus's first voyage. In another sense it did not. In both Mexico and Peru there is clear evidence of trading relationships before the conquest. Traders were a privileged caste under the Aztecs, their protection guaranteed by the state. Throughout the area subject to Aztec overlordship a single currency, the cocoa bean, had been established. In Peru trade was tightly regulated and an elaborate system of irrigation works enabled the local inhabitants to maintain a sustainable agricultural economy on very limited resources. The conquest disrupted these patterns, both deliberately, by establishing a new pattern of landownership, and accidentally, by introducing European diseases. Within eighty years the population of Mexico had fallen to a tenth of its pre-Columbian level and the indigenous population of Cuba and Santo Domingo had virtually died out. The resulting labour shortage led to the systematic introduction of African slaves who were to form the basis of a new plantation economy.

Meanwhile Spain, in pursuit of mercantilist objectives, had created a transatlantic closed market, in which production of primary goods for Spain was the main objective and purchase of goods in the Indies limited to Spanish industrial products.

By the end of the colonial period, however, smuggling was widespread and determined efforts were being made by British traders to penetrate the colonial market. It is important to emphasise, however, that with certain conspicuous exceptions the relations of Britain and other European states in the nineteenth century were based on trade alone. Though Britain asserted sovereignty over the Falkland Islands/Islas Malvinas in 1833, and established a protectorate over the Miskito a decade later, and the French attempted to turn Mexico into a protectorate between 1863 and 1867, there was no sustained attempt to extend existing colonial possessions in the region.

The struggle for physical resources

Conquest itself was a struggle to exploit a scarce resource, gold. Some parts of the former Spanish Empire lacked precious metals and settled down to a largely independent economic life based on agriculture and stock raising. In the colonial period the principal exports of both Argentina and Central America were high-bulk, low-cost products such as hides and tallow. Wherever possible, plantations were established to grow new high-value crops for export. In the colonial period the main product was sugar. With independence new sources of wealth, such as indigo and cochineal, were added.

In Argentina the wealth of the pampas not fully exploited until the invention of the refrigerated ship enabled chilled meat to be exported to Europe. From then on the pattern of development along the banks of the Paraguay–Paraná–Uruguay river system reflected geographical distance from Europe, with the higher reaches only used for canned beef. The Argentine railway network was set up in the first instance to facilitate the movement of cattle and grain to ports. Initially concentrated on both Buenos Aires and Rosario, the capital of the separate Argentine Federation, with the federalisation of the capital Buenos Aires became the main outlet, and the government-owned narrow-gauge network was extended to link directly with the capital. Since nationalisation in 1947 there have been constant complaints that the radial pattern of the railways benefited primarily the foreigners who built it. It did not, it is claimed, facilitate communications between neighbouring areas within Argentina. In fact the accusation is not factually accurate, since the greater part by distance of the network was built by the state. Moreover in so far as the radial

pattern reflects dominance, it could also, as in the case of London or
Paris, reflect the importance of Buenos Aires as both national capital
and commercial centre.

In Brazil a variety of minerals were known to exist but limited
exploration and poor communications limited the vast natural
potential of the country. Under the Empire, the great sugar boom of
the eighteenth century gave way to a new wave of economic prosperity based on the harvesting of wild rubber. The Amazon became
the main artery of commerce, and the export of seeds and plants was
prohibited to safeguard value of an economic resource, in the traditional mercantilist style. However at the end of the nineteenth
century the spread of the rubber trade into the Putumayo region of
Peru was still dependent on trade downstream on the Amazon, but
being wholly unregulated by the Peruvian government, led to an
outcry in Europe at the inhumane methods used to exploit the Indian
rubber gatherers. The scandal of 'red rubber' had one positive by-
product; it led to the setting up of the Brazilian Indian Service
(FUNAI).

We have already seen (Chapter Three) how the valuable nitrate
resources of Antofagasta were the cause of the War of the Pacific.
They remained the basis of the Chilean economy until after the First
World War, not only generating an enhanced standard of living for
its middle classes but also enabling Chile to live above its means as a
regional power. At the time of the Baltimore incident in 1892 it was
the United States that had to back down when the State Department
realised that the Chilean Navy was considerably larger than that of
the United States. Chile in consequence was seen as one of the three
major powers of South America (the ABC powers).

However when Germany was cut off from sources of natural
nitrate during the War, German scientists discovered process of
fixing nitrogen directly from the air. After 1920, therefore, Chile was
plunged into a sharp recession, this in turn leading to internal political instability, and as its population failed to grow it fell behind in the
race with Argentina. Ironically, in turn Argentina, too, was to lose its
way economically, and today rivalry between the two states still
leads to inordinate suspicion of one another's motives.

National and international economic strategies

Traditionally the state was seen as managing national economy exactly as a good landlord would manage his estate. In Spanish, the same term, *hacienda*, means finance and estate. Improvements in productivity were seen as landowners would see them, as the improvement of the national patrimony. They would take place only slowly and over a long period.

The notion of economic development in the modern sense was a product of the industrial revolution in Europe. The nature of that revolution conditioned assumptions about the possibility of economic development elsewhere. Limitations of technology led to the assumption that there was a single path to economic development: industrialisation, based on the technology of iron and steel. The big problem in Latin America was the irregular distribution of these minerals both between and within states. Of the Spanish-speaking states, only Mexico, which began production in the early years of this century, was known to have both, and even there the deposits lay on opposite sides of the Sierra Madre. Colombia had coal but not iron. Venezuela had vast deposits of high-grade iron ore but not (as far as was then known) coal. Coal has since been discovered in Venezuela, mostly in the State of Táchira, but before that happened it was a change in technology, the introduction of the open-hearth process, which turned the country into a steel producer. Despite this, almost all of Venezuela's very large iron ore production today is exported to be processed elsewhere.

Brazil under the Vargas government in the 1930s used heavy investment to set up the giant Volta Redonda project, which put it in first place among Latin American states for steel production. In the face of steep competition from East Asia, the Sarney administration was responsible for the construction in the late 1980s of a new 'steel railway' from the iron ore mines of Minas Gerais, the steel plant at Volta Redonda and the port of Sepetiba in the State of Rio de Janeiro.

In the late 1940s, in a belated response to Latin American pressures first put forward at the Chapultepec Conference in 1945, the UN Economic Commission for Latin America (ECLA or in Spanish, CEPAL) was created to promote economic growth. The new organisation attracted a group of bright, young economists, known often from the Spanish acronym of their organisation as the cepalistas, among whom the best known was the Argentine Raúl Prebisch. When he published his *Economic development of Latin America and its principal problems* in 1949, it became the starting point for the policies of a whole generation, and was to influence in particular the policies of Frondizi in Argentina and Kubitschek in Brazil.

Prebisch and the cepalistas took it for granted that the state would be the main instrument in promoting economic growth. It was for the state to provide the basic infrastructure of development, by orderly planning. Private-sector investment was welcomed and would be encouraged by the creation of a stable climate for investment. However it must be on the terms laid down by the host government.

Despite its initial hopes, Frondizi's government was marked by a stagnating economy with relatively slow growth. In Brazil Kubitschek had promised fifty years' development in five. It was said rightly by his opponents that what he had actually delivered was forty years' inflation in four. By the early 1960s the problem of economic development in Latin America was beginning to look much more complicated than had previously been thought. There were two principal responses.

One was to blame civilian politics for a failure to maintain consistent economic policies. Though the charge had a certain element of truth, the deduction that military governments could and would do better was to prove in the main to be false. But for the time being, the military belief that they alone could promote real economic growth was to lead to the emergence in Argentina (1966) of what Guillermo O'Donnell (1988) has termed *bureaucratic authoritarianism*. Given that the military are in fact 'armed bureaucrats', the term is quite appropriate, but it does not adequately stress the military, rather than the bureaucratic, element, and it omits the key factor of the desire for economic growth. For this reason the term *military developmentalism* is preferred here (see Chapter Two above and Calvert and Calvert 1990, pp. 117–18).

The second was to argue that the nature of the problem had been misunderstood. Mere will was not enough. Latin American economic development was constrained by structural factors.

Dependency and underdevelopment

Among civilian critics, therefore, the critique of developmentalism took a much more significant form. The *dependency* thesis (Love 1990; Roxborough 1979), as it has become known, originated with the Marxist analysis of Third World economies by Paul Baran (1957). It was Baran who first distinguished these and other Third World economies as being on the periphery of the world economic system, whose centre was in Europe and North America. But the dependency thesis was developed and popularised in Latin America, by a variety of writers not all of whom were Marxists, specifically in Argentina (Sunkel 1969; Sunkel and Paz 1970) and Brazil (Jaguaribe 1967; Cardoso and Faletto 1969, English translation 1979; Dos Santos 1969, 1970; Furtado 1970; Cardoso 1972; Ianni 1968, 1975a, b). It has since been widely adopted in other regions of the Third World. Though derived from Marxism, which ascribes primacy to classes, dependency theory makes the state the main unit of analysis. States are even seen as being stratified in the same way that classes are stratified, by some writers.

The dependency thesis argues that because the economies of Latin America are on the periphery of the world capitalist system, they have become *dependent* on the advanced industrialised countries. It rejects the developmentalist view that Third World states can in time undergo the same form of development as the existing industrialised states, for at least as long as the capitalist system exists in its present form. The reason, its adherents argue, is that the 'centre', the advanced industrialised countries, sets the terms on which the system operates, and hence both the terms of trade and the flow of capital is asymmetrical, tending to flow from the periphery towards the centre. This outflow is a structural constraint that ensures that the states of the 'periphery' are weak, open to penetration from the centre and with little or no scope for autonomous action (Bonilla and Girling 1973).

In one respect dependency theory is fully compatible with a realist perspective. Both hold that some states have considerable capacity for autonomous action; others very little. This has in turn led some writers to ascribe a special significance to what they term the *problem of the weak state*. It is this weakness, they argue, that makes Latin American and other Third World states peripheral (Migdal 1988). However the fact that a state has a considerable amount of autonomy does not necessarily mean that it is strong, nor does the fact that it lacks autonomy mean that it is weak. Military dictatorship has not proved a magic tool to extricate a country from dependency.

Inevitably there have been vigorous debates within the dependency school about how rigid the structural constraints on capitalist development actually are. In one extreme form, world systems analysis (Wallerstein 1974; cf. Skocpol 1977) seems to imply an unchangeable world capitalist order in which a country's economic role is determined by its position within it. On the other hand, Marxist dependency theorists have consistently suggested that a country can break out of its condition of dependency through a socialist revolution which would overturn capitalism itself. However the details of how this might be achieved in a world dominated by the advanced capitalist states have not been very specific.

An important sub-theme in dependency writing has been the *development of underdevelopment*, associated particularly with the work of André Gunder Frank (1966, 1967, 1969). Frank argues that developed countries were formerly 'undeveloped' but they have never been 'underdeveloped'. Underdevelopment for Frank is a process of structural distortion. The economies of underdeveloped countries have been partially developed, but in a way that enhances their economic value, not to their own citizens, but to the advanced industrialised countries. In this process, he, in common with other dependency writers, ascribes a special role to two agencies. The first is what he terms the 'lumpenbourgeoisie', otherwise generally known as the *national bourgeoisie* or for the Maoists, the 'comprador' bourgeoisie, from the Portuguese word for a merchant (Frank 1970, 1974). The ruling classes in peripheral states actively encourage the outflow of wealth from their countries by using their 'control of state power to protect the interests of multinational capital' (Kitching 1982). It is they who find their economic interests best served by an alliance with the second agency, the foreign corporation, to exploit their own fellow-countryfolk.

In more recent times, the consolidation of capitalism, most writers agree, has taken the form of the development of the multi-national corporation (MNC). In fact, 'multi-national' is in some respects a misnomer, as all corporations have to be registered somewhere. Hence the term 'trans-national corporation (TNC)' is often preferred. But in other senses it is very appropriate. MNCs are very large and they operate in many different countries at the same time. Their size gives them more economic power than the economies of many small states. Their scope enables them to play one small state off against another in their own self-interest. Their personnel come from many different countries, and hence are encouraged to replace their individual loyalties with one, their loyalty to the company they serve. The main purpose of that company is to make money for its shareholders in the advanced industrial countries; it will therefore demand the free movement of capital in order to repatriate its profits, which therefore pass out of the control of the country in which it operates without necessarily benefiting it in any direct way. Lastly they have the ability to arrange their business operations in such a way as to minimise their tax liabilities and in this process the smaller countries, who lack the resources adequately to police their activities, are the losers. The classic example is the case of 'the Seven Sisters', a nickname popularised by Enrico Mattei for the seven great oil majors which control the production and sale of oil throughout the world (Sampson 1980; see more particularly Philip 1982).

Such flexibility as there is in this view is to be found in the fact that, in common with other structuralist writers, the dependency theorists attach particular importance to certain *conjunctures* of events. At these periods of time, there exist certain possibilities for change which are not present otherwise. One such conjuncture is the moment of insertion of a country's economy into the global capitalist system. A second needs to occur at the point at which a country commences to industrialise; hence the process of capital formation within Latin America has been intensively studied (Anglade and Fortín 1985), within which key points in the development of labour movements and their relationship to political parties have been identified (Collier and Collier 1991). A third occurs at the point at which the state seeks to move from *import substitution indus-trialisation*, the mere production of goods for the internal market, to an export-led economy. However such conjunctures do not necessarily occur at the right time.

It has been argued, for example, that an important conjuncture occurred between the last stages of the Second World War and the full onset of the Cold War. During this time, a substantial demo-cratisation occurred, accompanied by a relatively high level of middle-class and working-class participation in politics and the emergence of workers' movements and left-wing political parties.

However only one of the regimes which emerged at the beginning of the period survived into the 1950s (Bethell and Roxborough 1992). Again in the early 1980s a group of military developmentalist regimes, which had been engaged in trying to restructure their economies regardless of their impact on the well-being of the people whose support they had initially elicited, crumbled in the face of the growing evidence of massive economic failure (O'Brien and Cammack 1985, pp. 184ff.)

There have been many critiques of the dependency thesis, both from Latin America and from the United States. Some of these critiques have been positive from sympathetic writers such as Bath and James (1976) and Caporaso (1978). Others have been negative in differing degrees. From the Marxist standpoint, the theory is suspect because of its failure to ascribe primacy to class forces (Oxaal *et al.* 1975). From the viewpoint of non-Marxists, the main objection is its failure to explain why some countries seem able to develop and others do not. These differences are generally explained by dependency writers as being caused by a process of *dependent development* (Cardoso 1973). Dependency, they say, does not result in the complete absence of all forms of development; rather the only forms of development that do occur are those that serve the interests of the international capitalist system. If an MNC wishes to transfer production to a Third World state to take advantage of cheap labour or other incentives, it will do so. The point is that the development will not be under the control of the host country, which remains dependent on decisions made in Wall Street. There is much truth in this argument. However it does not explain how Japan came to develop beyond this point to become the second-largest economy in the world, and the fact that Brazil is now already in tenth place suggests that it, too, has already already escaped from the limitations of history and geography.

There is also much truth in the second main line of criticism, which is that the explanations offered by dependency writers tend to remain at a very high level of generality and both the validity and the relevance of the historical examples which are used to support the dependency argument can be criticised (Smith 1978; Chilcote 1974, 1978; Chilcote and Edelstein 1974; Leys 1983). In this context it is interesting to note that Chile, whose elite prospered on the export of nitrates to Europe before the First World War, were at the same time able to resist all pressures to link themselves decisively into the world economic system by adopting the gold standard (Conoboy 1976).

A third line of criticism is that the theory assumes that the relationship between Latin America and the industrialised world is entirely negative. These criticisms are not, as is sometimes alleged, confined only to the United States – Ray (1973) criticises three major fallacies he identifies, and O'Brien (1973, 1975) argues that the dependency thesis is merely a new version of an old theme, the nationalist one that all the troubles of Latin America have been caused by foreigners. This view, he asserts, is not supported by the evidence: Latin Americans have taken an active role in creating their own problems.

However when Keohane and Nye (1973, 1977) argue that the real relationship is one of interdependence rather than dependency (cf. Morse 1969, 1970; Rosenau 1972), this argument clearly has its limits. The history of the 1980s suggests that a small and weak country like Honduras can exercise very little influence indeed on the United States. In fact, during the decade there was added to the overwhelming presence of the US fruit interests already mentioned, the continued presence of several tens of thousands of US troops, and the roads and air fields they built, and the money they spent, increased the dependence of the local population on the maintenance of this patron–client relationship (Lapper 1985, pp. 88–102). The only case in which a degree of genuine interdependence can be demonstrated is in the case of Mexico, where the cheap labour of Mexican immigrants has contributed markedly to US prosperity (Bilateral Commission 1989).

In addition, dependency is not just a matter of trade, but a matter of investment. With some important exceptions, of which Brazil is again the outstanding one, Latin American elites have not invested their wealth in their own countries. Hence in the international financial markets, it is the countries of the 'periphery' that borrow and those of the 'centre' that lend.

Relationship with world financial centres

When a country is unable to balance its income and expenditure out of taxation, it has to borrow to cover the deficit. A number of the newly independent Latin American states borrowed in this way to cover the immediate expenses of government. As new states, they received very bad terms, and most soon went into default. Mexico, for example, in 1825, from a loan of 16 million pesos received only 5.4 million pesos, the balance being withheld as a security against future interest payments at rates reflecting the riskiness of the operation (Cumberland 1968, p. 14). This established an ominous precedent for the future.

Towards the end of the nineteenth century, however, existing debts had been settled or written off, and an increasing amount of European and US money flowed into Latin America to finance productive enterprises, such as railways, tramways, docks and harbours, mines, factories etc. At the same time, in South America and Mexico, political stability superseded long periods of uncertainty and turbulence. The result was that the credit rating of some countries improved substantially. In the early years of the twentieth century the governments of Argentina, Uruguay and Mexico could borrow on the world financial markets at 4 per cent. In 1931 first Bolivia and then Peru defaulted on their debts, through a combination of depressed commodity prices, the general economic depression and the unwise way in which the debts had been invested, and Peru was to remain in default until 1946 (Carey 1964, pp. 79–80). However the military coup in Argentina in 1930 occurred before the Argentine economy had been affected by the crisis, and in Mexico, which had reached a settlement with its creditors in 1923, following the turmoil of the Mexican Revolution, the main fear was that US banks in the southern states would collapse, taking a great deal of Mexican funds with them (Slarke 1985).

The situation was very different in Central America, where a combination of political and economic rivalry both within Europe and between Europe and the United States enabled weak governments to default with impunity. As late as 1913 Britain threatened to use military force to make the government of Guatemala pay up (Calvert 1971). However US intervention, the Roosevelt Corollary and the financial stabilisation plans of the mid-1920s gave investors assurances that their money would be reasonably safe, and the dictatorships of the 1930s brought an illusion of stability.

At the end of the Second World War as part of the Bretton Woods system set up by the United Nations in 1944 new financial organisations were created on a multilateral basis. The most important of these were the International Monetary Fund (IMF) and the International Bank for Reconstruction and Development (IBRD, usually called The World Bank).

The main purpose of the International Monetary Fund is to provide short-term finance to correct temporary balance of payments problems and so to enable the world financial system to function smoothly. Countries that are members of the Fund pay into it according to quotas. The bulk of the quotas are held by the advanced industrial countries, some 20 per cent by the United States alone. Any member may borrow up to 25 per cent of its quota on demand and a further 25 per cent on an assurance that it will make reasonable efforts to correct its balance of payments problems, which amounts to the same thing. Beyond that it can only only borrow on condition that it presents the Fund with a stabilisation programme embodying a set of performance indicators that it will meet at fixed times. It is the standard set of conditions that is usually recommended by IMF staff that is often referred to as 'IMF conditionality'.

The problems that follow stem basically from the fact that the IMF was set up to maintain the equilibrium of the world financial system, not with the specific brief of promoting economic development in the less-developed countries (LDCs). IMF terms, such as a devaluation of the currency and sharp cuts in public expenditure are designed to limit domestic consumption in the short term. This in turn is intended to cut back on imports and to promote exports. However though Latin American Finance Ministers sometimes secretly welcome this, as it enables them to blame the IMF for decisions they have neither the political strength nor the political skill to take themselves, the social effects are still serious, since they are not cushioned by the welfare systems that exist in the advanced industrialised countries.

In practice many Latin American states, notably Brazil, have failed regularly to meet most of their IMF targets, though they have often put on a very good show of doing so. The Fund has often claimed that countries which seek its assistance as soon as possible will benefit from doing so. Hence in 1982 Brazil was praised for seeking IMF support as soon as its economic difficulties were obvious, while Mexico was criticised for not doing so. And it is of course the case that this was precisely what the Fund was set up to do. However few countries like going to the Fund – Britain did so in 1976 and the Conservatives have never stopped criticising the decision ever since. They do tend to try to put off the evil hour as long as possible, and as in Mexico's case end up with a great deal of short-term debt at inordinately high rates of interest which they then have in a year or two to ask their private creditors of the so-called 'Paris Club' to reschedule.

Few have tried to reject the terms altogether, and those that have done so soon find that private lending institutions use IMF approval as their benchmark for deciding whether or not to grant loans. It is no longer possible, as before 1914, to go from one country to another, knowing that if the French, say, are not prepared to offer a loan, the Germans will do so. When in 1985 the incoming Aprista government of Alan García in Peru refused to accept IMF terms and stated instead its intention of limiting debt repayments to 10 per cent of annual export earnings it was not long before it realised its mistake. Within a short period Peru found that it was totally unable to find any other source to supply the funds it wanted to borrow, and that its ultimate economic plight was much worse than if it had accepted IMF terms in the first place.

The World Bank has quite a different function. It does exist to lend funds for the construction of specific development projects, many of which are in Third World states. Criticism of the World Bank centres on the fact that it has tended to support very large-scale projects, in particular, huge dams and irrigation projects, which are increasingly seen as having very serious environmental consequences, and that as late as 1985 it did so without regard to the wider environmental impact of such programmes. On the other hand, if it does not do so, private finance is often available to pick up the bill, and even if it costs more, the country concerned knows that at least it will not be required to take too much heed of environmental considerations. In recent years, therefore, the World Bank has not only reviewed its position and argued that environmental considerations are good economics (World Bank 1993), but has instituted a new fund, the Global Environment Facility (GEF), 'to maximise experience in addressing – through promising approaches and technologies – the problems of biodiversity loss, global warming, and the pollution of international waters'. By June 1992 23 per cent of the resources so far allocated under the GEF were in Latin America and the Caribbean (World Bank 1992).

The Inter-American Development Bank (IDB), which was established in 1959 after Vice-President Nixon's ill-fated tour of Latin America, was designed to perform a very similar function specifically for countries in the inter-American system. Set up with the fear of

Communism very much in mind, it has from its inception been much more ready to extend 'soft' loans for less spectacular but socially useful projects such as low-cost housing, education and land reform.

There followed two substantial waves of investment in Latin America generally. The first was in the period 1950–65, when the developmentalists were in power in many Latin American states and the United States economy was strong. The second came after the first 'oil shock' of 1973, when the price of crude oil multiplied fivefold in a year, sending shock-waves through the world markets. The huge increase in the flow of 'petrodollars' to oil producing states created the need for new places to invest the revenue, and Brazil and Mexico were high up the list of places that looked attractive. Banks both in Europe and in the United States competed fiercely to offer loans at competitive rates. When in August 1983 Mexico announced that it would be unable to meet the repayments on its national debt, it proved to be only the beginning of what was speedily termed 'the debt crisis'.

The debt crisis

The debt crisis, it should be said, was not just a debt crisis, and it was by no means a problem peculiar to Latin America. It had three main aspects.

The first problem was the sheer *size* of the debts. In gross terms Mexico and Brazil led the world. Both owed their creditors more than $100 billion. By the end of 1988 the gross debt of Brazil had risen to over $115 billion, and Mexico had fallen slightly owing to the strenuous efforts of the de la Madrid administration to impose austerity.

The second problem was that *inability to pay* did not result simply from the original circumstances of the loans or the way in which they were used but also from economic policy choices in the United States. By the beginning of the 1980s rising inflation in the United States had led to a sharp rise in interest rates, which were to remain at historically very high levels throughout the decade. The result was that the very rapid accumulation of interest consistently outpaced the effects of stabilisation programmes.

The third problem was that the debts of the 1970s and 1980s had been incurred in haste from a variety of private lenders. The *role of the banks* in responding to the crisis was crucial, therefore.

Unfortunately under the law of their own countries those banks were required to remain solvent. Indeed US banks who had to demonstrate solvency at the end of every ninety days soon found themselves in the bizarre position of lending money to their creditors for a day or so at the end of each quarter so that they could temporarily pay them back. Faced by irate shareholders who had become habituated to the absurd idea that dividend payments would continue to rise indefinitely, they had to bargain toughly for every cent, and certainly could not easily admit that any part of their outstanding loans might not be repaid, for fear of a stampede. In the end it was the decision of the major US player, Citicorp, to cut its exposure and mark down the book value of its debt in 1987 that paved the way for the safer disengagement of other banks. Within months it had led to the Brazilian government signing an agreement with its creditor banks (2 November 1988) to make a $3 billion payment of interest on account – the largest interest payment ever made. In 1988 by a variety of methods Brazil reduced its indebtedness by some $6 billion, while Mexico retired $5 billion of public-sector and more than $10 billion of private-sector debt (*Keesing's* 1989 37017).

In the 1990s the Brady Plan, so called because it was originally put forward by President Bush's Secretary of the Treasury, enabled Latin American countries to implement, by agreement, more ambitious plans not just of debt management but of debt reduction. Several countries – Mexico, Brazil, Venezuela – have taken advantage of these schemes to reduce their capital debt by converting it into various forms of equity.

Different problems . . .

The interesting thing about the debt crisis is that although the problems and the local reaction to them were much the same in each case (Thorp and Whitehead 1987), the way in which the debts had been incurred in the first place was significantly different. In each case, however, the state of the world oil market was a significant factor.

It was a particular irony that Mexico should have been the country where the crisis first showed itself (Martínez Cantú 1992), for long before 1975 Mexico was a substantial oil producer, producing far more than its growing needs. At one time it had been the second-largest oil exporting nation in the world, but that came to an end in the early 1920s, and after the nationalisation of oil in 1938 for a long time production levels remained fairly static. However in the early 1970s deep drilling techniques revealed that under the existing oil fields of the Isthmus, extending far offshore from the coast of the Yucatán peninsula and southwards under northern Belize and Guatemala, there was an even larger untapped reservoir yet to be exploited.

The leap in oil prices in 1973 proved a temptation too great for the government of Luis Echeverría (1970–76) to resist. Concerned that the long period of growth that Mexico had enjoyed since 1940 was being outpaced by the rising expectations of a rapidly growing population, and heedless of the effect of inflation, the fateful decision was taken in 1975 to embark on a programme of state-led economic development, to be funded by borrowing in anticipation of vastly increased oil revenues. The tripling of the country's known reserves at a stroke seemed adequate guarantee to the banks and they lent heavily. The result was that by 1979 the government of Gustavo López Portillo (1976–82) had increased debt to record levels but there were still no returns from the new field. In fact the US Department of Energy had refused to pay Mexico's asking price for gas in 1978, and as a result plans to draw additional revenue from that source had to be scaled back after huge expenditure on pipelines had already been incurred.

Mexico had of course not been alone, even in Latin America, in seeing oil as the means by which major economic advance could be achieved painlessly, with considerable political benefits for the political incumbents. The government of Carlos Andrés Pérez in Venezuela, Latin America's largest oil producer and its only full member of the Organization of Petroleum Exporting Countries (OPEC), had used its windfall profits from the first 'oil shock' to embark on the nationalisation of both the petroleum and the electricity industries. Now it had to meet the costs, and, what was worse, to do so on falling production levels. However the other really big discoveries of the decade, by an unfortunate coincidence, were made not by the OPEC states, but by the United States on the Alaskan North Slope and by the United Kingdom and Norway in the North Sea. Assisted by the economic recession generated by free-market policies, there was a decisive downturn in oil prices in 1982 and it was this that led directly to Mexico's default.

Argentina was not an oil exporter, but its state-owned oil industry produced enough from its fields in Mendoza and Tierra del Fuego to satisfy domestic demand, and at the beginning of the 1980s it was regarded as 97 per cent self-sufficient in energy resources. However from 1976 to 1983 it was ruled by an authoritarian military government which regarded itself as being engaged in a full-scale war against communism and internal subversion. It was this military government that added more than $20 billion to Argentina's national debt in less than six years. Some of the causes were obvious. Enormous sums were spent on high-technology weapons, many of which in the event proved to be quite useless. There was heavy spending on prestige capital projects, much of which was wasted, as when the Buenos Aires to La Plata highway was abandoned. An overvalued currency during the heyday of Finance Minister Dr José Martínez de Hoz, the so-called *plata dulce* ('easy money') period, resulted in massive losses. Free movement of currency then meant capital flight set in at the first sign of difficulties. of funds overseas. However, though detailed investigation by the authorities after 1983 disclosed what had happened to some $10 billion, the rest, amounting to another $10 billion, has never been recovered, and if anyone in Argentina knows where it has gone, they are not saying.

Brazil's problems stemmed from the fact that, despite many years of exploration, by the end of the 1970s it still had virtually no oil of its own, and was having to pay hugely inflated prices for every imported litre. The military government from 1964 onwards gave top priority to economic growth, which it saw as a matter of national security. Its free-enterprise model for development was dependent on encouraging heavy investment from overseas. When the authorities found that lack of oil had left their country vulnerable to the oil shocks of 1970s, therefore, they had very little alternative but to grit their teeth and try to bluff their way through. But with the general recession in foreign trade in the early 1980s, it was by no means easy to find anything that would enable the country to export enough even to pay the dollar cost of its oil imports. Brazil's oil imports during the 1980s amounted to US $58.5 billion. Its net foreign debt in the same period increased by $38.6 billion.

The government sought a variety of remedies for its predicament. They encouraged the opening up of the Amazon basin to cultivation, encouraged crop diversification, eliminated non-tariff barriers to economic growth, such as trade unions and labour legislation. They stepped up the search for oil, which eventually bore fruit, and embarked on an innovative energy substitution programme, based on the distillation of alcohol from sugar cane. In 1991 dollars, Brazil invested $10.7 billion in the *proalcool* programme. By the end of 1991 it had saved the equivalent of $20.3 billion on oil imports and was meeting over half its needs for fuel with ethanol (Brasil: AIAA/ Sopral 1992). Though it was by then also meeting a substantial proportion of its petroleum needs from offshore production, the fact that all the costs of the ethanol programme could be met in national currency gave it a considerable advantage which the government argued was not adequately represented by comparison litre for litre with the spot price of oil FOB Rotterdam (Governo do Brasil 1992b).

The enormous size of the Brazilian economy also gave it leverage with its creditors; a kind of reverse influence. There were genuine fears in Wall Street that if Brazil and Mexico went into total default, the world economy would collapse. (As events in October 1987 were later to prove, it was quite possible for it to collapse without this happening.) Hence Brazil's insistence that the banks must be prepared to negotiate, which enabled the Brazilian government to make rescheduling of its debts virtually an annual event. One Finance Minister went so far as to state openly that the banks knew perfectly well that they would never get their capital back, it was just a question of arguing about the interest. Fear was publicly expressed that if Brazil and Mexico were not humoured they might lead the formation of a 'debtors' cartel' that could dictate terms to the lenders. The banks were however soon to realise two things: that they need not be frightened of this possibility, as each government hoped to do a deal before its neighbour, and, furthermore, that they could insulate themselves from the catastrophic scenario by putting pressure on the smaller countries and trading off losses against their home market. And with time their position became stronger, not weaker. The Brazilian moratorium of 1987–88, for example, was believed to have cost the $1.5 billion alone of much-needed capital and with government absorbing 80 per cent of the credit available there was less and less available for private enterprise.

By the end of the 1980s Colombia, with a total external debt of only $17 billion at end-88, was the only Latin American country that had not defaulted and indeed had not had to reschedule its debts. There were a variety of reasons for this. First of all, Colombia had benefited from demand stability for its main export, very high quality coffee, and by good fortune, its oil production was expanding and not contracting like that of Venezuela. The relative diversity of the Colombian economy and a large subsistence sector in the rural hinterland also acted to insulate it from external forces. Last but not least, the Colombian oligarchy had been able despite strong challenges from the left, to maintain political stability over a long period and so very conservative fiscal policies. One drug baron, Pablo Escobar, is said to have offered to pay off the entire national debt if he was allowed in from the cold. However the offer was refused.

In the Commonwealth Caribbean new states found themselves, by contrast, in a very weak position. Jamaica's dependence on sugar has declined but it still needs a world-wide market for bauxite. Bauxite, the raw material from which aluminium is extracted, is a very common mineral (it takes its name from Les Baux in France). Aluminium processing is an expensive process, requiring a huge input of electrical power. Few LDCs have the necessary generating capacity to make it practicable to produce finished aluminium ingots; they therefore have to depend purely on the revenue from a low-value, high-bulk export. Hence Jamaica shares with many other countries a dependence on large foreign corporations, whose inter-connection with local political interests gives them an important say in internal politics.

In his first period in office (1972–80), Michael Manley spent heavily in order to try to extricate his country from what he saw as this condition of dependence (Manley 1979). In international affairs he aligned himself with Cuba, which sent construction brigades to help build public housing and other projects, and at the same time incurred the deep suspicion and hostility of the United States. When Manley's government ran into economic difficulties, he initially ignored them. Then when he could get no more credit and had failed the performance indicators required by the IMF, he took the high-risk strategy of defying it. In the resulting economic crisis, his government was voted out of office and succeeded by a right-wing government committed to free-market solutions (Thomas 1987, pp. 146–97).

The new Prime Minister, Edward Seaga, did not let the grass grow under his feet. He was the first foreign leader to visit President Reagan when he entered the White House in 1981 and in return received extensive aid from the United States government. Despite this, he would probably not have survived the next election had

Manley, with uncharacteristic ineptness, not decided that his party should boycott the elections. US generosity stopped, however, when Jamaica was hit by a hurricane (Payne 1989). In 1989 Manley was decisively returned to power, but this time took a much more cautious path.

Given the previous history of Jamaica, it was hardly surprising that when in 1979 a coup placed Maurice Bishop and his left-wing New Jewel Movement in power in Grenada, Washington should similarly have been suspicious of its overtures towards the Soviet Union and Eastern Europe. When the Reagan administration took office, Grenada's Provisional Revolutionary Government (PRG) was cut off from further sources of credit controlled or strongly influenced by the United States (Searle 1983). Help, though in very limited quantities, was however given by the European Community (EC) for the PRG's most important project, the construction of a new airport at Point Salines (Thorndike 1985, p. 124–7), and, unlike Jamaica, Grenada had not had time to run up a large foreign debt. After the events of 1983, which ended in US military intervention and the installation of a conventional government led by Nicholas Braithwaite, US aid was resumed on a large scale, with the obvious intention of turning Grenada into a showcase for capitalism (Thorndike 1985, p. 174; see also Ferguson 1990b). The government relies on tourism and on the large number of remittances by Grenadians living overseas to balance the trade deficit which has persisted since 1979. Total external debt stood at $80.9 million in 1987 – a large sum for an island with a population of only some 100,000 inhabitants.

. . . *similar consequences*

For Latin America the 1980s were a decade in which development stood still. Though it is not a wholly fair comparison, it is sobering to realise that more was paid out by Latin American states in interest during the decade than came in as new investment (though in fact this is hardly surprising when the interest on the original loan was not being paid). Coupled with the impact of IMF conditionality on restructuring programmes designed to cut inflation by severe restraint on public expenditure, much too little was spent on the social needs of the poor, with a direct result in terms of a general decline in living standards for Latin Americans at a time when

Europe, the United States and Japan were all enjoying boom years.

Five problems needed solution and none was solved. Most conspicuous to visitors (though not to Latin American elites who had got used to ignoring them) was the poor housing of families and the rapid spread of shanty towns, some of which, as in the case of Lima, Peru, could clearly be seen spreading across the hills above the city. This, however, was in turn only the visible evidence of urban poverty, stemming from very high rates of un- and underemployment, which in Mexico, for example, meant that something of the order of 40 per cent of the population in 1989 was either un- or underemployed. Malnutrition was an inevitable consequence. Though low, life expectancy generally continued to rise during the decade, lagged far behind developed states, and – more surprisingly – well behind some Third World ones with no greater economic resources, such as Sri Lanka. A clear division had emerged between the richer states of the Southern Cone, where people tended to die of the diseases of the developed world such as heart attack and cancer, and the poorer Andean and Central American states, where the main causes of death were the diseases of poverty, notably gastroenteritis, which by the end of the 1980s was in virtually all cases easily treatable by simple and inexpensive rehydration therapy. Inadequate education and illiteracy in countries of rapid population growth meant in addition that their peoples suffered from their inability to make use of the facilities of a democratic society. However it was noteworthy that literacy rates in the Commonwealth Caribbean were very high by almost all Latin American standards, suggesting that low literacy standards had a cultural rather than a purely economic explanation.

A major factor common to all the traditional Latin American states (except Mexico and Costa Rica) plus Suriname and Guyana (but not Belize and the rest of Commonwealth Caribbean) was the dominant role of the armed forces in government. The strengthening of the military hold on the continent in response to the Cold War and the Cuban Revolution of 1959 had very widespread social consequences, leading as it did to repression of legitimate political activity, concentration of wealth and landownership, corrupt and inefficient government and overcentralisation of decision making.

Military ascendancy was a major factor in governments, adopting, and compelling their citizens to adopt, the neo-liberal model of economic development promoted by the United States. Again the effects of the neo-liberal model of economic development favoured by these authoritarian governments in the 1970s and early 1980s fell mainly on the poorer sectors of society. In both Brazil and Chile statistics show clearly a widening of the gap between rich and poor; the poor simply failed to benefit significantly from any of the economic growth that took place around them. The sharp contrast between rich and poor, as in Colombia, where beggars accost visitors to the celebrated Museo d'Oro (Museum of Gold), produced the greatest social unrest, in turn leading for new pressures for military involvement in politics.

One obvious way for individuals to try to escape this trap is to migrate to another, wealthier, country in search of work. For two generations the pressure along the 2,000-km frontier between Mexico and the United States has been acute. During the Second World War the need for additional labour in the United States was so great that a special programme, the *bracero* programme, was set up to organise the importation of Mexican labour. In the immediate postwar period, migrants continued to arrive, as in those days Latin Americans were exempt from the quota system imposed in 1924 on immigrants from other parts of the world. It was not until 1965 that this exemption was ended by the Johnson administration, with the obvious result that there was a sudden jump in the number of illegal immigrants, popularly known as 'wetbacks'. Since most of these were what were later termed 'economic migrants', that is, those who, like the original settlers in the American colonies, had gone there is search of a better life, they were not in the main able to claim the protection of international law accorded to those fleeing their countries in fear of persecution.

However when the Nixon administration tried to clamp down on wetbacks, cross-border trade came to a halt and in less than two weeks the measures were rescinded. In their place an elaborate network of wire, lights, electronic detection devices and mobile patrols was set up to track down 'illegals' when they had already crossed the frontier. The use of technology to patrol the frontier, however, proved to have its limitations: vehicular traffic remained the real weak point and organised crime syndicates were able to facilitate successful illegal entry. Once in the United States, and clear of the border area, the illegal immigrant was able to lose him/herself in the informal sector of the US economy. This was a very unsatisfactory state of affairs. Under the Bush administration an amnesty was offered but at the same time it became an offence knowingly to give employment to an illegal immigrant. There is no evidence that this law is effectively enforced.

The case of so-called 'economic migrants' points up the limitations of the economic liberal model of free trade as a motor of economic growth. On a purely economic argument, it should have been not only maintained but encouraged. In this case, it was political objections that were successful in imposing new obstacles to a stream of migration that had been economically convenient for both Mexico and the United States. The fruit growers of California were able to exploit cheap labour when it was not needed in Mexico; the Mexican government was relieved of the pressure to provide work for the migrants and the balance of payments benefited from the substantial remittances they sent back to their families.

An additional political benefit was that political refugees from the conflicts in Central America did not stay in Mexico, but instead became a problem for the United States. Since Mexicans considered US intervention in Central America to be largely responsible for the problem in the first place, they did not feel very sympathetic for their difficulties, if any. Central Americans soon learnt that it was better not to claim to be refugees fleeing from persecution, since as the United States was supporting the governments that were persecuting them that meant they were in great danger of being labelled 'Communists' and returned to the vengeance of militant right-wing governments. Far better to say they were Mexicans, and simply to be put in a bus for a free passage back to Tijuana and the chance to try again the next day.

Relationship with creditor countries

Inevitably during the so-called debt crisis, Latin American relationships with creditor countries suffered. Prime hostility was, naturally enough, directed towards the United States. The Reagan administration's high-interest policy was seen as directly causing misery. Its strategy of armed intervention in Grenada and Central America fuelled suspicion of its imperialist motives. The inept handling of President Bush's intervention in Panama created extreme hostility throughout the continent, and as part of series of extraordinary claims of the rights of US courts to extra-territorial jurisdiction in support of its anti-drugs campaign it fuelled nationalist resentment. Lastly the US eradication programme hit at poor Andean farmers, and created anti-Americanism even in Bolivia, which previously was one of the few countries in the region in which it was virtually unknown.

In Europe, West Germany, which was not seen as having a colonial past, was favoured (Pearce 1982). Here traditional links with immigrants helped. Immigrant links also favoured Italy; in Argentina the Italian banks are not seen as foreign while British banks, irrationally enough, are. The British habit of conducting diplomacy and finance separately did not help create goodwill anywhere. It was clear that Mrs Thatcher, with her unthinking enthusiasm for the virtues of the free market, failed to see that there was a relationship between Latin American financial problems and British foreign policy. Even before the outbreak of the Falklands Crisis, she had created quite unnecessary hostility in usually sympathetic Brazil, by an incautious remark that it was up to 'these countries' to pay their debts, and this 'hands-off' attitude was explicitly shared by Mr Lawson (cf. Ferguson and Pearce 1988, pp. 21, 23). Conversely French diplomacy saw the close relationship between finance and foreign policy and exploited it with great success, and other European countries were quick to move into the space which Britain had vacated (Durán 1985).

Cuba, too, was able to make skilful use of its advocacy of a rival model of development to gain friends and influence people in other Latin American countries. Isolated from trade with the rest of the then OAS countries in 1964, by 1968 it had been successful in breaking the embargo. Interestingly enough, though the country that first resumed trade relations was Chile, it was not under the Marxist government of President Allende (1970–73), but under the Christian Democratic government of President Frei (1964–70). Against strong US resistance, however, it was still several years before the 1964 embargo was finally rescinded. The United States insisted that any lifting of the embargo be conditional on two conditions, neither of them economic. Cuba must unambiguously renounce the export of revolution to the rest of the region, and it must give up its military dependence on the Soviet Union. At the Fifteenth Meeting of Foreign Ministers of the OAS in November 1974, twelve Latin American states voted in favour of lifting the embargo, two less than the necessary two-thirds majority. The United States chose to abstain rather than vote against, and at the Sixteenth Meeting in July 1975 voted for a similar resolution, which was carried by 16 votes to 3 with 2 abstentions.

The Cuban alternative

Though it is the political role of Communist Cuba in world affairs since 1961 that has attracted the headlines, Cuba's influence as an alternative model for economic development is easily under-estimated. Each of its first three stages reflects current economic thinking about the possible route open to a small Third World state in escaping from a position of economic dependency on the capitalist West.

Cuba had traditionally been dependent on a single crop, sugar, which was exported to the United States. In December 1960 President Eisenhower set the Cuban sugar quota for the first quarter of 1961 at zero. The Soviet Union, China and the other socialist states had already agreed to take some four million tons in 1961. With this assurance, in the first stage (1960–65) of their economic programme, all major industries were nationalised. The provisional government placed strong emphasis on Soviet-style industrialisation and Ernesto 'Che' Guevara was appointed head of INRA, the agency created for this purpose. It was not, however, a success. Cuba lacked both the basic raw materials needed and significant energy resources with which to process them. The nationalisation of the oil refineries, which had brought about the breakdown of relations with the United States, left Cuba heavily dependent on the import of oil from the Soviet Union, though in fact, because of the international nature of the oil industry, the oil came from Venezuela and the oil from the Soviet Union went to Franco's Spain.

In the second stage (1965–70), Cuba sought to break out of the thrall of dependency by increasing its self-sufficiency on the Chinese model. The strict system of rationing imposed in the early years was maintained, and the system of state control was extended to small businesses as well as large ones. However priority was now given to the countryside, since the first objective was to make the country self-sufficient in food. Unfortunately this clashed with the need to earn foreign exchange, something that was becoming increasingly difficult as a result of the US-sponsored boycott of Cuba products. Hence in 1968 the decision was taken to go back to the plantations and increase the production of sugar to hitherto unheard-of levels. This process culminated in the celebrated 'Harvest of the Ten Millions' in 1970. For months the whole effort of the regime went into reaching the target figure, and schools and factories fell silent while all available labour was directed into the fields. Even the Soviet Ambassador and the crews of Soviet vessels in port were encouraged to lend their fraternal support in the cane harvest. The irony was that a record harvest was achieved: 8.3 million tons, substantially more than had ever been harvested before. But because the target figure had been even higher, it was seen as a failure, and strong Soviet pressure was exerted to abandon the Maoist experiment and to adopt their systems of economic planning instead (Mesa-Lago 1981).

Castro had become adept in manipulating his relationship with the Soviet Union. Hence though there was an immediate return to economic incentives, and the militia was dissolved and replaced by worker brigades, it was not until 1975 that the First Congress of the Cuban Communist Party was finally held and an East European-style Constitution adopted. Its spectacular intervention in Angola in the same year distracted attention from the extent to which Cuba had now been locked into the East European economic system, COMECON, later CMEA, as a primary producer of tropical products. The wheel had come full circle and Cuba was again dependent on a single external market.

Ironically, this new stability was increasingly disturbed by events in the Soviet Union itself. In 1985–86 there was a brief flirtation again with the concept of the 'New Man' motivated by moral rather than economic incentives. However Castro soon became very concerned about the potential political effects of the Gorbachev notions of *perestroika* and *glasnost*, returning abruptly to a Stalinist line. The collapse of the Soviet Union in 1991 made plain what had already become probable, that Cuba would either have to come to terms with the United States or it would have to survive on its own very limited resources.

The New International Economic Order (NIEO)

At UNCTAD III (United Nations Conference on Trade and Development) at Santiago, Chile, President Luis Echeverría Alvarez of

Mexico proposed a Charter of Economic Rights and Duties of States, which was later accepted by the Third World majority on the UN General Assembly (Anell and Nygren 1980; Lozoya and Estevez 1980). The main planks of what was to become known as the New International Economic Order (NIEO) were: fair terms of trade for developing countries, a new world currency linked to the price of primary materials and the abolition of IMF conditionality as a requirement for new loans. Though it was carried by 120 votes to 6 with 10 abstentions, it was in fact totally opposed by the US and the advanced industrialised countries and so was effectively a dead letter (Thomas 1985, p. 65–6).

The Mexicans voiced the feelings of most Third World governments when they criticised the prevailing terms of trade. They saw themselves as being condemned by the existing system to export large quantities of primary products at low prices, and to import the manufactured goods they needed at very high ones. Hence the demand for an arrangement that would link producer prices to changes in the price of manufactured goods.

It was an irony that before the Charter could be adopted, the oil-rich states of the Middle East had already chosen to short-circuit the negotiations by unilaterally raising the price of crude oil. However this was not to be an omen of better things for the future for the Third World, many of whose countries, lacking the essential mineral, found that their balance of payments had been abruptly tipped against them. The difference was so great that the promise of Mexico and Venezuela to supply their smaller Caribbean neighbours with oil at preferential rates did little to counter it.

Commodity agreements

In fact, in the 1980s the terms of trade for developing countries of Latin America actually worsened as one by one the international commodity agreements or cartels that had been created since the 1930s to stabilise the prices of various primary products on the world market were systematically demolished. After the first 'oil shock' of 1973, many Third World states came to believe that their control of primary products could be used to dictate terms of trade to the developed countries of North America and Europe, and tried to establish new producer cartels for individual products.

A number of such arrangements already existed for agricultural produce, covering such products as cocoa, coffee and sugar (Gordon-Ashworth 1984). These producer cartels did have some effect in slowing down the swings of the economic cycle. However none of these products was absolutely essential to human life, let alone industrial development, and their perishable nature made them difficult substances to stockpile. In addition the creation of such cartels had a significant effect on the internal politics of the countries concerned. To regulate production, it was necessary not only for each country involved to abide by external quotas, but also to have an organisation sufficiently powerful to impose internal quotas on its own growers. In the case of a country like Colombia this gave the coffee growers' organisation, the Cafetera, great power in internal politics, which in turn reinforced the influence of the major growers of the Department of Antioquia (Espejo 1981). However though the International Coffee Agreement signed in 1962 did achieve a measure of stability, it was allowed to expire in 1973. The Central American countries in particular found that they could not afford to limit their production because the imposition of internal quotas generated politicial effects that they were not able to handle.

The coffee agreement was not an exceptional case. The power to impose quotas inevitably tended to squeeze the production of smaller growers and to extend the power of larger growers, thus strengthening the power of the state and of the corporatist organisations it had set up. The Brazilian sugar industry was a classic case (Gordon-Ashworth 1978). What cartelisation did not do was to increase greatly the power of the producing countries in face of the determination of buyers to keep the price down, and in fact it tended to prolong the very dependence on a few primary products that had got their countries into trading difficulties in the first place.

Even weaker was the position of the banana producers. A Union of Banana Exporting Countries (UPEB) was formed in the mid-1970s to try to put pressure on the giant corporations controlling the world banana trade. However joint action, seriously weakened when Ecuador refused to join the Caribbean states, collapsed altogether when Honduras agreed not to levy the additional 25 US cents per box UPEB was demanding. Shortly afterwards, the suicide of Eli Black, head of United Brands, revealed that a high official, easily identifiable as the President of Honduras, had been paid $500,000 shortly before the climb-down. Within a week of the news reaching Honduras the President was overthrown by a military coup, but of course it was too late to do anything to improve the lot of the banana growers (see also Lapper 1985, p. 68).

The outlook for industrially significant minerals looked much better. Until the collapse of the International Tin Agreement in 1985, which brought the end of deep-mined tin production in Bolivia, it had seemed to be a model of its kind. The first Agreement had been signed as long ago as 1931 by Malaya, Nigeria, the Netherlands East Indies and Bolivia to meet the crisis of the Great Depression. In the immediate postwar period the demand for tin had been strong and the United States opposed any cutback in production, so when in 1956 a new ITA was signed and the ITC reformed there was considerable enthuiasm for the idea of bringing the consumer countries into the agreement. However when in 1976 the United States joined the organisation on the occasion of the signing of the Fifth Agreement it soon became clear that it would use its very considerable voting weight and the sales of its stockpile to keep the ceiling price down, while the Council's buffer stocks would be used to manage the floor. The new Reagan administration in the US refused to take part in the Sixth Agreement signed in 1982, and Bolivia, by now desperate for foreign exchange, had little choice but to do likewise, but as the highest-cost producer it was to lose most when the agreement finally collapsed in 1985 (Crabtree 1987, p. 43). Meanwhile, however, in 1967 the Intergovernmental Council of Copper Exporting Countries (CPIC) had been established. Chile and Peru were members, together with Zambia, Zaire and Indonesia. As in the case of tin, the end of the Vietnam War was followed by a sharp reduction in the demand for copper and a heavy fall in its price to near-uneconomic levels, which the new organisation proved to be able to do little to alleviate. Indeed the 1973 coup in Chile gave that country a government which refused to take part in such collective measures as for example Peru might have been willing to contemplate. Despite this, there is no evidence that US support for the coup stemmed from economic motives rather than fear of communism (Sigmund 1993). In 1974 an International Bauxite Association was set up, consisting of seven countries controlling 63 per cent of world production. Three of the seven were Guyana, Jamaica and Suriname. In the same year agreement was reached at New Delhi to establish a similar organisation for iron ore, and in 1975 the Association of Iron Ore Exporting Countries (AIEC) came into existence. It comprised 13 countries controlling some 70 per cent of production, with Venezuela a major participant. However both proved to have fatal weaknesses. Both aluminium and iron are very widely distributed on the world's surface, and are to be found in the industrialised as well as the less industrialised countries. Stockpiling is difficult on account of the bulk of the ore and so costly. It was therefore very easy for the major companies to switch production to less troublesome areas.

The basic problem was that primary producing countries are not in general in a strong bargaining position. There are too many commodities. Very few of them are absolutely essential and most of these, like oil itself, are available from a number of different suppliers in different parts of the world, each of whom has a strong interest in bargaining separately for special favours. In fact, after their experience with OPEC in the 1970s, the advanced industrialised countries were able to develop substantial new sources of petroleum production, outside OPEC control. They also found that they could save a great deal on their fuel bills by using fuel less wastefully, and that their electorates were prepared to support them. Ironically, the recession created by the impact of the oil shock actually made things easier for them, as it reduced their consumption at the same time.

In Latin America the country that gained least was Ecuador, where a new military government had foolishly set out to renegotiate the terms under which the oil companies operated, before first ensuring that they had brought enough wells in, or that adequate transport facilities existed to handle the volume of output already planned, let alone what might be envisaged for the future. In any case Ecuador was in a poor negotiating position: its production costs were high, the quality of the oil produced was not exceptionally good, and, because all the oil would have to be shipped via Panama, transport costs were not competitive with the Middle East, let alone Mexico or Venezuela. As a result, all further exploration simply ceased and no applications were received for fresh licences (Philip 1982; Jaeger Calderón 1988).

The Lomé Conventions

The Lomé Conventions offer the best example of the only alternative to cartelisation so far on offer: an agreement between producer and consumer states, in this case between the European Community (EC) and some of the world's poorest countries. The French Overseas

Departments (Départements d'Outre Mer: DOM) and the remaining British and Dutch dependencies (OCT) in the region are for many purposes treated as part of the Community and enjoy the highest levels of aid. Relations between the Community and the countries of the Caribbean area which were formerly colonies of Britain, France or the Netherlands are governed by the *Lomé Convention*, the latest in a series of multilateral trade agreements granting such countries (and some others) preferential trade rights.

The system grew haphazardly out of the existing system of preferences given by France and Britain to their former colonies in Africa, the Caribbean and the Pacific (hence commonly referred to for short as the ACP countries). Ninety per cent of the countries benefiting from the Lomé regime were in Africa South of the Sahara (SSA) and were very poor. The Caribbean states were usually very small, island states.

The First Lomé Convention (Lomé I) was signed at Lomé, Togo on February 1975 and came into effect on 1 April 1976. It replaced the earlier Yaoundé Convention between the EC and its former colonial territories and the Arusha Declaration, and has since been replaced three times. The centrepiece of Lomé I was a system of stabilisation of export prices, commonly called 'Stabex', under which intervention by the European Community (EC) to keep up producer prices in a number of specified commodities could be triggered by two 'thresholds': the degree of dependence of the country on the commodity in question, set at 2.5 per cent in the case of island states, and a fall of export earnings by 2.5 per cent compared with a benchmark figure consisting of the average export earnings over the previous four years. Commodities covered included bananas, coffee, cocoa and cotton. Under Lomé II (effective 1981), Minex (Sysmin), a similar but more complex facility covering minerals such as bauxite, copper and tin, was added (Thomas 1987, pp. 80–4).

Separate from the Convention there are three Protocols which give Caribbean countries preferential access to the European market: the Sugar Protocol, which guarantees access for agreed quantities of tropical sugar at the European intervention at a price determined by the Community – which has however historically been substantially above the world price; the Banana Protocol, which benefits principally the Windward Islands by maintaining a price above that accorded to Latin American bananas, whose access to Britain and France (though not to Germany) is thereby restricted; and the Rum

Protocol, which is of limited value to both sides owing to the low demand for the product in Europe. A considerable amount of Community aid is also channelled into the Caribbean states, in general in proportion to their need, and both trade and aid policies appear in the main to have been beneficial from the point of view of the recipients, though this is not to say that they do not continue to share a sense of dependency and powerlessness (Payne and Sutton 1984).

Needless to say, there have been many criticisms of the Lomé system. Some of these arise from the fact that it is not a genuine bilateral agreement but a concession by rich nations to poor ones. However it is certainly better than no concession at all, and for the countries that qualify for it it opens the way to other benefits, such as loans at preferential interest rates outside the IMF system. A second set of complaints arise from the complexity of the conditions, but many of these arise from the fact that the budget allocated to the system is too low to make the stabilisation measures fully effective. A third set comes from countries outside the system. Since 1975 the importation to the EC of many products from the Latin American states has been strictly regulated, and in the case of fresh chilled or frozen beef, formerly a major export of Argentina and Uruguay, prohibited altogether. However investment by Community countries in the region has become increasingly important, and with the accession of Spain and Portugal to the Community the Latin American states hoped in their turn to obtain a better trade deal. In 1987 both Haiti and the Dominican Republic applied for admission to the Lomé Convention, but were admitted in 1989 only after it had been made clear that the decision would not be a precedent for other countries of the region.

Lomé III, signed in December 1984, came into effect on 1 March 1985, and Lomé IV, signed in December 1989, came into effect in March 1990 and unlike its predecessors will run for ten years. Of the 68 African, Caribbean and Pacific countries parties to Lomé IV, fifteen are in the Caribbean: Antigua & Barbuda, Bahamas, Barbados, Belize, Dominica, The Dominican Republic, Grenada, Guyana, Haiti, Jamaica, St Kitts-Nevis, St Lucia, St Vincent and the Grenadines, Suriname and Trinidad and Tobago. The latest agreement increases the proportion of grants to loans in Community aid, though falling far short of that demanded by the ACP countries. It also contains important provisions on sustainable development, support for ACP economies in face of short-term economic fluctuations, action on debt imbalances, detailed provisions for technical co-operation, additional concessions on the access of ACP products to the Community, extension of certain provisions of the convention to minerals and metals in addition to agricultural products, simplification of the rules of origin and improvements to Stabex.

Conclusion

Latin American economic conditions play a major part in determining both the capabilities for and limitations on action in the international arena. Awareness of these led Latin American writers to play a major role in developing the theory of dependency and Latin American politicians to call for the creation of a New International Economic Order. The debt crisis of 1983 demonstrated just how far they had failed to change the terms of trade or the conditions of borrowing imposed by the IMF and other lending agencies.

Since that time most of them have resorted to a policy of 'muddling through' which has in the course of time resulted in serious measures being taken both for debt rescheduling and, more recently, for debt reduction. Cartelisation proved an unsuccessful strategy for forcing a change in the terms of trade, and the Lomé system, though in many respects beneficial for the very small island states, and a possible model for the future, is costly and unlikely to be capable of much further extension at present. One area of promise, however, has recently emerged. South America has the richest and most diverse flora in the world, and its biological diversity, if it can be sustainably exploited for the benefit of its peoples, could not only bring them measurable increases in wealth and comfort, but increased bargaining power against the rich countries of the north. Sadly, given the power of the international drug companies, the benefits are likely to go instead to the rich countries of the north.

Chapter Five

The intellectual environment

The intellectual climate

According to Raymond Aron, there are two sets of human actors in international relations: soldiers and politicians. As has already been noted, it is characteristic of Latin American states that their destinies have been set by a small intellectual elite. A degree of internationalism in such an elite is natural in these circumstances, particularly when the fashionable models, in politics as in everything else, have been sought from Europe and/or the United States.

Though the civilian members of this elite are citizens of a specific country, they are at home almost anywhere in the continent. They read the same books and discuss the same problems. For those who have dared to criticise conditions in their own countries, exile has been a rite of passage of their political development. Hence the concept of Latin America and its relations to the outside world has been shaped by the distinctive role of Hispanic culture, but always in competition with new influences from outside. In the past century this concept of modernity has taken the form of 'liberal internationalism' derived from modern Europe and North America (Calvert and Calvert 1989).

As for the military members, they too live in an environment which is in some senses more open to the outside world than it is to what is going on in their own countries. A significant number of junior officers attend military academies in other Latin American countries, or in the United States. Those selected for accelerated promotion may look forward to a term as an aide-de-camp to the President, or to a period as a military attaché. Since the Second World War those who aspire to the top of the pyramid of promotion will have studied at specialised academies such as the Escola Superior de Guerra (ESG) of Brazil or the Centro de Altos Estudios Militares

(CAEM) of Peru, where they will be trained to grapple with the fundamental social and political problems of their respective countries according to the prevailing view of how these should be tackled. At this level the armed forces call upon the services of leading civilian academics, so that the civilian and military traditions have become even more closely interlinked.

Both civilian and military links between the ruling elites of Argentina and Peru played a significant part in the diplomacy of the Falklands Crisis and the South Atlantic war that followed. Within days of the Argentine occupation of the islands, the Peruvian Minister of Defence, General Luis Cisneros, who was a soldier in a civilian Cabinet, had expressed strong support for the Argentine position. The general's enthusiasm for his cadet days at the Argentine Military Academy was such, in fact, that among his fellow officers he had acquired the nickname of 'El gaucho'. The civilians, too, had their own links with Argentina. The Prime Minister of Peru, Manuel Ulloa, had spent a great deal of the 1970s in exile in Buenos Aires, where he had spent much of his time in nightclubs in the company of Dr Costa Méndez (*Lima Times*, 7 May 1982; *The Times*, 5 May 1982). In such circumstances, it was hardly surprising that when the so-called 'Peruvian peace plan' was proposed, requiring Britain to withdraw its forces from the South Atlantic, it was initially not taken very seriously in London.

Latin American political thought

Political thought as it emerged in the Early National Period was characterised by the great nineteenth-century struggle between liberalism and conservatism.

Conservativism was authoritarian, pro-clerical, centralising, 'hispanic', nationalist, state centred. It derived from the Catholic tradition, in which the idea of universal Christendom was made manifest in the structure of a hierarchical Church and a monarchical state backed by divine authority. In the tradition of the mediaeval theologians, notably Aquinas, conservatives accepted the notion that law was of divine origin, though interpreted through the application of reason. They also found useful the related Thomist beliefs of the right to resist tyranny and the doctrine of the just war (Aquinas 1959), as in their eyes liberalism was both subversive and heretical and acceptance of liberal rule was scarcely to be tolerated.

Liberalism, as a term, originated in Spain, but was soon adopted both in Europe and the Americas to refer to those who believed in the principles of the French Revolution. After 1815 it developed under the influence of the Frenchman Henri de Saint-Simon, the British philosophers David Hume, Jeremy Bentham and John Stuart Mill and the British economists Adam Smith and David Ricardo. It stood for constitutionalism and limited government and was anti-clerical, federalist, 'European' and laissez-faire. However the modern tendency to use 'liberalism' to refer solely to laissez-faire economics would give a very misleading impression of the vital importance of political liberalism in shaping a Latin America which was republican, secular and, to a limited degree, constitutional.

In Argentina, the main influence on the creation of modern republic was that of the 'Generation of '37' and in particular of Juan Bautista Alberdi (1810–1884). Published at the fall of Juan Manuel de Rosas in 1852, his *Bases and points of departure for the political organization of the Argentine Republic* (Alberdi 1980) is still seen as the main influence on the 1853 Constitution. Still in use today, this is now the oldest working Constitution in Latin America. Otherwise the American states have generally characterised by two problems: *faction constitutionalism* and *governmental instability*. Faction constitutionalism refers to the inability or unwillingness of liberals and conservatives to agree on a common set of governing principles. The governmental instability that resulted was manifested in a series of military rebellions, coups and pronunciamientos, interspersed with brief periods of civilian rule.

Until 1930 Argentina was fortunate in avoiding both of these problems, which were inadvertently to help create so many new states. A possible reason for the success of the Constitution was that Alberdi pragmatically accepted that the 'possible' republic would precede the 'true' republic. Though he admired the United States, especially in its policy of remaining aloof from Europe, he saw that the main difference between it and Argentina was in the extent to which it had successfully increased its population through immigration. His maxim, 'To govern is to populate', simply stated in short form the basic truth that the new republic of the Southern Cone, in common with most Latin American states, faced the urgent task of *filling the national territory*.

The view that this was to be done by the colonisation of the barbarous rural hinterland and imposing on it the norms and culture of the Europeanised urban elite, was exemplified in Argentina by Domingo Faustino Sarmiento (1811–88). His *Facundo* (1845), in the guise of the denunciation of a provincial caudillo from La Rioja, was in fact a coded attack on the all-pervasive dictatorship of Juan Manuel de Rosas (1785–1877). Following the fall of Rosas and the constitutional creation of modern Argentina, Sarmiento became President of the Republic 1868–74, and as such fulfilled his role as the great educator.

In Chile the 'Generation of '42' led by Andrés Bello (1781–1865), first Rector of the University of Chile, offered a model of a stable 'European' state to be obtained through the creation of an educated elite. It was not until well on in the latter half of the nineteenth century that the most advanced Latin American states followed in the footsteps of the United States in adopting the principle of free, univeral public education, and to this day there is nowhere in the Spanish-speaking states (except possibly in Cuba) where it has been effectively implemented. Otherwise, as noted earlier, only the most advanced states come near the standards of literacy of former British territories in the Caribbean such as Jamaica, Barbados and Trinidad.

Conflict was largely internal in large South American states, though political ideas did to some extent condition attitudes towards neighbouring states. For example, Rosas in Argentina was deeply hostile towards Artigas of Uruguay, not only because he had challenged his own authority but because he saw him as a disintegrating, disuniting force and was concerned at the potential danger he represented to Buenos Aires. The broad concept of citizenship inherited from the colonial period continued into the new and uncertain age of competing states and indeed never really disappeared. There were attempts by new consitutional arrangements to maintain the last vestiges of colonial unity in New Granada (or at least in Gran Colombia – modern Venezuela and Colombia including Panama) and to create a Peru-Bolivian Confederation, both unsuccessful. Federalism was adopted in Argentina and later also in Brazil, as a successful compromise between centre and periphery.

In Central America, the conflict between Liberals and Conservatives resulted in 1828–39 in the secession of Guatemala under a conservative caudillo and the disruption of the Republic. There was a tendency, however, for the rest of the century to form alignments on the old basis, with a series of attempts to reunify the old Central

America. Two factors have been very noticeable. On the one hand, a succession of leaders have sought to take advantage of and even to create a climate favourable to reunification by intervening in neighbouring countries. On the other, countries have sought to protect themselves against such pressure by seeking allies elsewhere. In 1881 Justo Rufino Barrios of Guatemala was killed in battle in El Salvador leading the Liberal forces for re-unification. Later the conquest and incorporation of the Atlantic coast by a nominally Liberal dictator, José Santos Zelaya (President 1895–1909), created a Nicaragua that had never existed in colonial times, and gave it new regional ambitions. Neighbouring Honduras had failed to develop economically until the growth in the early twentieth century of an 'enclave economy' of banana plantations in the north around La Ceiba and San Pedro Sula. Hence Honduran Liberals, led by their caudillo Policarpo Bonilla, were only too keen to obtain Zelaya's support against their own Conservatives. Eventually US opposition to Zelaya on the grounds that he was assisting Liberal insurgents in Honduras and other neighbouring countries led to his overthrow at the hands of a Conservative revolt backed by the US.

The last serious attempt to reunify Central America came in 1920–21 after the fall of the 22-year dictatorship of Manuel Estrada Cabrera in Guatemala. On that occasion agreement had been reached between all the states when a military coup in Guatemala itself broke the accord. In the next few years US hegemony over the Central American states was consolidated.

The impact of positivism, 1850–1910

With the spread of secularism, the Church was no longer a unifying force. After 1850 there was in its place a growing influence of the positivism of the French thinker Auguste Comte (1798–1857). For Comte, the positive philosophy meant that full understanding of society could be attained by the scientific method. To him we owe the term sociology, the study of human society. For Comte the understanding of human society represented the third and highest state of understanding. In his later years, however, it became for his followers a quasi-religion, claiming evolution towards sociological consciousness, under the motto: 'Love, order and progress'.

Positivism had a much more long-lasting impact on Latin America than on Europe. It had a special impact in Brazil, where the national motto, 'Order and Progress' ('love' may have been intended to be on the far side of the globe), reflects the ascendancy of positivist ideas of progress in the armed forces after their experience of the Paraguayan War (1865–70). Ruy Barbosa (1849–1923), the civilian leader of the republican movement, which gained its first objective with the abolition of slavery in 1888 and its second with the proclamation of the Republic on 15 November 1889, became Minister of Finance in the provisional government, which within months was in serious economic crisis. He was to have a continuing influence on both domestic and foreign policy up to and including the creation of the League of Nations in 1919. However, the Constitution of a federal republic which he presented to the consitutent assembly and which took effect in 1891 was modelled on that of the United States and, dominated as it was by the army, fell far short of the powerful centralised government which he and his colleagues had originally intended.

The self-confidence of the Republic showed its strongest manifestation in the work of Euclydes da Cunha (1868–1909), the author of epic *Os Sertões* (1902) reflecting consciously the Portuguese tradition with its theme of the navigation of and settlement in the interior 'sea'. There was at this stage little consideration for the wishes of the local inhabitants, and as recently as the military governments of 1964–85 Amazonia was openly regarded as simply a vast interior space to be exploited in the name of economic progress. At one stage, large tracts were given away by the government, free of charge, to anyone who undertook to construct the necessary communications with the outside world. Meanwhile the construction of the Transamazonica signalled to Brazil's neighbours a new desire to project power out towards and even across their borders.

In Chile the new ideas led to a relatively gradual transition from conservatism to liberalism, culminating in the election of Domingo Santa María, who had been foreign minister during the War of the Pacific, to the presidency in 1881. But in defeated Peru, with militarism in temporary abeyance, there was a strong nationalist resurgence which found in the positivism of Manuel González Prada and his contemporaries the logical justification for a programme of industrial development.

Positivism was no less central to the creation of the Porfiriato in Mexico in the last three decades of the nineteenth century. It replaced

Catholicism as the philosophical basis of the new secular education system created by the liberals after the Reform (1857). The Reform in turn led to the Three Years War between liberals and conservatives (1857–60) and then to the conservative-backed French intervention, which placed a Habsburg, Maxmilian of Austria-Hungary, on the revived imperial throne (1863–67). Benito Juárez (1806–72), who received the title of Benemérito de las Américas from the government of Colombia for his resistance to the invader, paradoxically led the liberal government that destroyed the traditional collective basis of property and first consciously began to open up Mexico to foreign investment. In 1868 he appointed Gabino Barreda, who had studied in France under Comte himself, as the first head of the Escuela Nacional Preparatoria.

However the Europeanising tendencies of liberal thought were much accentuated under Porfírio Díaz (1830–1915; President 1877–80, 1884–1911). Under the so-called 'científicos', who attained power in the last two decades of his rule, led by José Yves Limantour, Secretary of Finance 1892–1911, positivism became the guide and justification of their ascendancy. They believed that under authoritarian rule they could use their superior knowledge of society to promote steady economic growth, through the opening up of Mexico's economy to foreign capital. This, in turn, would ensure the continued stability of the existing order. In fact, however, their analysis was deeply flawed, since it took no account of the uneven distribution of wealth and the envy generated by a rich elite in a poor country.

Two critics of the Porfiriato drew attention to the impoverished state of the impoverished mass of Mexico's indigenous population. The first was Andrés Molina Enríquez (1866–1940), author of *Los grandes problemas nacionales* (1909). The second was Francisco Indalecio Madero (1873–1913). A spiritualist, a vegetarian and a homeopathic healer, this youthful scion of a rich northern family published in 1908 a manifesto in favour of constitutional government, entitled *La sucesión presidencial en 1910* (Madero 1911). Instead he became the leader of the national revolt against Díaz (20 November 1910). Chosen as President in 1911 after the fall of the dictatorship, he was killed 'trying to escape' after Huerta's coup in February 1913, and became for millions who fought for the Constitutionalist cause the 'Apostle of the Revolution'.

Like Madero, the key leaders of the Revolution, 1910–40, were educated under Porfiriato and so retained many positivist attitudes. The 'Líder máximo' of the Revolution, Plutarco Elias Calles (1877–1941), who served as President 1924–28, had been an inspector of schools under the Porfiriato, among other things, and must therefore have been regarded as ideologically sound. However, the fragmentation of Mexico during the early phase of the revolution stems from the fact that, with the rejection of the positivist model, there was really no one doctrine that united the revolutionary forces. They followed leaders rather than ideas. After 1920, socialist ideas were increasingly invoked as the basis of the authority those leaders sought to wield. These became part of the impact of the Revolution abroad, carried not by academic texts on political philosophy, but by the novel of the Mexican Revolution and the visual message of the art of Rivera, Orozco and Siquieros. However, the growing ascendancy of the United States to the north meant that its political influence on its immediate neighbours was very limited.

The impact of socialism, 1900–80

Given the overwhelmingly rural character of much of Latin America, socialism was seen as having little relevance until well into the twentieth century. Its rapid spread throughout the continent however illustrates clearly the permeability of frontiers to new ideas, especially in the age of the railroad, the steamship and the printing press. Ultimately, after the Second World War concern about the influence of Marxism was to lead to major confrontation between left and right in the age of the Cold War, and this took the form of international as well as domestic conflict – in fact, by the 1980s the difference between the two was hard to establish.

1900–20

Lack of industry meant weak workers' movements. At the beginning of the century the main influence, from Spain and Italy as from the United States, was that of anarchism and anarcho-syndicalism. In Argentina, such ideas, brought by the *golondrinas*, migratory workers who worked in the Southern hemisphere during the northern winter, attracted new attention after the financial crisis of 1890. In 1891 they influenced the foundation of the Unión Cívica

Radical (1891) by Leandro N. Alem (d. 1896) and his nephew Hipólito Yrigoyen (d. 1933), who became Argentina's first popularly elected President in 1916 and served 1916–22 and 1928–30.

In Mexico, the 1906 strike at the Cananea copper mine and the Rio Blanco textile workers' strike in the following year are seen as precursors of the Revolution to come. Both were put down by forces brought in from the United States, where the use of private armies to suppress strikes was already well established. The liberal movement of Ricardo Flores Magón in Lower California 1910–11, on the other hand, was also linked to the International Workers of the World (IWW) in Los Angeles, California. The first workers' central, the Casa de Obrero Mundial formed in Mexico City in 1913, was suppressed by Huerta, but its members formed the core of the 'Red Batallions' who fought for the constitutionalists under Obregón in 1915–16. In return they received formal guarantees of workers' rights in the Constitution of 1917, though it was not until the 1930s that they were actually implemented.

In some countries socialist ideas were adopted by the dominant liberals, notably in Colombia under the reforming governments of Alfonso López Pumarejo (1934–38, 1942–45) and in Cuba under the short-lived provisional government headed by Ramón Grau San Martín (1933–34).

The 1930s elsewhere saw the emergence of various charismatic leaders, such as Luis Sánchez Cerro in Peru and Germán Busch in Bolivia, who did not base their power on working-class movements but appealed to workers and peasants with programmes of social action which can be loosely grouped as 'populist'.

Populism is a term which defies definition. The term arises from its use by the People's Party, which achieved a modest electoral success in the United States of the early 1890s, but was eventually swallowed up in the Democratic Party (Hicks 1961). Slightly earlier, a group of intellectuals in Russia had called themselves the *narodniki* – a term usually translated as 'populist'. Both believed in the proposition that 'virtue resides in the simple people, who are the overwhelming majority, and in their collective traditions' (Wiles 1969, p. 166). There the possibilities of agreement end. No one now describes themselves as a 'populist'.

In the Latin American context, a populist movement has been defined as:

A political movement which enjoys the support of the mass of the working class and/or peasantry, but which does not result from the autonomous organizational power of either of these two sectors. It is also supported by non-working class sectors upholding an anti-status quo ideology. (di Tella 1965)

For Conniff the most important characteristics of Latin American populism are that it is 'urban, multiclass, electoral, expansive, "popular," and led by charismatic figures' (Conniff 1982, p. 13). However, as di Tella implies, it is stretching matters to suggest that populism is urban rather than rural, and in practice the term has come to refer to any movement characterised by three things:

1 An assertion that the people are always right.
2 A broad, non-ideological coalition of support.
3 A charismatic leader, often lacking any specific ideological commitment.

Dix has argued that there are two distinct forms of populism: authoritarian and democratic. For him, the authoritarian form is characterised by leadership from the military, the upper middle class, landowners and industry, support from a 'disposable mass' of urban/unskilled workers, and a short-term, diffuse, nationalist, status-quo-oriented ideological base. The democratic form is led by professionals and intellectuals, its support comes from organised labour and/or peasants, and its ideological base is more concrete and reformist, with its nationalism more articulate (Dix 1985). Yet again, in practice, populist movements are both democratic and authoritarian in differing degrees. Canovan derives from actual examples a typology of no less than seven types of populism, but these, too, are 'ideal types', and actual movements may well overlap more than one of her categories (Canovan 1981, p. 13). The importance of them is precisely how clearly they demonstrate that the main characteristic of populism is its *fluidity*. It was this that provided a vehicle for the mobilisation of masses in support of their governments, thus bringing a volatile and unformed public opinion into play in helping shape (or, more particularly, limit) the range of options in international relations.

1920–40

Populism is characteristic of Latin America precisely because the lack of industry precluded the emergence of strong workers' movements that could have formed a basis for socialism. The spread of specifically internationalist forms of socialism after 1920 became in itself an important factor in international relations, though it was not to have its full effect until well after 1945. Already in the 1920s travellers entering Paraguay were held up for fear that they might be communist agents. The result was that in the 1930s in many states power fell into the hands of old-style military caudillos determined, as they saw it, to resist all foreign influences. This was particularly the case in the Caribbean area. Leaders such as Fulgencio Batista y Zaldívar in Cuba, Rafael Leonidas Trujillo Molina in the Dominican Republic, Maximiliano Hernández Martínez in El Salvador, Jorge Ubico in Guatemala, Stenio Vincent in Haiti, Tiburcio Carias Andino in Honduras and Anastasio Somoza García in Nicaragua, made use however of a combination of populist techniques and old-fashioned physical force to dominate their countries whether or not they formally held the office of President. It was during this period that the foundations were laid for the re-emergence of the political right after the Second World War (Rachum 1993).

The Mexican Revolution had already been under way for seven years and the Constitution of 1917 had already been promulgated before the fall of the tsar, let alone the Bolshevik Revolution. However the spread of Marxism among the relatively tiny Latin American elite was relatively rapid. In 1920, when the Comintern was formed, the recently created Argentine Communist Party was a founder member.

In Chile the success of the new doctrine owed much to the influence of one man, Luis Emilio Recabarren (1876–1924), who was the founder of both the Chilean Socialist and the Chilean Communist Parties. When constitutional government broke down in the mid-1920s, Carlos Ibáñez became a virtual dictator, but the impact of the Great Depression brought down his government. In the unstable period of shifting governments, a short-lived *Socialist Republic* was proclaimed by a group of junior officers headed by Air Force Colonel Marmaduque Grove.

The outbreak of the Spanish Civil War in 1936 had an even more profound impact. Between 1937 and 1941 an elected *Popular Front* government held power in Chile. However the growing influence of the communists in the government led to the withdrawal of the socialists, led by Marmaduque Grove, and to the disintegration of the front. Despite the election of an anti-communist president, Juan

Antonio Ríos, in the election that followed, during the rest of the Second World War the communists were represented in government. It was not until 1948, with the onset of the Cold War, that they were abruptly expelled and the Communist Party banned. However their political support was simply transferred to the rival Socialist Party, which in the course of the next few years was to find itself well to the 'left' of the old Communist Party.

As so often, developments in Chile found echoes in both Bolivia and Peru, though in a very different political context they produced vey different results. After Bolivia's forces had been trounced by those of Paraguay in the Chaco War (1932–38), a bloodless coup led to the deposition in 1936 of the civilian president by a military junta led by the chief of staff of the army, Col. David Toro. Supported by the veterans of the Chaco, Toro was soon elected President and announced a far-reaching programme of socialist reform, only to be ousted in a military coup by the populist right-winger Germán Busch in the following year. Though he himself was unsuccessful, Toro's example was to contribute to the success of the populist Gualberto Villaroel (1943–46) and ultimately to that of the Revolution of 1952.

Since the rise of the USSR to superpower status after the Second World War, it has been easy to forget that in the 1920s Mexico too was an avowedly socialist country. Under Plutarco Elias Calles (1877–1941) in 1924 the Mexican Labour Party founded by Luis Morones, leader of the Confederación Regional de Obreros Mexicanos (CROM), was the main basis for government support. In 1929 the Partido Nacional Revolucionario (PNR) was founded as an official party to direct the continuing revolutionary transformation of society. After a brief interregnum, in 1934 Lázaro Cárdenas (1895–1970) became President. He initiated a far-reaching agrarian reform, based on the collective *ejido*, or co-operative farm, and, while implementing the new Labour Code passed in 1933, replaced the CROM by a new centralist trade union organization, the communist-backed Confederación General de Trabajadores (CGT), led by the Leninist and anti-imperialist Vicente Lombardo Toledano (1894–1969). In 1937 Cárdenas allowed Trotsky to take refuge in Mexico. Though he was murdered by a Stalinist agent in 1940, this confirmed Mexico's status as a 'revolutionary' country. After the fall of the Spanish Republic in 1939, a great many Spanish refugees also went to Mexico.

1940–80

The Mexicans were very sensitive about outside interference in their affairs. The first Soviet ambassador to Mexico, Alexandra Kollontai, was soon replaced by Stalin with a less diplomatic successor. Diplomatic relations were broken off by the Mexican Government in 1929 and not restored until 1942, by which time Mexico, like the USSR, had entered the war. Meanwhile, on the other hand, Mexico, by nationalising all foreign-owned oil companies, both British and American, had proclaimed its economic independence (18 March 1938).

Other prominent early Marxists included José Manuel Fortuny in Guatemala under Arbenz (1950–54); Blas Roca Calderio (d. 1987) in Cuba, who despite having openly supported Batista (President 1940–44, 1952–59), made his peace with the new regime and lived to serve it as Vice-President of the Council of State and as President of the National Assembly of Peoples Power; and, less probably, Rómulo Betancourt (b. 1908) in his early years as a student leader in Venezuela. Later in exile Betancourt was to found his own party, Acción Democrática (AD), and to return to lead Venezuela's new civilian regime as President 1959–64.

In the 1960s, just as its popularity dramatically increased throughout Latin America, Marxism was divided, both by the schism between the USSR and China and, more importantly, by the aftermath of the 1959 *Cuban Revolution* led by Fidel Castro Ruz (b. 1926). However, the Cuban Revolution had a dramatic impact on international relations in two ways:

1   The belief that revolution could be achieved voluntarily, through guerrilla warfare, encouraged many groups in a large arc from the State of Guerrero in Mexico to north-east Brazil to try to do the same.
2   The Cuban government aligned itself with the USSR, leading to the belief in the United States that these movements formed part of a single strategy for world revolution.

In 1960, the Argentine Ernesto Guevara de la Serna, known as Che Guevara (1928–67), who had fought with distinction in the Cuban Revolutionary War, published *La guerra de guerrillas*. In this he advanced three propositions which were to become the basis for rural guerrilla movements throughout the region:

1 Popular forces can win a war against the army.
2 It is not necessary to wait until all conditions for making revolution exist; the insurrection can create them.
3 In underdeveloped America the countryside is the basic area for armed fighting.   (Guevara 1967, p. 2)

For a brief period it looked as if the Andes, in Castro's phrase, might become 'the Sierra Maestra of South America' (Gott 1970). By the Declarations of Havana, the Cuban government sought not only to inspire emulation in Latin America, but throughout the world (Government of Cuba 1962). However, instead a wave of military coups spread across Latin America, in reaction to what was perceived by the armed forces as the Cuban threat (Lieuwen 1964). In 1967 Guevara himself was captured and killed trying to lead a guerrilla movement against the Bolivian government of Col. René Barrientos. The subsequent publication of Guevara's diaries showed all too clearly the fundamental weakness of his position (Mercier Vega 1969). He and his Cubans were seen as bearded conquistadores; on the other hand, Barrientos, although he had seized power in a coup, was a military populist who was the first leader of his country to speak Quechua. In 1965 by sending troops into the tin mines he had already quelled the possibility of a successful left-wing revolt based on the formidable power of the tin miners and the Central Obrero Boliviano (COB) (Debray 1965).

The new impetus that the Cuban Revolution had given the revolutionary left was, however, still far from exhausted. From 1967 onwards small groups tried, as in other parts of the world, to wage 'urban guerrilla' campaigns (Oppenheimer 1970). Their spectacular tactic of kidnapping businessmen and ambassadors was aimed both at exerting pressure on their own countries through the international capitalist system, and at securing admissions of 'guilt' for the way in which that system worked (Jackson 1973). The immediate effect, however, was to bring about a strong reaction and the extension of military dictatorship, through the anti-guerrilla campaign of General Arana in Guatemala (1967), the intensification of repression by the Fifth Institutional Act in Brazil (1968), a right-wing coup in Bolivia (1971) and the 'soft coup' which brought Uruguay under military domination (1973).

There was one major exception. In 1968 a new military government seized power in Peru. Its strategy was, as its leader, General

Juan Velasco Alvarado put it, to seek a 'third way' between capitalism, which had failed, and communism, which would not work. However, in the context of the Americas, the wholesale nationalisation of the great estates and all major business enterprises, and the institution of a system of 'social property' for medium-sized and small enterprises, resembled the nearest thing that had been seen on the mainland to a controlled socialist revolution, which it resembled both in its idological coherence and its fondness for corporatist measures (Stepan 1978; Booth and Sorj 1983).

Two years later, in 1970, the leader of the Chilean socialists, Salvador Allende (1908–73), was elected president of Chile in a free election. Before he was overthrown in a savage coup in 1973 and replaced by a right-wing dictatorship under General Augusto Pinochet Ugarte, there had been a short-lived military socialist government in Bolivia in 1971 and, in 1972, Michael Manley (b. 1924) had been elected Prime Minister of Jamaica (1972–1980). Despite their very different backgrounds and styles, these 'constitutional' Marxists shared a common belief that the social problems of their countries stemmed from the nature of capitalism and were exacerbated by the neo-imperialism of the world financial order dominated by the United States.

By the mid-1970s Marxist revolutionaries seeking to overthrow the dictatorship of Anastasio Somoza Debayle in Nicaragua were divided into three groups, reflecting the contending views of the strategy to be followed. One group favoured a mass uprising, Russian style. A second, influenced by Mao Zedong and the Chinese, favoured a rural guerrilla movement and 'prolonged popular war (*guerra popular prolongada*: GPP). The third, the *terceristas*, led by Daniel Ortega Saavedra (b. 1944) favoured a pragmatic alliance with all other anti-Somoza groups, whether Marxist or not. It was under their leadership, and with the support of democratic Costa Rica and the populist military government of Panama, as well as of Cuba, that the Sandinista National Liberation Front (FSLN) led the coalition that deposed the younger Somoza and inaugurated the Nicaraguan Revolution of 1979, under the leadership, however, of a cross-party coalition and with a joint programme which they hoped that the United States would feel able to accept. In the same year, Maurice Bishop (1944–83) and the New Jewel Movement seized power in the Commonwealth Caribbean island of Grenada, openly proclaiming their support for the Soviet Union.

This was to be the high-water mark for the left in the Caribbean region. In 1980 Manley, whose government was in serious financial difficulties, was voted out of office. The following year President Reagan took office in the United States and ordered a clandestine campaign against the Sandinistas, which he and his followers persisted in regarding as a Marxist-Leninist movement controlled by Moscow through Cuba (Pastor 1987; see also Child 1986; Di Palma and Whitehead 1986; Best 1987). Under pressure from the United States, the PRG in Grenada splintered. Maurice Bishop was deposed and killed by a military coup in 1983, and this in turn formed the pretext for the US intervention in Grenada, which had been planned and practised for since 1981.

Indigenismo

In line with developments in the United States and elsewhere, recent thought has given increasing prominence to the role of the indigenous inhabitants of the Americas. Indigenismo is the name given to the political doctrine based on the primacy of the interests of the native Americans. Though it is no less relevant in, for example, Guatemala and Bolivia, its development in its present form owes most to Mexican and Peruvian writers and publicists. Its relevance to international relations stems from two facts. Firstly, it is the one major political tradition that, by definition, rejects the colonial boundaries which, admittedly in very much modified form, continue to exist between present-day states. Secondly, whereas in the 1920s and 1930s socialist ideas, written in Spanish, were accessible only to the literate elite, in the 1960s and 1970s, broadcast in Guaraní, Quechua or Quiché from the powerful transmitters of Radio Havana, they reached for the first time the poor and the dispossessed to whom they were primarily of interest.

In Mexico the very existence of the country is bound up with the conflict between Spaniard and Indian. In the Grito de Dolores (1810), the first leader of the Mexican independence movement, Miguel Hidalgo y Costilla, called on his parishioners to fight to reclaim the lands taken from them by the Conquest. However independence was actually achieved at the hands of a conservative movement seeking to retain conservative, Hispanic values in face of the liberal challenge from Europe. Hence Mexicans tended to accept the prevailing notions of a European superiority based on what later became known as 'Social Darwinism': the application to social life of the biological concept of the 'survival of the fittest'.

The career of Benito Juárez (1806–72), the great leader of the Reform and of Mexican resistance to the French, who was a pure-blooded Zapotec Indian from the State of Oaxaca, did not dispel these ideas and the dictatorship of the Zapotec Porfirio Díaz emphasised the Hispanic and not the Indian element in Mexican tradition. The reason was the influence of a new elite, who had found in French positivism the scientific certitude they yearned for as a substitute for the religious faith they had rejected. Their repeated references to 'science' as the basis of their authority was reflected in the derisory term, 'scientists' (*científicos*) applied to them by their political opponents.

At a higher intellectual level, the científicos used their belief in 'social Darwinism', the belief that progress resulted from successful struggle of one group against another, to promote the role of education in creating a better society. Justo Sierra (1848–1912), who gave a definitive voice to his ideas in 1903 in his *México y su evolución social*, was in 1910 to be responsible for the refounding of Mexico's National University. The humanism of Antonio Caso and his followers of the *Ateneo de la Juventud* was paralleled, too, by the work of Alfonso Caso to disentangle Mexico's complex archaeological past.

However, a cruder version of the same themes was much more widespread. Francisco Bulnes (1849–1924), a well-known journalistic apologist for the Porfiriato, who in 1904, in *El verdadero Juárez*, debunked the great leader of the Reform period, by contrast praising the achievements attributed to Porfirio Díaz, developed an idiosyncratic theory of race based on diet: the wheat-eaters, he believed, were destined to dominate the maize-eaters, who made up 90 per cent of the Mexican population. The only consolation was that both, he believed, were destined to dominate those who lived mainly on rice. There does seem to be some link between these theories and the new interest the Mexican government showed between 1892 and 1909 in strengthening their position in Central America. Unfortunately for them, after early successes in extending their southern frontier at the expense of Guatemala, their further expansion in this direction was to be checkmated by the interest of a more powerful rival, the United States.

The Mexican Revolution (1910–40) resulted in a mass

mobilisation of the peasantry. As a result, in the 1920s there was a revival of Náhuatl as a language and of interest in Mexico's archaeological and anthropological diversity. In official circles, this in turn gave rise to the doctrine of the three cultures: the view that Mexican culture is neither Hispanic, nor Indian, but a unique and powerful mixture of the two, with its own dynamic qualities.

In Peru, too, the majority of the population had been excluded from the political process by the Constitution of 1860, which made literacy (in Spanish) a requirement for voting. In fact it was not until the 1970s that the military government of 1968 made Quechua an official language, thus enabling a significant fraction of their population to address their rulers in their own language.

Manuel González Prada (1848–1918) was influenced not only by the positivism of Comte and the scepticism of Renan, but also by the racialism of Gumplowicz. However, as already noted, it was he who, after the disaster of the *War of the Pacific (1879–84)*, did most in intellectual circles to revive Peruvian nationalism. In his *Horas de lucha* (see González Prada 1985) he became the first Peruvian writer to draw attention to the competing cultural elements in the Peruvian tradition.

The most important figure in twentieth-century Peruvian political thought was unquestionably José Carlos Mariátegui (1895–1930). In 1919 he was converted to Marxism in Europe. Before his early death from tuberculosis, he had not only helped found the Peruvian Communist Party, but had published in 1926 his *Siete ensayos de interpretación de la realidad peruana* (Mariátegui 1955). In this work, he calls for Peru to return to the *line of pre-Conquest development*. Just as Marx himself believed that Russia could evolve into a socialist society on the basis of the primitive Russian commune, the *mir*, so Mariátegui saw the Inca *ayllu* as the basis of a distinctively Peruvian form of socialism, with a strongly anti-imperialist flavour.

Víctor Raúl Haya de la Torre (1895–1980) shared Mariátegui's anti-imperialist and pro-indigenista outlook, but not his Marxism. As a student leader, he was exiled by the Leguía dictatorship in 1923, and took refuge in Mexico, where he was strongly influenced by mexican indigenismo. In exile in 1924 he founded the Alianza Popular Revoluctionaria Americana (APRA), which was intended to be a continental movement to free what he termed 'Indoamerica' from foreign domination. In 1930 when he was able to return from exile, he formed in Peru the Peruvian Aprista Party (PAP). Since this was the only Aprista party ever officially formed, it was later simply called Apra, and the original significance of the title was lost.

The military government that had succeeded Leguía regarded Apra with the greatest suspicion. When in 1932 Apristas were implicated in a revolt at Trujillo, Apra was blamed and the revolt was savagely suppressed by the army. Thereafter, as long as Haya lived, the army ensured that he and his movement were denied any access to political power. In 1948 he took refuge in the Colombian Embassy after the coup led by General Odría. For six years he was a prisoner, being denied the traditional safe conduct into exile, and became so well established in his position that he showed a succession of new Colombian ambassadors round their own Embassy. At the fall of Odría he was released.

It was not long before it was clear that Haya's views had shifted sharply to the right. The old denunciations of imperialism were muted and he reached out for an alliance with the followers of the same man who had put him in prison. In the 1962 presidential election Haya won, but the army intervened again and in a short interregnum (1962–63) changed the rules to ensure that he could not be elected. Between 1968 and 1979 Peru was again under military government. In 1979, when he was already over eighty and in poor health, Haya was elected President of the Constituent Assembly that wrote the new Constitution. In 1980 he died. It was five more years before in 1985 Alan García became the first Aprista President of Peru.

Haya de la Torre was a charismatic speaker and a prolific writer. Two of his most important works, embodying his distinctive, earlier philosophy, are *A donde va indoamérica? (1935)* and *Y despues de la guerra qué? (1946)*. In them he combines well established Marxist ideas of revolution and social progress with his own distinctive notion of Indoamerica and what might be termed 'Social Einsteinism', the concept of *historical space-time (relativity)*, which gave a scientific veneer to his basic determination that Peru should pursue its own distinctive route to socialism (Alexander 1973).

In keeping with its continental ambitions, Apra had a maximum programme for the whole of Indoamerica as well as a minumum programme for Peru itself. The maximum programme has as its planks:

1   Action against Yankee imperialism.

2   Political unity of Latin America.
3   Nationalisation of land and industry.
4   Internationalisation of the Panama Canal.
5   Solidarity with all peoples.

(Kantor 1953)

The minimum programme for Peru itself was much more specific: the secret ballot, a proper statistical survey, decentralisation of power, judicial autonomy, honesty in public office, planning of the economy, formation of the Bureau of Indian Affairs, annulment of usurped titles and the expropriation of estates. By 1985 many of these aims had already been achieved, by the left-wing military government of Velasco Alvarado. Hence the return to civilian government was not universally welcomed. In 1980 a new revolutionary force emerged, the Maoist movement *Sendero Luminoso*, led by a former professor of philosophy, Abimael Guzmán Renoso (b. 1935), alias 'Presidente Gonzalo'. Its name, 'The shining path', is taken from a phrase of Mariátegui describing Marxism. Its tactics were extremely violent, rejecting all forms of collaboration. The conflict lasted for twelve years and cost some 23,000 lives. In September 1992, after President Fujimori had suspended constitutional government, Guzmán was arrested. Interestingly, he was not captured by the army but found by efficient police work in a 'safe house' in Lima. Following his arrest he was exhibited to journalists in a cage in the central police station in Lima before being sentenced to life imprisonment. In the months that followed many of his key followers were also captured, though violence continued in the rural areas.

The Caribbean area

Although (as noted above) Aprismo as such was confined in the event to Peru, aprismo has had a significant influence on four other political parties in the region. In Paraguay, with its large Indian majority, the Partido Febrerista, a splinter-group of the army, emerged in 1937 but failed to make headway and remained a minority faction under the long period of Colorado-dominated military dictatorship. In Venezuela, on the other hand, Betancourt's Acción Democrática (AD) became the dominant political party after 1945 without any special need to take account of the relatively small indigneous minority. In Cuba, the indigenous population had completely disappeared in the colonial period, and the Partido Revolucionario Cubano (Auténtico) was swept away by the Cuban Revolution.

In Central America the ruling dictatorships viewed the possibility of a successful indigenista movement with varying degrees of hostility. In Guatemala, despite the initial electoral success of the Partido Acción Revolucionario, the government of Juan José Arévalo was able to make only tentative steps towards land-reform. The bolder efforts of Arévalo's successor, Jacobo Arbenz, were terminated by the US-sponsored revolt and military coup of 1954. Subsequently any movement to rectify the historic injustices of the Conquest was labelled as subversive. After two major campaigns against rural guerrillas had failed, a full-scale race war exploded and following the Panzós massacre of 1978 the army made a determined effort to extirpate Indian resistance to the confiscation of their remaining lands by the new military elite. Despite the dangers, peaceful resistance did continue, and in 1992 the award of the Nobel Peace Prize to the human rights activist Rigoberta Menchú was seen worldwide as recognition that the long-term effects of the Encounter of 1492 had still to be put right (Menchú 1984).

The Latin American contribution to international law and practice

The Rationalist view of international relations, that the rulers of states, aware that they share a common history or sense of their destiny or both, are bound by certain rules, norms or practices that operate within a common social framework for the resolution of disputes (Grotius 1964), is strongly supported by the strong sense of commitment shown by the Latin American states to the concepts of international law and organisation. The practical outcome of this, the inter-American system and the Latin American role in the world community, will be discussed further in Chapters Six and Seven respectively. Here the main strands of thought which have guided action will be considered in turn.

Multilateralism

Within the South American system, isolated as it was from all but occasional political contact with the rest of the world, the joint influences of a common culture and a similar legal training were most deep rooted. Since the time of Simón Bolívar (1783–1830) and the abortive Panama Conference of 1826 the hope that a new continental solidarity could be created under constitutional means remained alive, if only just.

Early moves towards pan-Americanism took the form of a series of conferences held for specific purposes. Representatives of the Spanish American states met and agreed on measures for common resistance to foreign aggression at Lima in 1849 and at Santiago de Chile in 1856. At the Second Congress of Lima in 1865 representatives of all the existing states except Brazil, Paraguay and Uruguay met and signed a Treaty of Union and Defensive Alliance. This treaty, which would have provided mutual guarantees of independence and territorial integrity, was never ratified.

In 1880 Chile and Colombia sponsored the idea of compulsory arbitration of territorial disputes. Their draft Continental Treaty proposed that in the event of the powers being unable to agree on an arbitrator, the dispute be referred to the arbitration of the President of the United States, whose prestige among the Latin American states was then at its height following the successful expulsion of the French from Mexico. However it was not until the United States took the initiative and called the First Inter-American Conference at Washington in 1889–90 that a plan of regular arbitration was actually agreed. Though it too was never ratified, a regular series of general meetings had begun and the notion of an inter-American community started finally to take concrete form.

Following the Paraguayan War (1865–70), the Argentine Alberdi published *The Crime of War* (1870). Under General Roca and the 'Generation of '80' the so-called Conquest of the Desert extended Argentine power into Patagonia and ended the possibility of Chilean expansion there. In Brazil, the war brought the army into the centre of politics. But there too it strengthened the idea of seeking new routes to the peaceful solution of disputes. Ruy Barbosa (1849–1923), who had been a key influence on the proclamation of the Republic, took a key part both in the First Hague Conference (1899) and later in the creation of the League of Nations. It was partly as a result of this, and partly through the good offices of the United States, that all the Latin American states received an invitation to the Second Hague Conference.

Regionally, impetus for multilateralism took shape with the transformation in 1910 of the Bureau of American Republics into the Pan-American Union. At the Fifth Inter-American Conference at Santiago de Chile 1923 delegates agreed the text of the Pan-American Treaty for the Pacific Settlement of Disputes, commonly called the Gondra Treaty after its sponsor, the Paraguayan statesman. At the Sixth Conference at Havana in 1928 the Pan-American Union was officially established on a treaty basis (see Chapter Six).

Globally, the idea of a League of Nations to resolve disputes by general discussion originated with an academic, Goldsworthy Lowes Dickinson, in Britain in 1916, and was soon taken up by Woodrow Wilson, then President of the United States, to whom the idea is generally attributed. The leaders of many Latin American states were enthusiastic about the possibility, since the new organisation would accord all states formal equality in a way hitherto unknown. Their enthusiasm for the League soon waned, however, when they found that they were not, after all, going to have much say. However after the early departure of Argentina, other states soon realised that the League did have one major advantage: the United States was not a member.

The League was successful to a limited extent in helping solve international conflicts in the later years after the Good Neighbor policy had signalled US reluctance to intervene. However it did not replace the inter-American system (see Chapter Six) and indeed its successor organisation was to incorporate it in a way which both strengthened and prolonged the hegemony of the United States in the Western hemisphere (see Chapter Seven).

Arielismo

The Spanish–American War of 1898 was the decisive event that transformed admiration into hostility towards the United States. This strengthed sentiments of nationalism in many states. Adjustment to the new might of the United States, and the relative weakness of states such as Colombia and Venezuela, to say nothing of the new client states of Cuba, Panama, Nicaragua etc., took various forms.

One response was to deny the importance of the change. Latin America remained superior in culture and spiritual qualities. The gross materialism of the United States in the 'Gilded Age' was not to be envied. The Uruguayan José Enrique Rodó (1872–1917) was the first and most important writer to develop this theme of Latin American spirituality versus US materialism in his book *Ariel* (hence '*arielismo*'), first published in 1900. With its echoes of old religious disputes, this struck an answering chord among Latin American intellectuals and is still conventionally popular. Another and perhaps more practical response was pan-Hispanism – the belief in collective solidarity against the 'Coloso del Norte' – as voiced by such writers as Rufino Blanco Fombona of Venezuela, Manuel Ugarte of Argentina and José Vasconcelos of Mexico. As the political career of the last was to demonstrate, a practical difficulty with this attitude was the very wide range of political standpoints that it had to encompass. In the course of two decades Vasconcelos, who had served as an agent of the nascent Mexican Revolution in Washington, a mission which he described in graphic detail in the (unexpurgated) version of his quasi-autobiographical 'novel' *Ulises Criollo* (Vasconcelos 1958), changed from being a propagandist of revolutionary socialism as Minister of Education under Alvaro Obregón (President 1920–24) into a violent reactionary and sympathiser with the Spanish Falange after his own failed presidential bid in 1930.

The two attitudes often co-existed, as in the case of the Nicaraguan poet, Rubén Darío (1857–1916), who had an all-too-clear awareness of the physical power and military might of the United States. But it is at this point that the sharpest differences between the Caribbean and South America emerge. On the one hand, even the biggest states in the Caribbean area have had little alternative but to keep in line with US policy, since in the last analysis they lacked the physical strength to resist. On the other hand, the island states are generally too small to attract much US attention, and the fact that most of them have until recently formed part of a European empire has given them a healthy disrespect for US attitudes of superiority, which they have not yet lost.

Only Cuba, the largest of the island states, under the leadership of Fidel Castro, and in very special historical and geographical circumstances, has translated the prevailing dislike of US hegemony into successful rebellion. The three larger states of the region have all, however reluctantly, come to terms with US hegemony. For Colombia, the guiding principle since the 1920s has been 'respice polum' ('follow the north star') (Espejo 1981). In Venezuela there has been a bipartisan consensus on foreign policy between the two main political parties, both of whom, between 1959 and 1974, adhered to the Betancourt Doctrine of uncompromising hostility to dictatorial regimes of both left and right. But despite Carlos Andrés Perez's rapprochement with Cuba and vigorous attempts to make friends worldwide among the non-aligned (see Chapter Seven) and in the smaller Caribbean states, with the accession of Jimmy Carter to the Presidency of the United States he soon found himself, in a different context, back in an old role for Venezuelan Presidents, advising a new US President on Latin American affairs (Martz 1984). And since the 1960s, while holding formally aloof from the United States, successive Mexican governments have played a very similar role, which has now culminated in Mexico's decision, under Carlos Salinas, to enter into a North American Free Trade Area with the United States and Canada.

In South America the great contrast is between Brazil and the rest. Brazilians, as such, do not seem to feel any particular hostility towards the United States, though there is naturally quite a lot of criticism of US policy from the left. The United States has been content to allow Brazil to operate as a regional power under its hegemony, sometimes, as under Richard Nixon (President 1969–74) quite explicitly.

Militarism

There is a similar intellectual justification in military circles and others for militarism: the belief that the soldier is an 'armed priest', superior to other people, maintaining the true spirit of the nation (Nunn 1992). For an alternative reaction to the new power of the United States was to seek to match it in military strength, something that, given their remoteness from the United States at the beginning of the century, was still perfectly sensible for several of the major South American states.

The armed forces had long served as a vehicle for rapid social advancement. The army was, in fact, virtually the only institution which transcended the combined structure of race and class, and which enabled a Porfirio Díaz to become leader of his country. The introduction of universal military training in the 1890s however raised the stakes. In turn Peru, Chile and Argentina, all adopted the new idea. They sought to create modern, efficient military forces, but they did so in a way that had the added advantage, to the officer corps, of enabling them to propagate the military ideal and their own concept of their mission among large sectors of the male population.

As a result, Latin American politics has historically been pervaded not only by what Alfred Vagts has termed 'military militarism' – the belief in their special mission of the armed forces themselves, but also by 'civilian militarism' – the belief among civilians that the armed forces are well-deserving of the nation, leading in extreme cases to 'self-immolation on the altar of violence' (Vagts 1959, p. 22).

The majority of the Latin American states, including Argentina, Bolivia, Chile and Paraguay looked for their military model, and, more significantly, for their instructors, to Prussia. With the rise of the nazis in Germany (1933) itself, these military associations became a significant route for German influence in South America, and sympathy with Germany (not necessarily with the nazis) was a significant factor in both Argentina and Chile refusing to join in hemispheric solidarity with the United States in December 1941–January 1942. Chile finally yielded to US pressure and broke off relations with the Axis in January 1943. Soon afterwards the military government of Maj. Gualberto Villaroel, which had come to power by insurrection in Bolivia in December 1943, sought to re-establish relations with the Axis, but found itself barred from recognition by the United States. The Bolivian forces which had fought in the Chaco War in the 1930s had not only been trained, but even commanded, by German officers.

The armed forces of both Brazil and Peru continued to maintain older associations with France, which were to be less controversial. Sigificantly, perhaps, in the post-war period only Peru was to experiment with left-wing military-led reform under the government of General Velasco Alvarado (President 1968–75). Since, until after the end of the Second World War, navies tended to look to the United Kingdom for their instructors, a very different ethos prevailed in naval circles, but only in Chile was the navy traditionally of sufficient political importance to make its constitutionalist views felt. It was, after all, perhaps the only navy in the world that has ever defeated its own country's army, when in the Civil War of 1891 the Congressional side, supported by the navy, successfully outfought the presidential side, supported by the army, and established the Parliamentary Republic that lasted until 1924.

After the Second World War both navies and armies turned to the United States for their instructors, and a number of countries, beginning with Brazil in 1950, entered into formal bilateral military agreements which created a closer working partnership between their services. A very conspicuous result of this partnership was the emergence of a militant anti-communist orientation among Latin American officers, and subsequently of what was to become known as the 'national security paradigm', examples of which were Argentina, Brazil, Chile, Guatemala and Uruguay.

The military leadership of Argentina between 1976 and 1983, for example, saw their prime purpose as being to defend the 'Western and Christian world' against communist aggression. In this worldwide conflict they would retain a traditional military role, to defend the South Atlantic, if possible in a South Atlantic Treaty alliance with South Africa and other right-wing regional states. However one major player held aloof from the SATO concept, and that was multi-racial Brazil, which since 1960 had been steadily building up its links with Africa South of the Sahara. To avoid damage to these links, its military government put forward instead the notion of a 'zone of peace' in the South Atlantic, though this in turn fuelled Argentine suspicions of Brazilian imperialism (Selcher 1984).

The Argentine military government, in pursuit of its goals, gave active support to General García Meza's coup in Bolivia in 1980, to prevent a left-wing contender being elected (and also to secure a reliable ally against Chile in the event of war over the Beagle Channel islands) and was actively collaborating with the United States in counter-insurgency operations in Central America by the beginning of 1982. But the main battleground of the new conflict was within Argentina itself. For them, the Third World War had already begun, in the form of attack from within by 'subversive' elements. By the so-called Process of National Reorganisation they sought to extirpate subversion and by doing so to save Western civilisation, much as their ancestors had done in Spain during the seven hundred years of the Reconquest. Early in 1982, while visiting Washington, General Leopoldo Galtieri put this view concisely:

> The First World War was one of armies against armies, the Second World War was one of weapons against weapons, the Third World War is one of ideology against ideology. (Jessel 1983)

Brazilian military governments after 1964 (and more particularly after 1968) gave priority also to countering internal subversion, which they did in a much more systematic way, but by the same means, by imprisoning or killing known 'subversives'. However at the same time they placed more emphasis on the social causes of discontent and saw the means to counter them as being to bring about economic development, within a military-led context. In the 1980s 'the internal social and political effects of the foreign debt, high international interest rates, export problems, and petroleum prices' (Selcher 1984) emerged as the major threats to Brazil's national security.

Legalism

In South as well as Central America, there was growing concern about the danger of US intervention. Though fronting on the Caribbean, Colombia, which lost Panama, and Venezuela, where the US tried vigorously to dislodge Cypriano Castro, were both substantial South American states.

Since intervention often resulted from an appeal to a great power to enforce performance of a contract, an early attempt to avert intervention took the form of including a clause – the so-called Calvo clause, after its Argentine inventor – in any contract with an overseas contractor. This clause required the contractor to pledge in advance not to appeal to their own government to enforce any claims they might have. However, the governments of the great powers, led by Britain and the United States, held that the contractor might be bound by the clause, but they were not, and they therefore retained the right to intervene if they wished. In 1902 German, British and Italian forces jointly blockaded Venezuela to compel its government to pay its debts.

The Argentine Foreign Minister, Luis M. Drago, noted that investors invariably took into account the risk involved before deciding to lend their money to a Latin American state. In November 1902, therefore, he proposed the adoption of a new principle of international law, 'that the public debt cannot occasion armed intervention nor the actual occupation of the territory of American nations by a European power' (Dozer 1962, p. 475; Borchard 1930). Initially the 'Drago doctrine' as such was ignored and indeed derided by the US popular press. Then the idea behind it was adopted unilaterally by the United States in the Roosevelt Corollary in 1904, and, in the form of the Porter resolution, proposed successfully by the United States at the Second Hague Conference in 1907. However it was not until 1936 that steady pressure for the establishment of the non-intervention norm was finally conceded by the United States at the special Pan-American Conference at Buenos Aires. In Chapter Six it will be seen how the United States later reasserted a right of intervention in very different circumstances to those originally envisaged.

Ironically, the United States itself took the lead in asserting the principle of the peaceful resolution of disputes by an international court. The idea originally arose from the agreement between the presidents of El Salvador and Guatemala in 1906 aboard USS *Marblehead*. In 1907, at the invitation of Presidents Roosevelt and Díaz, representatives of the five Central American states met in Washington. There, at the urging of Theodore Roosevelt's Secretary of State, Elihu Root, they agreed to establish a Central American Court of Justice to settle all future controversies between them.

Initially the Central American Court was successful. Unfortunately in 1916 Costa Rica appealed to the Court to settle a question arising out of the Bryan-Chamorro Treaty of 1914 by which Nicaragua granted to the United States in perpetuity the right to build a canal across its territory making use of the waters of the San Juan River, and granted it both a 99-year lease on the Great Corn and Little Corn Islands in the Caribbean and the right for the same period to establish a naval base on the Gulf of Fonseca in the Pacific. This treaty, Costa Rica argued, contravened the rights of navigation of the river ceded to it by Nicaragua in a treaty of 1858, which also gave it the right to be consulted before any canal was built. At the same time El Salvador complained that the treaty violated her rights on the Gulf of Fonseca. The Court ruled that it was unable to pronounce on the validity of the treaty itself but that in agreeing to it Nicaragua had undoubtedly violated the rights of both Costa Rica and El Salvador. Since both Nicaragua and the United States refused to accept this judgment, their support for the Court was withdrawn, and in March 1918 it was formally dissolved.

This, however, was not quite the end of the story. In 1979 the Provisional Government of Nicaragua formally denounced the Bryan-Chamorro Treaty on the grounds that US forces had been stationed on its territory at the time that it had been agreed. With the accession of Ronald Reagan in 1981 the United States initiated a covert war against the Sandinistas, and when it seemed on the point of stalling, stepped up its campaign. On 3 January 1984 irregular forces co-ordinated by a US warship attacked oil facilities at Puerto Sandino. On 25 February similar attacks on the Atlantic port of El Bluff and the Pacific harbour of Corinto were accompanied by the laying of mines which damaged four freighters, one of Soviet registration. On 5 April the US vetoed a UN Security Council resolution condemning the mining of the ports. Meanwhile at a press conference President Reagan had complained that the Nicaraguans were 'exporting revolution'. 'We are going to try and inconvenience the government of Nicaragua until they quit that kind of action', he promised (*Guardian*, 6 April 1984; Calvert 1988b).

By this time the principle of settling international disputes by adjudication had long since been accepted by the world community. Nicaragua therefore took its case to the World Court. In an act of remarkable cynicism, the United States, which had been one of the chief architects of the World Court, announced that it would no longer be bound by its jurisdiction. However, on 17 June 1986 the International Court of Justice delivered its judgment in the case of *Military and Paramilitary Activities in and against Nicaragua (Nicaragua v. United States of America)*. By a large majority the judges found in all fourteen counts in favour of Nicaragua, holding that 'the United States of America, by training, arming, equipping, financing and supplying the Contra forces . . . has acted, against the Republic of Nicaragua, in breach of its obligation under customary international law not to intervene in the affairs of another state' (ICJ Communiqué 86/8 of 26 June 1986). Fortunately for Nicaragua, in the meantime by the Boland Amendment the US congress had cut off further military aid to the contras, the news of the Iran–Contra scandal had broken in Washington and the danger to Nicaragua had, as a result, already been sharply scaled down.

Conclusion

The fact that a common language exists throughout much of the hemisphere has facilitated the free movement of ideas in Spanish-speaking America, and Brazil has shared in this movement. The influence of European ideas continued to dominate intellectual thought well into the twentieth century. *Arielismo* co-exists with a continuing disrespect for the United States as the cultured, modern nation which in fact it is.

These facts have given an international dimension to Latin American politics generally, but more particularly in Central America, where the myth of unity still survives in an attenuated form. However since 1920 the hegemony of the United States has limited the efficacy of left-wing ideas and movements, with the sole exception of Cuba. The Latin American contribution to international peacemaking and peacekeeping has, ironically, proved to be more enduring than its most famous contribution to world thought, the theory of guerrilla warfare.

Chapter Six

The inter-American system

The inter-American system

The origins of the inter-American system go back to the colonial period and to Bolívar's abortive Congress of Panama in 1826. In the constant re-writing of history, it is easy to overlook the strength of feeling in Latin America for continental co-operation and to regard the present-day inter-American system as simply a tool of US imperialism. The very existence of the system, to say nothing of the multiplicity and complexity of regional and sub-regional organisation within it, is a powerful argument for a rationalist rather than a realist model of international relations, while the theories of both functionalists and neo-functionalists find some support in the way that the system has expanded from relatively modest beginnings.

Certainly it was a North American, James G. Blaine, US Secretary of State, whose initiative in calling the First Conference of American States at Washington in 1889–90 forms the starting point for all later developments. His primary motive was to facilitate commerce and trade. However the fact that most of the other American states thought it worthwhile to send delegates, suggests that they too thought that such an initiative deserved support. As was seen in Chapter Five, earlier conferences called for specific purposes at the initiative of individual Latin American states had paved the way for a more regular series of meetings, while Blaine's initiative came at precisely the moment when the prestige of the United States stood at its highest in the rest of the hemisphere.

The Second Conference took place in Mexico in 1901–2. In the meanwhile the Spanish–American War had put a final end to the Spanish presence in the Americas and the United States had emerged as the strongest and best armed power in the region. It was decided that future conferences would be held at five, rather than at ten-year intervals, but the Third Conference took place at Rio de Janeiro in 1906 and the Fourth, to coincide with the centenary of the start of independence, at Buenos Aires in 1910.

These early meetings, like the first, were primarily concerned with trade matters. However in 1914 the United States for the first time called a regional conference for a political purpose, mediating in the conflicts of the Mexican Revolution. It consisted of representatives of the United States and of the so-called ABC powers (Argentina, Brazil, Chile), and was held at Niagara Falls, NY. The conference was not a success, and broke up when the other delegates came to the correct conclusion that the United States had a secret agenda, to prolong discussions until their favoured faction had emerged victorious.

At the end of the Great War regional considerations gave way for a time to interest in the formation of the League of Nations (see Chapter Seven). It was only after the United States Senate had voted not to join the League that voices were again heard calling for the creation of a new regional alliance against attack from outside the hemisphere and the series of inter-American conferences was resumed.

It proved relatively easy to agree to the peaceful resolution of disputes between the American states. At the Fifth Conference at Santiago de Chile in 1923 the United States supported the negotiations for the first inter-American peace treaty, the Pan-American Treaty for the Pacific Settlement of Disputes (the Gondra Treaty). Growing concern among the other states at the steadily increasing involvement of the US in central America, however, led to the first moves of Latin American delegates to the Sixth Conference, held in Havana in 1928, to try to establish the principle of *non-intervention*, which would bind the United States as well as the other states of the region.

However the main result of the Conference was the formal decision to establish the Pan-American Union (PAU) on a treaty basis, with a permanent secretariat based in Washington, DC. The idea of a regular organisation or alliance against attack from Europe had been on the agenda for some time, and for many it was seen as the only logical alternative to relying on the United States to use the Monroe Doctrine. In 1921 President Baltasar Brum of Uruguay had called for 'a defensive alliance between all the American countries ... with reciprocal obligations and advantages for all of them', under which the countries of the region would 'formulate a declaration, similar to that of Monroe, in which they would engage to intervene in behalf of any one of them, including the United States, if, in the defense of her rights, she should find herself involved in war with an extracontinental nation' (Dozer 1962, p. 532). However in the 1920s the United States was strongly isolationist and not ready to enter into such a commitment, and was still actively engaged in maintaining a series of protectorates in the Caribbean Basin. It was not until after the Clark Memorandum of 1928 that it was realised that the Monroe Doctrine was not, as many in the United States had come to believe, a general principle of international law, nor was it intended as a statement of US policy towards Latin America, but of US policy towards Europe; a realisation which was to pave the way towards a radical reappraisal of US policy towards Latin America.

From the Pan-American Union to the OAS

The Seventh Conference, which took place in Montevideo in 1933, followed the election of Franklin D. Roosevelt to the Presidency of the United States and his declaration that in future relations between the United States and other states of the hemisphere would be guided by the principle of the 'Good Neighbor' (Wood 1961). By the adoption by the Conference of the Convention on Rights and Duties of States, the United States accepted the principle of the juridical equality of states and subsequently renounced both her right of intervention and her privileged position within the Pan-American Union (Connell-Smith 1966, p. 308).

There remained, however, a sharp division between the United States and the other states over the role of the League. It was only after the apparent failure of the League to put an end to the Chaco War, that a Special Conference was convened at Buenos Aires in 1936 to try to arrive at a common position of neutrality. It agreed only on the principle of regional consultation in the event of a threat to the peace of the continent.

The deteriorating situation in Europe in 1937–38 finally awoke delegates to the real possibility of a new world war. However the reaction was still only partial, and very much coloured by fear of renewed US intervention in the guides of hemispheric solidarity. Hence, though at the Eighth Conference at Lima in 1938 delegates adopted the first of a long line of multilateral declarations, the

Declaration of Lima, the Declaration reaffirmed the right to sovereignty of the various states and their determination to defend themselves against 'all foreign intervention or activities that might threaten them', there was still no agreement to act, rather than simply to hold consultations. However the Declaration's statement on sovereignty was believed by the other delegates to constitute a major concession by the United States, a formal commitment to the principle of non-intervention.

Despite this emphasis on consultation, it was soon to become clear that, as the other states had feared, the United States interpreted the Declaration rather differently from the other states. At the outbreak of war in 1939, Roosevelt proclaimed a zone, not only around the United States itself but around the two American continents south of Canada, any violation of which it would treat an attack on itself. This 320-km (200-mile) wide zone, which soon became known as 'the Hemispheric Safety Belt', was endorsed by the First Meeting of Consultation of the Foreign Ministers at Panama in September 1939, but almost immediately violated by the German cruiser *Graf Spee*, when it fled into Uruguayan waters to escape Allied pursuit.

The Hemispheric Safety Belt inevitably included a range of colonial possessions of various European powers, and these were to become an issue following the fall of France in June 1940. A Second Meeting of Consultation at Havana later the same month voted to take over French colonies in the Western hemisphere in the event of a German threat to annex them. In this event they would administer them under trusteeship for the ultimate benefit of the people of the colonies. In the destroyer/bases deal with Britain in December 1940, the United States gained a series of bases in these territories, confirming its hegemony over the Caribbean Basin by completing its outer defensive perimeter.

The US government was already working to try to eliminate possible nazi influence in South America and if possible to win the friendship of Brazil. US economic interest in Brazil had begun to displace British influence during the 1920s, largely as the result of the development of the automobile (Downes 1992). More recently, the Vargas government, eager further to reduce British influence and nervous of the intentions of its Spanish-speaking neighbours, had been angling for military collaboration with the United States. In October 1940 Britain's high-handed action in impounding the Brazilian freighter *Siquiera Campos*, loaded with German arms for

Brazil, caused fury in Rio. Though they were released on United States insistence, Brazilian coolness towards Britain lasted throughout the war (McCann 1973, pp. 208–12).

It was another eighteen months, however, before, as a result of the Japanese attack on Pearl Harbor, the United States and its nine small Caribbean allies were abruptly to find themselves at war, first with Japan, and then, within days, also with Germany and Italy. Collectively they joined in signing the United Nations declaration on 1 January 1942.

The speed of events was such that the Third Meeting of Consultation at Rio de Janeiro in January 1942 met after these crucial decisions had already been made. Despite this, or because of it, the meeting was unable to agree to do more than to recommend member states to break off diplomatic relations with the Rome-Berlin Axis, because of the resistance of Argentina and Chile. At the same time the United States, together with the ABC Powers, insisted on the peremptory settlement of the simmering boundary dispute between Ecuador and Peru, embodied in the Protocol of Rio de Janeiro, of which they became the guarantors – a piece of *Realpolitik* which was to be bitterly resented by Ecuador and so continue to compromise the integrity of the inter-American peace process for decades to come.

Colombia and Mexico had already broken off diplomatic relations with the Axis, and Brazil, Ecuador, Paraguay and Peru had stated their solidarity with the United States. All these states, as well as Bolivia, Uruguay and Venezuela, now broke off diplomatic relations. Both Brazil and Mexico were shortly afterwards to enter the war and to take an active combatant role. A third large South American state, Colombia, declared war on 28 November 1943, while the outcome was still very much in doubt. The remaining states remained neutral until the fighting was nearly over. Their role was to act as sources of strategic war materials for the Allied cause, and in Chile, for example, the local elite recognised how far they were dependent on the US market and collaborated willingly. The limits to US hegemony were clearly shown by the fact that efforts to get Argentina to enter the war backfired: the pro-Allied stand of the Castillo government led to the military revolt of 1943 and a pro-Axis government (Francis 1977). However even Argentina was eventually encouraged by the United States to enter the war so as to take an active part in the postwar settlement.

Two very different views of the future of the inter-American system became apparent in 1945 at a Special Conference of the American States held at Chapultepec Castle, high above Mexico City, the former residence of the Viceroys of New Spain. The United States saw the United Nations as the guarantor of world peace for the future. However the other states were concerned that the new organisation was going to be too much like the former League. They wanted major changes in the organisation: two permanent seats on the Security Council, stronger powers for the General Assembly and an effective International Court. They also wanted substantial funds for economic development. However for the moment they got neither, and by the time that the next Conference was held the Cold War had already begun and the United States had other pre-occupations.

By the Act of Chapultepec, however, a new basis for regular regional consultation was established. There were to be full Conferences every four years, with annual meetings of Foreign Ministers in the interim. The American states reaffirmed their commitment to peace. They also reaffirmed the principle of non-intervention established in 1936, though the new democratic government of Guatemala also gained support for a resolution to defend democracy and to oppose anti-democratic regimes.

With the onset of the Cold War, two major changes transformed the inter-American system.

At Rio de Janeiro in September 1947 the United States and the other American states replaced the 1938 Declaration of Lima by a formal military alliance. The Inter-American Treaty of Reciprocal Assistance (in Latin America usually referred to by its Spanish initials TIAR, but in English colloquially as 'the Rio Pact'), obliged signatory powers to come to each others' aid in the event of an attack from outside the hemisphere, and it was backed by a series of bilateral military aid agreements between the United States and various countries, starting with Brazil.

At Bogotá in 1948 the Ninth Inter-American Conference agreed to replace the Pan-American Union by a new regional organisation within the United Nations, to be called the Organization of American States (OAS/OEA). Its Charter embodied in Articles 15 and 17 the by now well established concept of non-intervention, in a most specific form. Article 15 reads:

> No State or group of States has the right to intervene, directly or
> indirectly, for any reason whatever, in the internal or external affairs
> of any other State. The foregoing principle prohibits not only armed
> force but also any other form of interference or attempted threat
> against the personality of the State or against its political, economic
> and cultural elements.

This explicit statement, which expands the Additional Protocol of
Buenos Aires to cover also collective intervention, is reinforced by
Article 17's insistence on the principle of territorial inviolability.
Territory of any state 'may not be the object, even temporarily, of
military occupation or of other measures of force taken by another
State, directly or indirectly, on any grounds whatever' (Connell-
Smith 1966, pp. 201–2). Unfortunately, from the rationalist point of
view, the Charter also contained provisions on regional peace keeping which in practice were to give the United States a freedom to
intervene which it was not intended to have and did not have
elsewhere. However this does not mean either that this was a
deliberate intention of the United States, or that the Latin Americans
were wrong to believe that their only hope of being able to maintain a
degree of independence of the United States was by imposing
restraints on its freedom of action within the inter-American system.
As Farer puts it:

> Why would political leaders in countries so sensitive to the risk of
> American intervention have promoted institutions that, according to
> the critics, would serve merely to cloak or even thinly to legitimate
> American threats to their political independence? The simple answer,
> of course, is that they would not and did not. They devised the
> institutions of the Inter-American System not to legitimate but rather
> to contain American power. Containment was their dominating pur-
> pose. And the charter and the treaty were its imperfect expressions.
>
> (Farer 1979, p. xvii)

Much to the disappointment of the Latin American delegates, the
idea of a Marshall Plan for Latin America was turned down by none
other than Secretary of State Marshall himself. What they did get
was support from the United States for the formation of the UN
Economic Commission for Latin America (ECLA) and the Point
Four programme to foster private US investment in the region.

The Organization of American States (OAS)

The purpose of the Organization of American States, the first regional organization to be established within the United Nations, is to further peace, security, mutual understanding and co-operation among the states of the Western hemisphere. There were 21 founder members. To that number were added in due course most of the newly independent states of the Commonwealth Caribbean and Suriname. Canada continued to hold aloof, but finally acceded in January 1990 as the 33rd member state. At the General Assembly held in Washington, DC, on 8 January 1991, Guyana and Belize formally became the 34th and 35th members of the organisation. Their membership had for many years been delayed by the claims on their territory of Venezuela and Guatemala respectively. Cuba is still officially a member of the organisation President Castro once described as 'a heap of dung' but it has been suspended from all activities since 1962.

The main organ of consultation of the OAS today is the annual meeting of the General Assembly, a full-scale conference of Foreign Ministers held in a different national capital each year, and not always at the same time of year. The permanent secretariat, where the Permanent Council sits and Meetings of Consultation of Ministers of Foreign Affairs are normally held, is in Washington, DC, in the old Pan-American Building. The Permanent Council consists of representatives of each of the member states with the rank of Ambassador. The chair rotates among the representatives in alphabetical order, three months at a time, and the current Secretary General is João Clemente Baena Soares of Brazil.

Originally the centrepiece of the organisation was to be the conference itself, but the Tenth Inter-American Conference was delayed until 1954, when the fact that it was held in Caracas, then under the dictatorship of Marcos Pérez Jiménez led to it being boycotted by democratic Costa Rica. US Secretary of State John Foster Dulles came to that meeting, however, with the sole objective of getting delegates to accept a strong anti-communist resolution (see also US Department of State 1977). A modified version, the Declaration of Solidarity for the Preservation of the Political Integrity of the American States against the Intervention of International Communism, more commonly known as the Declaration of Caracas, was eventually passed, though without the support either of Mexico or of

Argentina, which had already shown that if the Soviet Union were opposed to the United States, then it would be prepared to look favourably upon it (Vacs 1984). A few months later it became the basis for the clandestine intervention of the United States in Guatemala which resulted in the fall of Arbenz. The Guatemalan government on that occasion tried to appeal to the UN Security Council rather than to the OAS, but was referred back to the regional organisation which, as Inis Claude observed, 'was prepared to treat Guatemala as the defendant, not the plaintiff' (Claude 1964). After further delay a Special Meeting of the Council on 28 June summoned a meeting of Consultation to meet at Rio de Janeiro on 7 July 1954. Two days later the Arbenz government collapsed and the Meeting never took place (see also Chapter Seven). It was to prove to the the the first step in what has been aptly termed 'the dismantling of the Good Neighbor policy' (Wood 1985).

After that fiasco, the Eleventh Inter-American Conference, scheduled for Quito in 1958, was indefinitely postponed, and by default the major forum of the organisation became the regular meetings of Foreign Ministers. It was the Sixth and Seventh Meetings of Consultation, held at San José, Costa Rica, in August 1960, that delegates voted sanctions against Trujillo in the Dominican Republic, while showing a clear reluctance to criticise Castro's regime in Cuba. The following year many governments voiced strong criticism of the abortive Bay of Pigs expedition and of the US role in it, since it constituted a clear breach of Articles 15 and 17 of the Charter of the OAS. However the use later in 1961 of US warships to drive the Trujillo family out of the Dominican Republic was tacitly condoned, while with an effective combination of pressure and inducement the Kennedy administration succeeded in persuading the Eighth Meeting of Consultation of Foreign Ministers held at Punta del Este in January 1962 to exclude Cuba and to impose a general embargo on Cuban trade. This decision was highly controversial. It was carried by 17 votes to 7, a bare two-thirds majority of the membership, but among those states not supporting the resolution, apart from Cuba, were Argentina, Bolivia, Brazil, Chile, Ecuador and Mexico (Morrison 1965).

As it happened, it did not matter, since for many of the uncommitted the issue was subsequently decided for them by the Cuban Missile Crisis of October 1962. Treating the confrontation not as one between the United States and Cuba, but between the United

States and the Soviet Union, President Kennedy did inform the OAS on this occasion of his intention to impose a 'quarantine' around Cuba, but only after the decision had been fully worked out, the forces had been deployed and he had announced on television when the blockade was going to begin. This time there was little formal complaint from the other American states. The Council was immediately transformed into a Provisional Organ of Consultation and, at the request of the United States, adopted a resolution sanctioning the use of armed force under the Rio Pact. It called for 'the immediate dismantling and withdrawal of all missiles and other weapons with any offensive capability' and voted:

> To recommend that the member states, in accordance with Articles 6 and 8 of the Inter-American Treaty of Reciprocal Assistance, take all measures, individually and collectively, including the use of armed force, which they may deem necessary to ensure that the Government of Cuba cannot continue to receive from the Sino-Soviet powers (*sic*) military material and related supplies which may threaten the peace and security of the Continent and to prevent the missiles in Cuba with offensive capability from ever becoming an active threat to the peace and security of the Continent.
>
> (Connell-Smith 1966, p. 257)

Although all states except Uruguay (whose collegiate executive had not come to a decision) voted in favour of the first proposition, Brazil, Bolivia and Mexico abstained on the second, as an indication that they did not support an armed invasion of Cuba. In the event it did not matter. The United States had already made it clear how it was going to act and the OAS was simply invited to act as a rubber stamp. The fact that it did so only because the situation was viewed as a crisis was soon apparent, when in 1963 the United States abandoned plans to ask the OAS to declare an economic embargo against Cuba.

However after Venezuela had charged Cuba with both aggression and intervention in its internal affairs, and an OAS investigating committee had substantiated the charges, the Ninth Meeting of Consultation of Foreign Ministers, convening in Washington, DC, in July 1964, voted to break off diplomatic relations and the embargo on Cuban trade established in 1962 was reinforced by a clear warning that if Cuban aggression continued the other states might resort to 'the use of self-defense in either individual or collective form, which could go so far as resort to armed force' (Connell-Smith 1966,

p. 262). Three months before, in April 1964, the Brazilian Revolution had transformed the largest state in South America from a
consistent opponent of the United States into its most enthusiastic
supporter (Black 1977, p. 51). Its influence was decisive. This time
only four states failed to support the resolution: Bolivia, Chile,
Mexico and Uruguay. By the end of the year only Mexico retained its
links with Cuba.

In this, as in other respects, the inability of the OAS to handle
effectively conflicts arising outside the hemisphere was misleading.
In a number of inter-American disputes it had continued to work
effectively throughout the period, though often with little recognition from outside. In 1955 acting as a Provisional Organ of Consultation the OAS Council sent an investigating committee to both
Nicaragua and Costa Rica after the latter complained that she had
been invaded by troops from the former. Costa Rica subsequently
asked for military assistance, which, on the request of the Council,
was afforded by the United States. Though the Government of
General Anasastio Somoza García asserted its innocence, it had in
fact been forced to withdraw, although it was not subsequently
censured (Connell-Smith 1966, p. 238).

In September 1955 Ecuador complained to the Council that Peru
had built up a substantial concentration of troops on their common
frontier and had stationed ships close to the Ecuadorian coast, and
thus posed a threat to her territorial integrity. On this occasion,
however, the Council noted that the four guarantor Powers of the
Protocol of Rio de Janeiro had also been approached, and that
therefore the Rio Pact did not apply in this case.

In May 1957 Honduras complained that Nicaraguan forces had
invaded Honduran territory by crossing the Coco River, the area
concerned actually forming part of the disputed area awarded to
Honduras by the King of Spain in 1906 under an arbitration which
Nicaragua had refused to accept. In return, Nicaragua charged
Honduras with aggression and invoked the Rio Pact. Acting again as
a Provisional Organ of Consultation, the Council sent a mission to
the two countries. Once a cease-fire had been established, a special
committee established by the Council kept up pressure for the two
parties to determine the matter by arbitration, and eventually
Nicaragua agreed to allow the question to be determined by the
International Court of Justice. In its judgment, the ICJ held in
November 1960 that the original award had been valid and that

Nicaragua was obliged to give effect to it. Finally the Inter-American Peace Committee's good offices were secured to set up a Honduran-Nicaraguan Mixed Commission to give effect to the award, which was thus finally settled.

The complaint of Panama in April 1959 that its territory had been entered by a small group of insurrectionists from Cuba was only the first of a number of similar cases which gradually eroded Cuban support in the OAS. An investigating committee found that the invading forces had come from Cuba, but the Cuban government refused to admit responsibility and it was not censured. In June Nicaragua made a similar complaint about forces crossing its border from Costa Rica. On this occasion Venezuela supported Cuba in arguing that the forces were in fact Nicaraguan exiles, and after the investigating committee had found only that troops had crossed the frontier of Nicaragua from Costa Rica, Cuba announced that, while it sympathised with the efforts of peoples struggling against tyranny, it had taken effective measures to see that no such expeditions left its own shores. The following month, however, a similar complaint came from the Dominican Republic, which accused Venezuela of complicity with Cuba. Both governments denied the charges. On the advice of the United States, the Council decided to call the Fifth Meeting of Consultation of Foreign Ministers, which met in Santiago de Chile in August 1959. But it was not to deal with the specific complaint, which had by then been withdrawn, but with the causes of the tensions in the area, and the way in which the principles of non-intervention and collective security could be maintained. It was this meeting that recognised the Inter-American Peace Committee for the first time as a permanent part of the structure of the organisation.

Over the next two years a long series of complaints were lodged against the governments of either Cuba or the Dominican Republic, which were ultimately to lead to the Sixth and Seventh Meetings of Consultation at San José. The former had to deal with a formal complaint by Venezuela against the Dominican Republic for the assassination attempt that had nearly cost President Betancourt his life. It condemned the Government of the Dominican Republic for 'acts of aggression and intervention against the State of Venezuela' and imposed sanctions on it, the first time in the history of the organisation that this had happened. However the Seventh Meeting, which had been called to deal with a formal complaint by Peru against Cuba, failed to produce an explicit resolution of any kind, and certainly not the outright condemnation which the United States government had hoped for, though it was later able to use the precedent of the Sixth Meeting, after the Cuban Missile Crisis, to obtain an economic embargo against Cuba.

In 1962, when Chile built a tunnel to divert approximately half of the waters of the Río Lauca for irrigation purposes, there were violent protests in Bolivia, which broke off diplomatic relations with Chile. Bolivia eventually decided to take the matter to the OAS, where it was still outstanding at the time of the Cuban Missile Crisis. Despite Chilean support for the US position, Bolivia was persuaded to back it also.

The unilateral American intervention in the Dominican Republic in 1965 placed an even greater strain on the organisation. The intervention arose as a result of an unsuccessful revolt against the provisional government that had been installed when the military had deposed the constitutional President, Juan Bosch, on 25 September 1963. Their coup had been led by Colonel Elías Wessin y Wessin, and it was he who remained the 'strong man' behind the triumvirate that nominally headed the new government. Its US-supported figurehead, Donald Reid Cabral, promised elections in due course. But the colonel (now a general) did not wish to see Bosch re-elected, so Congress was dissolved and the promised elections did not materialise.

Late in the evening of 24 April 1965 constitutionalist forces began to seize strategic strong points in Santo Domingo. With the Presidential Palace captured, Reid Cabral resigned, and a member of Bosch's party, José Rafael Molina Ureña, was proclaimed President pending Bosch's return. However the following day Wessin's supporters in the air force started to bomb the presidential palace, starting a brief civil war. But though Molina speedily was forced to resign, constitutionalist resistance continued, led by the Secretary of the Interior, Colonel Francisco Alberto Caamaño Deñó. It seems clear that Washington was initially caught by surprise, having assumed that the Dominican Republic was in safe hands, and that their initial reaction was that the revolt would soon be crushed. When it became clear that the so-called 'loyalist' reaction was on the point of failure Washington abruptly decided to act.

On the evening of 28 April, to general surprise, President Lyndon B. Johnson sent in United States marines to protect the lives of

American citizens. He did not notify the OAS Council. In the event this did not matter, since it met on the following two days and decided only to convene the Tenth Meeting of Consultation of Foreign Ministers to study 'the situation created by the armed struggle in the Dominican Republic'.

It proved easier to intervene than to restore order, and as time went on President Johnson could not resist the temptation to issue more and more statements defending his actions. Soon he was claiming that a 'Communist threat' had existed, in terms that were so exaggerated that many US journalists became disillusioned and began to criticise the administration publicly. Meanwhile US diplomatic pressure ensured that on 7 May the loyalist Government of National Reconstruction gave full power to the loyalist general Antonio Imbert Barrera to suppress the constitutionalist revolt by any means possible.

The Tenth Meeting of Consultation had already convened on 3 May when the United States had belatedly asked it to endorse its actions by creating an Inter-American Peace Force (IAPF) which would create a legal basis for its intervention. In the event only 12 states joined the US in voting for the resolution, the 14th vote needed to secure a bare two-thirds majority being the vote of the defunct triumvirate's ambassador being counted as that of the disputed government of the Dominican Republic. With Cuba already excluded, Chile, Ecuador, Mexico, Peru and Uruguay voted against, and Venezuela abstained, but none of their representatives denounced the fiction by which the vote of the Dominican Republic was counted in favour of the resolution.

As a result, as Gleijeses points out, the soldiers of five dictatorships (Brazil, Honduras, Paraguay, Nicaragua and El Salvador) and twenty-one Costa Rican policemen joined US marines in restoring 'democracy' to the Dominican Republic by systematically massacring the remaining constitutionalists holding out in the slums of the *barrios altos*. When the last of them had been slaughtered, the OAS force remained to supervise the election of a provisional government chosen by the United States, which was eventually accepted by most of the major political factions for fear that civil war might be resumed (Gleijeses 1978, pp. 260–1, 262–4, 275–7).

Apart from the credibility of the OAS itself, the main casualty of 1965 was the idea of an inter-American peace force. As the events in the Dominican Republic showed, the new dictatorships of the 1960s were much more willing to collaborate with the United States than their democratic predecessors, but there were limits to what even they felt their people could stand, and, in any case, the guerrilla threat was already fading. It was noteworthy that, though a limited amount of pressure was exercised by the OAS against the dictatorship of Dr François Duvalier in Haiti, the dictatorship survived while the democratic government of the Dominican Republic was overthrown by its own armed forces. The notion that the inter-American system was an association of 'democratic' states was already discredited, but the failure of the OAS to act on the occasion of any of the numerous military coups of the early 1960s certainly did nothing to help its credibility in this respect.

However though the trend towards right-wing authoritarianism continued to strengthen in the 1970s in the traditional Latin American states, the emergence of the Commonwealth Caribbean and its incorporation into the system resulted in some building of bridges between the United States and Latin America by states such as Jamaica, Grenada and Guyana who shared the economic objectives of the Latin Americans but had democratic governments and spoke English like the United States. Partly in response to pressure for enlargement, in 1970 the Organization of American States was reconstituted on its present basis by the Protocol of Buenos Aires, and given a structure which much more closely resembled that of the United Nations itself than the previous cumbersome maze of meetings and committees.

The General Assembly, which met for its first regular session at San José, Costa Rica, in 1971, replaced the Inter-American Conferences and various councils. For many years it fulfilled a useful role in airing current political issues and through the work of its related agencies achieving important though less spectacular gains for Latin American co-operation. Co-operation with the United States reached a peak during the period of the Carter administration in the United States (1977–81). In 1977 Carter successfully concluded with General Omar Torrijos the Panama Canal Treaties by which the United States relinquished control of four-fifths of the former Panama Canal Zone and established a timetable by which the Canal itself would be progressively transferred to Panamanian control from 31 December 1999 (Latin American Bureau 1978; Jorden 1984; Zimbalist and Weeks 1991). It was less successful in its support for a positive policy of encouraging human rights (Farer

1979; Vincent 1986). In 1979 the Inter-American Court of Human Rights was established with its seat in San José, but the Tenth General Assembly was unable to go beyond naming Argentina, Chile, El Salvador, Haiti, Paraguay and Uruguay as countries of 'special concern' with regard to human rights when Argentina threatened to secede.

Worse still, since the Falklands War of 1982 open conflict between the United States and the majority of the Latin American states has effectively stultified much of the political work of the organisation. Four main issues have divided them: the Falklands Crisis itself, US policy towards Central America, the ambiguous US attitude towards the maintenance of democracy in Haiti and, more recently, the anti-narcotic campaign which led indirectly to the invasion of Panama and the fall of General Noriega.

The Falklands Crisis

The limits of regional peacekeeping when a country outside the region is involved, were clearly shown by the events following the Argentine occupation of the Falkland Islands on 2 April 1982 (Calvert 1982; Coll and Arend 1985; Beck 1988; Gustafson 1988; Charlton 1989; Danchev 1992). Initially the initiative lay with Britain, which took its case direct to the UN Security Council. At its meeting on 1 April it called on the governments of both Argentina and the UK 'to refrain from the use or threat of force in the region of the Falkland Islands (Islas Malvinas)'. When notified of the invasion the following day, constituting a breach of the peace, the Council was already aware that Argentine troops had actually been on the islands the previous day. With strong support from France and Ireland, Resolution 502 passed by 10 votes to 1 (Panama), with 4 abstentions, including that of the Soviet Union.

The resolution, which Britain had lobbied hard to obtain, demanded 'an immediate cessation of hostilities' and 'an immediate withdrawal of all Argentine forces from the Falkland Islands (Islas Malvinas)'. It also called on both governments 'to seek a diplomatic solution to their differences, and to respect fully the purposes and principles of the Charter of the United Nations.'

With Argentine forces securely in place, however, the initiative now passed to Argentina, while Britain dispatched a task force to the South Atlantic to strengthen its bargaining position and if that failed (as it did) to seek to recover the islands. Given that Britain had the power of veto in the Security Council it was inevitable that Argentina would wish to transfer the debate to the OAS, and the recapture of South Georgia on 25 April 1982 gave it an opening to do so. When Dr Nicanor Costa Méndez arrived in Washington for the Twentieth Meeting of Consultation of Ministers of Foreign Affairs, which had been summoned at his request for the following day, he told reporters that his country was 'now technically in a state of war with Britain'. His immediate aim was to call on the OAS for collective action against Britain. However among the thirty members represented at the meeting, twenty-one were also signatories of the Rio Pact, and Argentina had already indicated its intention in advance of the meeting of invoking Article 6 of that treaty, branding Britain, not Argentina, as an aggressor.

So the action in South Georgia was a perfect pretext. It might even be used to invoke Article 3 of the Treaty, requiring the signatories to give armed assistance in the event of an attack from outside the hemisphere on any of the states within the region listed in Article 4. Of course it had not occurred to the framers of the treaty that an American state would ever attack a state outside the hemisphere and then rely on the treaty for protection. In 1947 it had been communist aggression that was feared, and that, by definition, would always be unprovoked. In the event, the Argentine Foreign Minister, aware that he would not get the fourteen votes he needed for a resolution calling for armed support for Argentina, wisely did not ask the delegates to go so far. But the meeting did adopt on 28 April a resolution which gave the Argentine military and diplomatic position virtually all the support it required.

> That resolution urged the Government of the United Kingdom 'immediately to cease the hostilities it is carrying on within the security region defined by Article 4 of the Inter-American Treaty of Reciprocal Assistance, and also to refrain from any act that may affect inter-American peace and security,' and urged the Government of the Republic of Argentina 'to refrain from taking any action that may exacerbate the situation'.
>
> The same resolution urged the governments of the United Kingdom and the Argentine Republic 'to call a truce that will make it possible to resume and proceed normally with the negotiation aimed at a peaceful settlement of the conflict, taking into account *the rights of sovereignty of the Republic of Argentina over the Malvinas Islands*

and the interests of the islanders'.

(*The Times*, 29 April 1982; my italics).

Mr Al Haig, the US Secretary of State, was at that stage still trying to mediate between the contending parties. He received a cold reception from the other delegates, when he blamed Argentina for being the first party to use force, and said that the dispute should not be handled within the security framework of the Rio Pact. In the end, seventeen votes were cast for the resolution, none against, and the United States, together with Chile, Colombia and Trinidad & Tobago, abstained.

In the light of later comments in Britain that the Thatcher government should have accepted the so-called Peruvian Peace Plan, it is interesting to note that Peru was one of the strongest supporters of the resolution and had therefore no credibility as far as London was concerned. Chile abstained because of its unresolved dispute with Argentina over the Beagle Channel Islands; Colombia, because the Provisional Government of Nicaragua, which rather surprisingly was a strong supporter of the resolution, had in 1979 claimed the Caribbean island group of San Andrés and Providencia, which although it had always been Colombian and had been formally awarded to Colombia in 1929, lay close to the Nicaraguan coast (Calvert 1982, pp. 101–5).

The OAS played no further significant role in the gathering crisis until after the British landings at San Carlos Bay on 21 May. This brought an immediate reaction from Dr Costa Méndez, who asked for and obtained a meeting of the UN Security Council in New York. However though he obtained strong verbal support from Panama and other Latin American states which were not members of the Council, and the United States' position, as voiced by Dr Jeane Kirkpatrick, was equivocal, Britain had made it clear that it would veto any resolution calling for an immediate cease-fire and the only result therefore was one renewing the Secretary General's mandate to use his good offices to that purpose.

Before this happened, however, at Argentina's request, the Meeting of Consultation of the Foreign Ministers of the OAS had reconvened in Washington. Behind closed doors, Dr Costa Méndez denounced the United States for 'supporting the criminal colonialist, warlike adventure' of the UK and received a standing ovation. Mr Haig did point out that it had been Argentina, not Britain, that had rejected his mediation and the subsequent Peruvian peace plan, but received only limited support (*The Times*, 29 May 1982). Not surprisingly the meeting voted on 29 May for a resolution condemning Britain's attack on the islands, urging the United States to halt aid to Britain and calling on members to offer any aid to Argentina they thought appropriate. Only because of heavy US lobbying did it stop short of calling for mandatory collective sanctions against Britain. However the US did not go so far as to vote against the resolution, which was again carried by 17 votes to 0 with 4 abstentions (Calvert 1982, pp. 133–5).

Central America

Following the 1979 revolutions in Nicaragua and Grenada, there was euphoria on the revolutionary left, some of whose supporters failed to recognise the very special situation that had obtained in each of these countries. In 1980 civil war broke out in El Salvador. The military government there seemed unprepared and was soon in serious difficulties. However the Carter administration lent them considerable support and with the election and inauguration of President Reagan support to the Salvadorean government was stepped up (Dunkerley 1985).

The Reagan administration believed that the insurrection in El Salvador formed part of a world-wide Communist conspiracy, supported by the Soviet Union through Havana and Managua. In 1981, therefore, President Reagan gave authority for a clandestine force to be formed to launch a counter-revolutionary guerrilla campaign in Nicaragua. These soon became known to their opponents as *contras* (short for counter-revolutionaries) and this name stuck, though the anodyne title chosen by the CIA was the Nicaraguan Democratic Force (FDN) (Walker 1987).

With decolonisation now almost complete – Belize became independent in 1981, despite the fact that Guatemala had not yet abandoned its claims to its territory – the US government felt free to adopt a policy of 'rolling back the frontiers of Communism' (Calvert 1988b). Though the strategy was primarily military, it was backed by a limited amount of economic aid in the form of the so-called Caribbean Basin Initiative. But the situation in El Salvador proved intractable, and in October 1983 the US government took advantage of the fall of Bishop in Grenada to assert its capacity to carry out a successful military intervention, after it had already taken significant measures to destabilise the Provisional Revolutionary Government (Searle 1983; O'Shaughnessy 1984; Ambursley and Dunkerley 1984).

President Reagan objected on 3 November 1983 to the term 'invasion' to describe the US intervention in Grenada; it was, he said, a 'rescue' mission. In fact it was both an invasion and an intervention, and, more poignantly, a war. True, it was a very small war for those who started it: a 'Low Intensity Conflict' intended to give a costless victory to a world superpower to boost its world pre-eminence at a moment when its credibility was threatened by events in the Lebanon (Davidson 1987, pp. 162–3). 'The consequences of war are many. But essentially "War kills" ' and in Grenada, when the frothy rhetoric had died down and the facts emerged, at least 111 people died and 644 were wounded, the vast majority of them Grenadians (Tiwathia 1987, p. 116).

Analysis of the operation had very uncomfortable lessons for the United States, which later events were to prove had not been learnt. Despite the psychological build-up over the previous four years, and three full-scale rehearsals, virtually everything that could go wrong went wrong. It took a world superpower nine days to attack and subdue all opposition in an island of only 311 km². Bridgeheads were not secured because highly trained forces hesitated to land in face of small-arms fire. Intelligence was hopelessly wrong, though the information could have been had for the asking – a group of unarmed reporters landed peacefully on the quay at St George's in the middle of the fighting and were received with courtesy by the people their country was attacking. Most of the 135 US casualties were the victims of collision or mechanical failures resulting from overdependence on high technology. The paranoid belief that the island was full of armed Cuban soldiers had no foundation, yet was unquestioningly believed and led directly to the high level of Grenadan casualties through either overreliance on firepower, or a callous disregard for the enemy, or both (Tiwathia 1987, p. 117).

While the United States was still trying to put the Grenadian Revolution into reverse (Ferguson 1990b), a series of clandestine attacks took place on shipping and harbours along the Nicaraguan coast. Though these were represented as being spontaneous actions by the contras there was evidence of them being co-ordinated from a US warship. At this point the Nicaraguan government by-passed the

OAS and took its case directly to the UN Security Council. On 5 April 1984 the United States vetoed a Security Council resolution condemning the mining of Nicaraguan ports, and when the Nicaraguan government filed a case against them in the World Court four days later the US formally withdrew from its jurisdiction. It was at this point that for the first time President Reagan admitted the active complicity of the United States and tried to justify it. He told a press conference that the Nicaraguan government was 'exporting revolution' and promised: 'We are going to try to inconvenience the government of Nicaragua until they quit that kind of action' (*The Guardian*, 6 April 1984).

It was as a result of the US ability to manipulate the work of the OAS that the task of mediation in Central America was taken up by the ad hoc Contadora Group, made up of representatives of Mexico, Panama, Colombia and Venezuela. However this effort foundered in the face of US intransigence. When Nicaragua accepted a bargain with the other four Central American countries, the US pressured the latter to change their minds and to demand further concessions. In February 1985, after his re-election, President Reagan publicly called on the newly elected government of President Ortega to give in and to admit the contras to government. Meanwhile, faced by a hostile Congress that voted to cut off aid to the contras, the United States government initiated a rolling programme of 'exercises' in Honduras which amounted to a substantial arms build-up. However any further build-up in Honduras was halted by first the Contadora initiative and then the breaking on 25 November 1986 of the news of the 'Iran–Contra' scandal.

The meeting of the sixteenth General Assembly in Guatemala City in 1986 was effectively paralysed by the division between the United States and the Latin American majority on two issues: Central America and the Falklands/Malvinas. Britain's unilateral declaration of a fisheries conservation zone had prompted a request from Argentina for an emergency session of the Permanent Council, which in a compromise resolution unanimously adopted on 11 November urged Britain and Argentina to resume negotiations over the sovereignty of the islands and to refrain from further actions that could upset 'the already delicate existing situation'. In supporting this, the United States Secretary of State, Mr George Shultz, was understood to have headed off a much more toughly worded resolution condemning the British action and reasserting Argentine sovereignty, while he concentrated his attack on Nicaragua, where, he said, there would be 'civil war' until 'genuine democracy' was restored.

The resolution adopted by consensus on 14 November calling on the Contadora Group and its co-sponsors 'to persist in their efforts towards peace in Central America' was meaningless as long as the United States, through its allies Honduras and Costa Rica, was able, as it had consistently done in private, to frustrate talks with Nicaragua. An equally meaningless resolution on human rights was virtually the only other tangible outcome of the session. In effect the Falklands/Malvinas issue had served to deflect much criticism of the United States for its decision the previous month to resume overt aid to the 'contras' in Nicaragua, and it was not until a week later that news of the Iran–Contra scandal broke in Washington.

In 1987, a year dominated by events in Central America, the OAS continued to maintain its less conspicuous role. The Permanent Council called for restraint when President Lusinchi of Venezuela complained in August that a Colombian warship had infringed his country's territorial waters in the Gulf of Venezuela and dispatched troop reinforcements to the area. The Venezuelan Foreign Minister, Simon Alberto Consalvi, brushed aside Colombian proposals for mediation. The rejection of Bolivia's bid for access to the sea by Chile led the former to threaten to take its dispute to the OAS, but Chilean spokesmen made it clear that they would not recognise the organisation's jurisdiction.

Costa Rica, which had abolished its own army, and was under strong pressure from the Reagan administration to create a new one, next under President Oscar Arias took the leading role in bringing the Central American states themselves together to make peace. The Arias Plan, and subsequent agreement to it of the Central American states at Esquipulas II, resulted in extensive concessions by Nicaragua and prospects for at least relative peace (Arias 1987; see also Millán 1983). As a result, the meeting of the seventeenth General Assembly held in Washington, DC, in November 1987 was dominated by President Daniel Ortega of Nicaragua, who in his first visit to that city since taking office scored a substantial propaganda coup. The release of more than a thousand prisoners on the eve of his departure confirmed his acceptance of the Arias Plan. The initial refusal of Honduras to play its part in the peace process had been undermined by the finding in October of the Inter-American Court of Human Rights that at least 130 people had been abducted by the Honduran armed forces between 1981 and 1984. Hence when on 9 November, the Nicaraguan Foreign Minister, Fr Miguel d'Escoto, trumped a tentative offer of direct talks from the United States by accepting it, the Honduran Foreign Minister, Carlos López Contreras, responded with an offer to ban the contras from Honduran soil and establish joint border verification.

In the last years of the Reagan administration, the aftermath of the Iran–Contra scandal paralysed US attempts to increase pressure on Nicaragua. However the administration was still able to block any serious attempt to achieve a general peace. Fortunately the other work of the OAS and its related agencies went on despite its political paralysis. On 20 January Honduras, the first Latin American government to be arraigned before the Inter-American Court of Human Rights, was held guilty of maintaining army death squads responsible for the 'disappearance' of named civilians. Meanwhile the USSR under Gorbachev showed no real interest in the Caribbean area. Even before the collapse of the USSR Cuba could no longer count on Soviet economic aid, and the Cubans had made it very plain to the Nicaraguans after 1983 that in a showdown with the United States, they were on their own. If there was only going to be one Cuba in the Americas it was going to be Cuba and not Nicaragua.

In the event, 1990 saw free elections being held for the second time in Nicaragua. On this occasion, however, war weariness had set in (González 1990). The result was a new pro-US government led by Sra Violeta Barrios de Chamorro and the speedy disarming of the contras, ironically at the hands of what was still essentially the old Sandinista army led by General Humberto Ortega, brother of the outgoing President. Meanwhile the outgoing UN Secretary General, Sr Javier Pérez de Cuéllar, successfully brokered peace in El Salvador and there were even reports of a possible bargain between the armed forces and guerrilla groups in Guatemala. Significantly it was the United Nations, and not the OAS, that was called upon to oversee the demobilisation of the contras in Nicaragua, while Argentina deployed four unarmed Israeli-built patrol craft to patrol the Gulf of Fonseca on behalf of the United Nations' observer force, Observadores de las Naciones Unidas para Centroamérica (ONUCA) (Pugh 1994).

Panama

Initially, under the Reagan administration, the US government accepted the rise to power in Panama of General Noriega, and was content to make use of him as their agent. Noriega received commendation both from the US Drug Enforcement Agency (DEA) and Attorney General Edwin Meese for his collaboration with their campaign to stop drugs from reaching the United States. However the facts now available suggest a very different picture: that he was actively engaged in funding the US-backed contras through his drugs dealings (Scranton 1991; Zimbalist and Weeks 1991, pp. 140–1; Kempe 1990). When he had served his purpose and was becoming a public embarrassment, the Reagan administration took a series of steps to force him out.

In the early part of 1988, this led to the OAS being drawn into the tragi-comedy. At a Special Meeting of Consultation on 27 February, delegates invited to consider the 'crisis' in Panama voiced support for Noriega's puppet President Delvalle but failed to vote either for the United States or for General Noriega. Following the decision of the United States Senate on 26 June, which led to the recall of the Panamanian Ambassador and a diplomatic protest at US interference in Panama's internal affairs, an extraordinary session of the OAS convened at Panama's request resolved by 17 votes to 1 (the United States) that US activities in Panama now constituted 'unwarranted interference' in Panama's internal affairs – not at all the sort of response for which the US might have hoped (Zimbalist 1989).

President Bush succeeded President Reagan in January 1989. On 7 May 1989 elections took place in Panama but were annulled by President Noriega after widespread violence, leaving him in power. An extraordinary Meeting of Consultation of Foreign Ministers was held in Washington on 17 May which approved by consensus a resolution to send a delegation to Panama. An amendment specifically naming General Noriega, the Commander of the Panamanian Defence Forces, as responsible for 'grave events and abuses' which had curtailed the right to free choice and curtailed human rights was carried by 20 votes to two (Panama and Nicaragua) with seven abstentions (Antigua and Barbuda, Bahamas, Dominica, Grenada, Peru, Suriname, Uruguay). The delegation led by the Secretary General, João Baena Soares, visited Panama between 23 and

27 May and held talks with government and opposition parties, including General Noriega himself. It was unsuccessful in negotiating a resolution to the dispute.

A second Meeting of Consultation of the Foreign Ministers held in Washington, DC on 19–20 July called for a transitional government to be formed by 1 September when the presidential term of the de facto head of state, Manuel Solis Palma, was due to expire and fresh elections to be held as soon as possible. The US demand for the resignation of General Noriega was not however accepted, and when the mediation mission delivered its report at a further Meeting of Consultation on 23–4 August the US Deputy Secretary of State, Lawrence Eagleburger, denounced Panama in the strongest terms, stating that if power was not transferred by 1 September 'civilised nations' would have to declare the regime illegal. The Foreign Minister of Venezuela was subsequently dismissed for his strong line in support of the United States position.

In the event the Bush administration did refuse to recognise the interim government and broke off diplomatic relations. An unsuccessful coup attempt, which appears to have had US support, was frustrated. Meanwhile another consideration came to the fore. On 31 December 1989, under the Panama Canal Treaties, a Panamanian president of the Canal Commission was due to be appointed, marking a further stage in the transfer of authority over the Canal from the US to Panama. Bush made it clear that he would not accept any name proposed by the interim government. However, eleven days before this contingency actually arose, on 20 December 1989, US troops intervened to overthrow General Noriega.

As in the case of Grenada the intervention in Panama was met by resistance. In this case it came both from the Panamanian armed forces (FDP) and from the pro-Noriega militia, the so-called 'dignity batallions'. Military action, code-named 'Operation Just Cause', began when, at 1 a.m. local time on 20 December 1989, 13,000 US troops stationed in the Canal area, reinforced by 2nd Army Ranger Battalions and a brigade of the 82nd Airborne Division, flown in directly from bases in the United States, a further 9,500 men, with full support from aircraft, helicopters, tanks and artillery, seized key installations in six simultaneous thrusts at FDP installations from Rio Hato, 70 miles west of the Canal to Fort Cimarron, some 30 miles east of it (*Keesing's* 1989: 37452) FDP headquarters was destroyed, but not before General Noriega was able to broadcast a call to continue fighting. Hence though by 21 December the Defence Department claimed 'organised resistance' had been effectively crushed, in fact serious fighting between US troops and both the FDP and the 'dignity battalions' went on until 26 December. Hundreds of homes were destroyed by US action in the vicinity of the FDP headquarters, while fighting and looting spread to the town centres of Panama City and Colon. To combat this, a further 2,000 personnel were flown in from the United States on 23 December. At their peak, some 26,000 US troops were deployed, including the first US women to take part in armed combat.

Certainly 'Operation Just Cause' was far from bloodless. Casualty figures released by the US Department of Defense after the first stage of the fighting was over stated that 23 US soldiers had been killed and 323 wounded. Later the number of fatalities was revised to 26. On 9 January the Defense Department stated that 314 members of the FDP had been killed and 124 wounded (*Keesing's*: 37181). 'Collateral damage', as civilian casualties are officially termed in the Pentagon, was undoubtedly high, given the tendency to make maximum use of heavy firepower to minimise US casualties. Reliable figures indicate that more than 3,000 civilians were wounded in the operation, a fact which the official casualty figures seem to have ignored altogether.

After four days of resistance, General Noriega, who had hitherto evaded capture, took refuge in the Papal Nunciature. Guillermo Endara, sworn in as Head of State on a US base on the day of the intervention, established a new government. The Nunciature was immediately surrounded by barbed wire and US Marines who played very loud pop music at it through loudspeakers until the Papal Nuncio formally complained to Washington about the noise. Prayer and plain chant proved much less to the general's taste and on 3 January Noriega left diplomatic sanctuary and surrendered to US occupation forces (*Congressional Quarterly Weekly Report*, 48:1, 6 January 1990, 51).

President Bush did not attempt to disguise the fact that the United States had acted unilaterally. None of the four reasons he gave for the US intervention, however, warranted the open breach of the Charter of the OAS, and on this occasion the OAS did not accept them, even though there was nothing in practice that they could do about it. On 22 December 1989, while fighting was still going on, a Meeting of Consultation 'deeply deplored' the action and called for the immediate cessation of hostilities and beginning of negotiations, a resolution carried by 20 votes to 1 (that of the United States), with 6 abstentions (Antigua and Barbuda, Costa Rica, Honduras, El Salvador, Guatemala and Venezuela). However the surrender of General Noriega put an end to any further consideration of the issue and the new Endara government was, rather reluctantly, accepted as the legitimate government of Panama.

Thirty-four members attended the twenty-first General Assembly, held in Santiago de Chile from 3 to 9 June 1991, which endorsed the Declaration of Santiago, under which the Permanent Council was required to convene at once following 'any abrupt or irregular interruption of the democratic, political and institutional process, or of the legitimate exercise of power by a democratically elected government' of any member state. They rejected however the proposal that all states should immediately sever diplomatic relations with the state in question, supporting instead Mexico's traditional policy (the so-called Estrada Doctrine) of recognising any government shown to be in physical control of its national territory.

An admission that the United States had in the past made 'errors' in its Latin American policy by viewing the region through the 'sometimes distorting prism of the Cold War' was made by Lawrence Eagleburger, US Deputy Secretary of State, and was the more noteworthy for the fact that he personally had committed some of them.

Haiti and the preservation of democracy

Though with Aylwin's victory in Chile civilian government is now the norm in South America, there has been some spread of the military pattern to new areas of the Caribbean, for example, Grenada in 1983, Suriname currently. In Colombia the army have assumed new importance in face both of cocaine barons and renewed insurgency but both there and in Venezuela, where there have been two abortive military coups against the administration of President Carlos Andrés Pérez, civilians have held political power continuously since 1958. President Reagan himself took credit for the general restoration of democracy in the Hemisphere during the 1980s, though it began (under President Carter) before he took office and in most cases owed little or nothing to US assistance; indeed in the case of Nicaragua the US worked hard to displace a democratic regime which had substantial popular support evidenced in a free election. Otherwise the conspicuous exception in the Caribbean region has been Haiti, which has involved much of the attention of the OAS for some years, and is seen by many as a test case for the sincerity of US professions of support for democracy.

From 1957 to 1986 Haiti was under the rule, first of Dr François Duvalier ('Papa Doc') and then, on his death in April 1971, of his son, Jean-Claude Duvalier ('Bébé Doc'). Food riots which broke out in 1984 proved to be the prelude, first to the resignation of the hard-line Minister of the Interior, Dr Roger Lafontant, and then of a general uprising. The US government, concerned about a communist take-over, arranged for Duvalier to be flown into exile in France (February 1986), and power passed to an interim government headed by General Henri Namphy.

Unfortunately General Namphy had no intention of relinquishing power to a constitutional government, and after he had successfully frustrated two abortive attempts to hold elections, and the US and other governments had withdrawn their aid programmes in protest, he was deposed in a military coup in September 1988. His successor, General Prosper Avril, also tried to hold on to power, but was squeezed out by US pressure in March 1990. In the first free presidential election ever held in Haiti, in December 1990, Fr Jean-Bertrand Aristide, who had won huge popularity as the priest of the poor, was outright victor and took office in February 1991. In September 1991 the army, encouraged by the old 'mulatto' elite who saw themselves endangered by such a radical regime, deposed him.

A Meeting of Consultation of the OAS met to consider the situation and voted to impose sanctions in an attempt to secure the restoration of democracy. A mission consisting of six foreign ministers, and headed by the Secretary General, João Baena Soares, was sent to Port-au-Prince but was summarily expelled. However further painstaking negotiations did bring about a meeting between the contending parties in Bogotá on 22 November, but the settlement then negotiated was rejected by military and congressional leaders in Haiti on 8 January 1991, and it became clear that they would not in any circumstances accept a settlement that involved the return of Fr Aristide.

Hence at Nassau on 17 and 18 May 1991 a Special Meeting of Consultation of Foreign Ministers agreed to tighten trade sanctions, despite evidence that though the existing restrictions had already created widespread poverty in Haiti, the elite had prospered by evading them. The new measures banned the transport of goods to Haiti by sea and air, but foreign business in Haiti continued to operate and by ending the issue of travel visas the measures stopped refugees from escaping from the country and reaching the United States. On 28 May President Bush announced that the 'boat people' already intercepted by US Coastguards would be returned to Haiti forthwith, without a hearing, and by mid-August US Coastguard reported that 27,440 of the 37,381 people who had fled since the fall of Aristide had already been repatriated. Between 18 and 21 August the Secretary General, Sr João Baena Soares again visited Haiti at the head of a thirteen-member OAS delegation, following which on 17 September a small permanent OAS mission arrived to evaluate progress, a move generally taken as confirmation that the OAS had accepted de facto the military-backed government of Marc Bazin. The Secretary General was also the only dignitary of consequence to attend the five hundredth anniversary of the arrival of Columbus in the Dominican Republic, which was boycotted by all other Latin American leaders after violent objections throughout the region.

By contrast, the report of the OAS commission on the coup by President Fujimori of Peru on 5 April was non-committal. The President himself defended his actions to the meeting. He had already given pledges to hold a plebiscite and to allow local elections to go ahead as planned, and though Venezuela suspended diplomatic relations and Colombia trade links, no other action had followed. Now following warnings both from the US government and the OAS itself, though a special emissary, Héctor Gros Espiell, Foreign Minister of Uruguay, President Fujimori agreed to an elected constituent assembly within five months and to allow OAS observers to oversee the elections. In return, the meeting urged a swift return to democracy in Peru and did not impose economic sanctions. On 18 June the new Peruvian Prime Minister, Oscar de la Puente Raygada, travelled to Washington to explain his government's plan to postpone the municipal elections due on 8 November to March 1993, and the decision announced on 28 August to send observers to the Congressional elections was generally seen as acceptance of President Fujimori's position. However the Peruvian government's intention to re-introduce the death penalty was foreshadowed when it gave notice on 15 October of its intention to withdraw from the 1978 American Convention on Human Rights (the San José Pact).

The OAS paradox

The OAS works within the constraint of a basic paradox. The majority of its members wish to maintain the non-intervention norm, but, at the same time, they wish to make use of the organisation to promote their own objectives, and that in recent years has included the promotion of democracy in the region. The OAS has had a limited degree of success in this respect. Its most important role remains offering a forum in which issues can be discussed and contacts made in a multilateral framework, among nominal equals. On the basis of such informal contacts, it has been successful in promoting agreement between contending parties, but only, as the case of Central America shows, when and where the contending parties themselves eventually have come to recognise that a settlement was in their mutual interest.

The one area in which it has been conspicuously unsuccessful is where a conflict involves a party external to the hemisphere. The example of the Falklands Crisis is the most obvious, and it was also significant in the extent to which it called in question the traditional dominance of the OAS by the United States. But as the case of Cuba shows, this is not the only instance in which its ability to act has been constrained by its geographical limitations. Multilateral diplomacy, in any case, forms only part of a range of approaches to international peace keeping, none of which is likely to be successful except in combination with others.

Other regional organisations

Regional integration in Latin America has had a chequered history (Gauhar 1985). Creation of a *Latin American Free Trade Area* (LAFTA, or in Spanish ALALC) was envisaged by the UN Economic Commission for Latin America (ECLA) as early as 1955. The formal organisation, consisting of the states of South America together with Mexico, was created by the Treaty of Montevideo of 1960 which came into effect on 1 June 1961. However because of the very different levels of economic growth of the member states it failed to achieve its objective of promoting intra-regional trade, and by 1980 only 3 per cent of all concessions had been made since the treaty came into effect.

By a second Treaty of Montevideo LAFTA was therefore reconstituted on 12 August 1980 as the *Latin American Integration Association* (LAIA) or Asociación Latino-Americana de Integración (ALADI), with the more limited purpose of protecting existing trade arrangements. Members are divided into three tiers: most developed (Argentina, Brazil, Mexico), intermediate (Chile, Colombia, Peru, Uruguay, Venezuela) and least developed (Bolivia, Ecuador, Paraguay). The permanent directive body of the organisation is the Committee of Representatives, with representatives from each of the member states and a number of observers, subject to the overall direction of the Council of Ministers. The Secretariat has its offices in Montevideo, Uruguay. It has undoubtedly had a significant long-term impact by promoting the ideal of free trade. The fact that Chile has recently decided to enter into relations with the incipient North American Free Trade Area (NAFTA) has clearly been facilitated by the existence of regular contacts such as ALADI promotes.

Meanwhile a group of states, led by the Presidents of Mexico and Venezuela, had sought to create a new regional organisation which would not be dominated by the United States and which would include Cuba. The *Sistema Economica Latino-Americana (SELA)* or Latin American Economic System was founded in 1975 and now has 26 member states. Decision making is through regular annual conferences at Caracas, Venezuela, where its Secretariat is located. Its purpose is to promote regional economic co-operation and development through study and discussion of specific problems. It is fair to say that, despite the hopes of its founders that it would have a material effect in helping to bring about a New International Economic Order (NIEO), it has in practice had only a very limited impact on public debate.

Sub-regional organisations

The oldest of the sub-regional organisations in Latin America is, appropriately, to be found in Central America, which on account of its scale and poverty was excluded from the Latin American Free Trade Area. The Central American Common Market (Mercado Común Centroamericano – generally CACM, sometimes CACOM) was founded by the General Treaty for Central American Economic Integration, signed by the Central American states of Costa Rica, El Salvador, Guatemala, Honduras and Nicaragua at Managua on

13 February 1960. Policy is formulated by Ministerial Meetings of the five member states' Ministers of Central American Integration, and meetings of other ministers, presidents of central banks etc. The Permanent Secretariat (Secretaría Permanente del Tratado General de Integración Económica Centroamericana – SIECA) in Guatemala City supervises the working of the treaty and arranges meetings as required. There are several associated regional institutions, including the Fund for Economic Stabilisation founded in 1969.

Between 1962, when the treaty came into effect, and 1969, when its operations were disrupted by the so-called 'Football War' and the consequent withdrawal of Honduras in 1970 from the work of the organisation, there was a considerable increase in intra-regional trade, despite the largely similar nature of the five economies. In 1973 Honduras made bilateral arrangements with the other three states, but by the time that diplomatic relations with El Salvador were restored in 1980 civil war had broken out there and that and the Nicaraguan crisis led to a steep decline in intra-regional trade. An agreement to establish a Central American Monetary Union was signed in 1984 but has yet to be implemented. However since 1986 intra-regional trade has begun to pick up, and with the restoration of relative peace in the region is expected to increase further.

The *Andean Pact* group, originally the Andean Subregional Integration Agreement, takes its Spanish name – Acuerdo de Cartagena/Grupo Andino – from the Treaty of Cartagena signed by the governments of Bolivia, Chile, Colombia, Ecuador and Peru on 26 May 1969. In February 1973 Venezuela joined the organisation, but Chile withdrew from the organisation on 21 January 1977, officially because of its hostility to foreign capital but in practice because of the other members' hostility to the dictatorial regime of General Pinochet. Even after the Mandate of Cartagena in May 1979, which called for greater political and economic co-operation, regional issues continued to disrupt the working of the group; Bolivia briefly withdrew in 1980–81 after the seizure of power by General García Meza and Ecuador suspended membership in 1981 following a border clash with Peru.

The purpose of the group was and is to promote economic integration between the member states by progressive elimination of tariff barriers and the co-ordination of industrial development, and since its formation intra-group trade has grown significantly. At a summit meeting on 18 May 1991 heads of government approved the

Declaration of Caracas, committing the five states to a free-trade zone by January 1992, and envisaging a fully integrated common market by 1995. However on 26 August 1992, following President Fujimori's coup, the government of Peru announced its temporary withdrawal from the pact because of its failure to continue to receive multilateral aid. Given the earlier announcement that Bolivia had applied to join Mercosur, the outlook for the pact looked doubtful.

The supreme authority of the group is the Commission, made up of one ambassador from each member state. Foreign Ministers meet annually or as required to formulate external policy. The Andean Parliament (Parlamento Andino) of five members from each state has a purely advisory role but the Court of Justice established in 1984 settles disputes arising under the Treaty.

The *Caribbean Community and Common Market* (CARICOM) was created by the Treaty of Chaguaramas signed in Trinidad in July 1973, and replaced the Caribbean Free Trade Association (CARIFTA) created in 1965 (Payne 1980). The Caribbean Development Bank (headquarters at St Michael, Barbados) is an associate institution of CARICOM. Subject only to decisions of the Heads of Government Conference, which has met regularly since 1982, the work of the Common Market is directed by the Council, consisting of a Minister of Government from each member state. The Secretariat is located at Georgetown, Guyana. Present members are Antigua and Barbuda, Bahamas, Barbados, Belize, Dominica, Grenada, Guyana, Jamaica, Montserrat, St Kitts-Nevis, St Lucia, St Vincent and the Grenadines and Trinidad & Tobago. The purpose of the organisation is to promote intra-regional trade and development; however its work in this regard has been much hampered by unilateral decisions of member states and by lack of funds. In 1992 the leaders of the Central American Common Market took the decision to enter talks with CARICOM on the possibility of forming a larger regional organisation (see also Payne and Sutton 1993).

On 26 March 1991 the Presidents of Argentina, Brazil, Paraguay and Uruguay meeting at Asunción signed an agreement to create a new common market in the Southern Cone with its headquarters in Montevideo. The new grouping, to be termed the South American Common Market or *Mercosur*, formed a natural development from a series of bilateral accords between the participating states, such as the formal statement of intent signed during the visit of the President of Brazil, Fernando Collor de Mello, to Buenos Aires on 6–7 July

1990. With an estimated population of 190,000,000 and a combined GNP of $420,000 million, it aimed to achieve free movement of goods and services by 31 December 1994, commencing with a 47 per cent cut in tariffs in June. On 19 June its members signed a framework free-trade agreement with the United States and on 20 July the economy ministers met to discuss anti-dumping policy. The Presidents of Argentina, Brazil, Paraguay and Uruguay (with the President of Bolivia present as an observer) met on 26–7 June 1992 at Las Lenas, Argentina, to concert arrangements for the implementation of the Common Market (Mercosur) by 31 December 1994, as scheduled, and considered plans for improved communications between the participating countries.

In 1992 Mexico took the formal decision to enter into a *North American Free Trade Area* (NAFTA) with Canada and the United States. This project, which came into existence on 1 January 1994, will create a trading bloc of some 320 million people, significantly larger than the European Community (EC) as currently constituted. However though the Mexican government is undoubtedly strongly committed to the proposal, from which, despite traditional reservations, it expects very large economic returns for its people, political changes in both Canada and the United States are currently delaying further progress.

Conclusion

The growth and institutionalisation of the inter-American system, and the creation of the OAS, owes as much to Latin American efforts as to the impetus of the United States. The inter-American system owes its origins to rationalist notions of international relations. A rationalist interpretation of its growth and action is supported by many of the events described above. However nothing in this account is incompatible with the realist perspective, that, in an age of superpower confrontation, the OAS came in major issues to be heavily influenced and at times virtually controlled by the United States, while in no case has the solidarity of the Latin American states been effective against the hegemony of the United States as both a global and a regional power.

Sub-regional organisations have also been created, but have suffered from the limitations of the economies of which they are composed. The United States has, in accordance with its ideals of a liberal world economic order, traditionally preferred to keep economic and political issues separate, but has not hesitated to use political pressure to further its economic interests or vice versa. US pressure for the extension of the General Agreement on Tariffs and Trade, if successful, would preclude the effective operation of such sub-regional agreements, including, potentially, NAFTA itself. Nevertheless such agreements form a rationalist response to the economic situation in which most Latin American states actually find themselves, and the sense of political cohesion which they generate has proved functionally effective in generating and maintaining a wider sense of solidarity.

Chapter Seven

Latin America in the world

Latin America in the world

There has been a long argument between realists and rationalists as to how far, if at all, the world's less developed countries (LDCs) do participate in the world system. A cynical view is that they do participate – as victims.

Realism should suggest that there is enough truth in this to make it uncomfortable. However it should also tell us that, given their very limited capacity to project force, there would be very little that they could do about it. Rationalism, on the other hand, should remind us that the problems of Latin America are by no means the exclusive property of the outside world, nor are the countries concerned entirely without the ability to exert either direct or reverse influence on external powers. The Latin American states have therefore been able to maximise their capacity to influence events therefore, by co-sponsoring a world order in which they take maximum advantage of the opportunities afforded to them to gain significant bargaining advantages. Not surprisingly, this is precisely what the evidence suggests that they have tried to do.

Direct influence

Undoubtedly, in the main the direct influence of most Latin American states has been limited. Because of their sheer size, as well as other natural advantages, Brazil and Mexico could have been expected to emerge as significant regional powers, with some capacity for global reach. However, though both were recognised as such as early as the beginning of this century, for most of it they have been overshadowed by the United States. Only since the Second World War, in which it was an active participant, has Brazil taken a leading role inside South America. In part this has been with the active collaboration of the United States, which saw it as a regional support to its own continental hegemony.

However Brazil was once, if only for a brief period, the seat of a worldwide empire and since those days it has never ceased to think in global rather than regional terms. Hence the significance of its initiatives is that from time to time they have gone well beyond the limited objective of establishing or maintaining a regional power, with or without the support of the United States. Brazil took an active role in both world wars, and in the international peacekeeping that has followed. In the 1970s it embarked on significant diplomatic and trade initiatives in Africa South of the Sahara (SSA), where its key decision not to support a white South Atlantic project played a significant part in the eventual collapse of the Portuguese empire. Economically, the decision to use state power to further the transition to an export-led economy brought additional returns, for example, when the state oil company, Petrobrás, obtained licences to search for oil in the North Sea, and significantly, with the onset of the debt crisis, only Brazil was seen as being so important to the world economy that its credit lines had to be kept open at all costs.

Ironically, therefore, the most striking example of direct influence overseas in recent years has come neither from Brazil nor from Mexico, but from Cuba. Cuba's military interventions in Angola and Ethiopia are significantly different, both from the overseas involvement of other Latin American states, but also from one another. In Angola the Cubans themselves claim to have launched *Operación Carlota* spontaneously, returning to Africa the blessings of freedom of which their own ancestors had been unjustly deprived. Once there, Cubans fought independently or as part of Angolan government forces. In Ethiopia, on the other hand, Cuban troops fought as part of a Soviet formation under Soviet command, as noted in Chapter Two. However the fact that their intervention in the battle of Dire Dawa was generally recognised as decisive in the campaign to recapture the Ogaden from Somalia gave them a prestige in this part of the world also which had significant repercussions in terms of boosting Cuban influence in other Third World countries.

Blocked by the United States from assisting revolutionary movements in Latin America, Cuba's tricontinental strategy paid off in terms of goodwill and diplomatic influence out of all proportion to Cuba's relatively modest economic or military capability. The many instances of Cuban instructors supporting left-wing governments, as in Cabo Verde and Mozambique, and guerrilla movements in Africa, for example in Congo (Brazzaville), are by their nature harder to evaluate than the impact of direct military intervention. At the same time, Cuba took a leading role in the Non-Aligned Movement (NAM). But its attempt to convert its prestige as an antagonist of imperialism into support for the USSR, however, ultimately failed as the direct result of the Soviet intervention in Afghanistan, which directly undercut Castro's diplomatic initiative.

Owing to its proximity to the United States, Mexico has taken a neutralist line and avoided political involvement. Its major political contribution to international peace in the recent period has been its sponsorship of the 1967 Treaty for the Prohibition of Nuclear Weapons in Latin America (the Tlatelolco Treaty). Characteristically, however, this treaty, creating the first nuclear-free zone in an inhabited region, reflects the traditional Latin American tendency to seek isolation from the outside world, and its influence on the outside world has been indirect, by precept and example. However the direct influence of the governments of Mexico and Venezuela in pressure for a new international economic order (NIEO), exercised both through the NAM and the UN, should not be overlooked.

Reverse influence

The classic instance of a Latin American state exercising reverse influence on a major power outside the hemisphere, of course, is again that of Cuba, 1961–89. Its alliance with the Soviet Union committed that power to its maintenance, reinforced by Castro's bold declaration that Cuba was already a socialist state. Since according to the tenets of Marxism-Leninism, the stage of socialism, once achieved, could not be reversed, from that time on the Soviet Union was committed to a strategy of subsidising and supporting its outpost in the Americas. Ironically, this belief not only formed the implicit basis for the Brezhnev doctrine but was also widely believed in the West and indeed explicitly formed the basis for Jeane Kirkpatrick's notorious distinction between totalitarian regimes, which would not evolve into liberal democracies, and 'moderately repressive authoritarian governments', which would (Kirkpatrick 1982).

However as this argument shows, the United States, too, has found itself entangled into support for some very dubious regimes. In practice, it may matter little to the victims of such regimes whether their support has been deliberately sought, as when the Reagan administration courted the support of Argentina in El Salvador, or tacitly accepted as a fact of life, as when Harry Truman, asking of Anastasio Somoza Garcia if he were not 'an S.O.B.', received the terse reply: 'Yes, but he's our S.O.B.' (Diedrich 1982). But it does matter very much whether or not the countries they were living in were in the western hemisphere, since the hegemony of the United States necessarily limits the freedom of other countries in the region both to act and to be acted upon.

Growth of world involvement

The first emergence of Latin American states as members of world community came with independence. However, as we have noted, Spain itself was slow to recognise their right to exist, and most European powers paid little attention to them. The nineteenth-century world was strongly dominated by the European state system, and even the United States was not recognised as a fully fledged power until after 1898. Along with the United States, Mexico and Brazil were invited to the First Hague Peace Conference in 1899, but only the former attended. It is undoubtedly relevant to note that at the Paris Exposition of 1900 the soldiers forming the honour guard on the Mexican pavilion were chosen for their European complexion. It was, significantly, the United States that pressed for an invitation to be issued for all twenty Latin American states to attend the Second Hague Peace Conference in 1907. Only Costa Rica and Honduras failed to attend and several Latin America delegates played important roles in the discussions. However their position was still far from one of juridical equality. No Latin American state had ambassadorial relations with any country other than the United States until after the First World War.

At the 1907 Conference the Latin American states, led by Luis M. Drago, Foreign Minister of Argentina, took the initiative in trying to write the Drago doctrine into international law by proposing a resolution prohibiting the use of force to collect debts. However the compromise resolution eventually adopted, proposed by a US delegate named Horace Porter, allowed two major exceptions to the doctrine as Drago had originally presented it. Force could still be used if a debtor state refused to go to arbitration or failed to abide by the terms of an arbitral decision. Hence only four Latin America states ratified the convention and each made reservations refusing to recognise the validity of the exceptions (Mecham 1965, p. 99). Their caution proved well founded when Britain sent a cruiser to Guatemala in 1913 to force President Estrada Cabrera to pay his country's debts. However as the Council of Foreign Bondholders noted, there was at that time only one other country in the world with unpaid debts outstanding and that was the United States itself (Calvert 1971).

In the First World War, following the US decision to declare war on the Central Powers in April 1917, Cuba and Panama immediately declared war but did not take an active part on their own account. Both were effectively at the time American protectorates, and in the case of Panama, its strategic location made it of particular value to the US war effort. However, the Dominican Republic, Haiti and Nicaragua, which were also effectively US protectorates did not at this stage make any move towards involvement. In the remaining eighteen months of the war, however, two of these and a number of other states declared war: Peru on 6 October 1917, Uruguay on 7 October 1917, Brazil on 27 October 1917, Ecuador on 8 December 1917, Costa Rica on 23 March 1918, Guatemala on 23 April 1918, Nicaragua on 8 May 1918, Haiti on 12 July 1918 and Honduras on 19 July 1918. They did so for a variety of reasons, among those publicly stated being admiration of President Wilson's leadership, the desire to preserve continental solidarity, a feeling of cultural identity with the Allies and a belief that the Central Powers had violated fundamental principles of international law, specifically by interfering with the right of free navigation of the seas.

Of the belligerent states, however, only Brazil took an active part. Heavily dependent economically on trade with the Allied powers, despite substantial enclaves of German settlement in the South, the government of President Wenceslau Braz Pereira Gómes had broken off diplomatic relations with Germany when a Brazilian ship, the *Paraná*, was torpedoed off the coast of France on 5 April. However the United States had entered the war and several more Brazilian ships were sunk before the loss of the *Macau* off the coast of Spain in October 1917 led the government to declare war. However though

Brazil formally accepted responsibility for the security of the South Atlantic, she lacked the ships to make this effective, and although the size of the army was vastly increased by compulsory military service, forces took so long to train that only a small number of nurses and medical orderlies actually reached the Western front. Instead many of the troops were used to suppress demonstrations by some four hundred thousand German-Brazilians against the war, which led the government to proclaim martial law in the States of Paraná, Santa Caterina and Rio Grande do Sul.

Argentina, which had a much smaller German population and where British influence was at its height, took a generally pro-Allied position, although peninsular Spaniards generally supported Germany, as did the Catholic hierarchy in Argentina. However despite the sinking of a number of Argentine vessels the government of President Yrigoyen remained resolutely neutral, despite (or possibly because of) the incompetence of the German minister in Buenos Aires, whose correspondence, which fell into the hands of the US government in September 1917, described the Argentine foreign minister, Pueyrredón, as 'a notorious ass' (Dozer 1962, p. 478). Indeed, Yrigoyen in some respects anticipated the 'Third Position' of President Perón in advocating a continental policy of neutralism. Despite criticism from both sides, Yrigoyen can be said to have taken a Realist course, for his country benefited economically, under the forced-draught of import-substitution industrialisation which the circumstances of the war enjoined on it.

Chile, where the dominant sentiment was German until well after the entry of the United States into the war, similarly maintained a punctilious neutrality throughout the four years of conflict. They believed, correctly, that Admiral von Spee, commanding the German naval squadron in the South Atlantic, was getting naval intelligence from Chilean sources, but they were unable to prove it. On one occasion their neutrality was breached, when a German ship destroyed a British vessel at Juan Fernández Island in the South Pacific, but they sought and received a formal apology from the German government and no further action followed.

Germany's strongest diplomatic effort went into trying to persuade the Mexican Government to become an active ally against the United States. In anticipation of the declaration of unrestricted submarine warfare, Secretary of State Zimmermann sent a cipher telegram to the German chargé d'affaires in Mexico. The chargé was to seek an audience with the First Chief of the Constitutionalist Government, Venustiano Carranza, and invite him to join in an offensive and defensive alliance with Germany against the United States; the reward for Mexico, if successful, being the return of its 'lost territories' of California, Nevada, Arizona, New Mexico, Texas, etc. (Tuchman 1959).

A natural temporiser, Carranza put the chargé off with vague phrases, despite the fact that at the time US troops were still ranging over Mexican soil in fruitless pursuit of 'Pancho' Villa. What neither he nor Zimmermann knew, however, was that the telegram had already been deciphered by British Naval Intelligence, and that within weeks a clean copy of it was made available to President Wilson. In the event, the telegram was to have exactly the opposite effect to that intended. It helped precipitate the United States into the war, against Germany, while Mexico continued, perhaps wisely, to maintain a strict and often very prickly neutrality, in so far as its rather limited resources then allowed.

The League of Nations

Latin Americans played an important role in the rise and fall of the League, particularly after the United States decided not to take part. Seventeen – all but the Dominican Republic, Ecuador, El Salvador and Mexico – joined as founder members, making up some 36 per cent of the membership. The Dominican Republic and El Salvador joined in 1924; Mexico in 1931; and Ecuador in 1934, though Costa Rica withdrew in 1925 and did not return.

In keeping with Yrigoyen's interpretation both of Argentine nationalism and of active neutrality, Argentina did join the League. However it soon withdrew from the Assembly in 1921, indignant that it was not given a seat on the permanent Council, and refused to take any further part in its proceedings. It returned to full participation in 1933, after the fall of Yrigoyen's second administration in 1930 and the establishment of the Concordancia, and so was able to take an active role in the negotiations that led up to the ending of the Chaco War in 1938. Unfortunately, in the meanwhile in 1928 Brazil, which had been given a non-permanent seat on the Council and had taken a very active role in the organisation and debates of the new world body, decided to withdraw from the League. Within a year the collapse of its export economy had precipitated a serious political crisis, which was to lead to the rising of 1930 and the establishment of the 'authoritarian democracy' of Getúlio Vargas (President 1930–45). Strongly nationalistic, the Vargas regime tried hard to boost Brazil's economy by import substitution and the pursuit of economic autarky.

The League offered Latin American states formal equality in the new world system, and at a time when that had not yet been conceded within the inter-American system. The principles of nonintervention (formally embodied in Article X of the Covenant) and the peaceful settlement of disputes were congenial to them, and they hoped to use it to act as a check on the rising power of the United States. The problem was that the United States was not a member. Hence though the League was to be involved in both the Chaco War and the Leticia dispute, it was without much success, as the United States was successful in both cases in having them dealt with within the context of the inter-American system. Indeed its efforts to do so had received inadvertent support in the erroneous description of the Monroe Doctrine in Article XXI of the Covenant as a 'regional understanding' rather than a unilateral declaration of policy by a United States administration.

However most of the Latin American states stuck with the League and tried to make it work, forming a distinctive bloc for organisational purposes. This had its negative side, notably in the field of disarmament, where they favoured a regional approach which reflected their essential remoteness from the real problems of Europe. Only Venezuela (1928), Mexico (1932) and Chile (1935) signed the Geneva Protocol of 1925 during the lifetime of the League itself, though several other states have done so more recently. After the fiasco of Mussolini's invasion of Abyssinia (Ethiopia), Hitler's occupation of the Rhineland (1936) and the 'China Incident' of 1937, further attempts to bring about general disarmament were abandoned.

The United Nations

As with the League, membership of the United Nations was seen as a symbol of full equality in the world community. With the United States an active force in its creation, all twenty of the traditional

Latin American states were among the fifty-one founder members. Their 39 per cent of the total membership formed by far the largest coherent bloc in the new organisation. After 1962, when decolonisation began to take effect, their strength was reinforced by the admission of new states from the Commonwealth Caribbean, but at the same time there began a significant decline in their relative strength which has continued until the present day.

Using their strength as a bloc, meetings of which were formalised in 1953, the twenty original states had a decisive voice in the General Assembly until the mass admission of new states in 1955 and initially their support could be consistently expected to be thrown behind the United States. Thereafter, though they have retained sufficient strength to help block unwelcome resolutions, their alternative role as power brokers has become more important. It was undoubtedly their support for the United States at the beginning of the Cold War period that helped ensure that the UN was unable to get on with the work of international peace keeping as originally intended. From that time on, down to the Gulf War and the Bosnian crisis, the UN has been expertly sidelined and/or manipulated, especially (but certainly not exclusively) by the United States.

From the beginning, the Latin American states were sensitive to the fact that none of them had permanent representation on the Security Council, though almost at once it was established as a convention that they would have two seats and this informal position remained after the enlargement of the Security Council from nine to fifteen. There were two exceptions. For many years Mexico refused to take a seat on the Security Council at all, believing that by doing so it would risk compromising the principle of nonintervention. The US successfully opposed the election of Cuba after 1961, arguing that it should be represented only as a member of the Communist bloc. However, the Cubans, who had been excluded after 1964, were readmitted to the Latin American Caucusing Group in 1975 and have been active members ever since. Meanwhile the other states took turns to fill the two seats allocated by convention to the region, and all continued to vote as a bloc in elections. The US was not able to prevent the election of Sandinista Nicaragua, as the other Latin American states generally took its part.

Much of the strength of the bloc comes from the fact that Latin Americans have played an important role in the staffing of the Secretariat and other agencies. Sr Javier Pérez de Cuéllar, former

Foreign Minister of Peru, served two five-year terms as Secretary-General from 1982 to 1991. However he was chosen, in the tradition of U Thant, because the Great Powers did not want the United Nations to undertake an activist role, and his difficult term of office, which began with the Falklands Crisis and spanned the years of 'roll-back' and the collapse of communism in Eastern Europe, hence did not accurately reflect either his own abilities or the positive side of the Latin American contribution. From the Chapultepec Conference onwards the Latin American states pressed the other powers to make the UN an effective body in economic as well as political affairs. Their regional strength within the Economic and Social Council (ECOSOC) gave them the leverage they needed for the creation of the UN Economic Commission for Latin America (ECLA) in 1948.

The UN and the OAS

The United Nations Charter in Article 51 recognises both an individual and collective right of self-defence. The right was intended to cover only the limited circumstances of an attack by another state, and to be valid only until the Security Council could meet to consider the situation. However from the beginning it had other interpretations. The Latin American states collectively, led by Alberto Lleras Camargo of Colombia, pressed for the UN to recognise the right of regional organisation, and this article in some degree reflects the success of their lobbying.

Lleras, who had served briefly as President of Colombia, 1945–46, became Secretary General of the Pan-American Union in 1946, and oversaw its transformation into the Organization of American States (OAS) in 1948. He served as the first Secretary-General of the new organisation 1948–54 and a full term as President of Colombia 1958–62, under the power-sharing system instituted by the Pact of Sitges. There can be no doubt that his proposals were intended in the spirit of the 'Good Neighbor' policy to result in the peaceful settlement of disputes in accordance with juridical equality between states. However the result, in the new age of the Cold War, was to be highly unsatisfactory.

Since 1948 the UN has shown a marked reluctance to become involved in inter-American conflicts and has been content to leave that task to the OAS. Not by coincidence, this has been eminently convenient for the United States, which, as the hegemonic power in the Western hemisphere, has been free to act within its own 'sphere of influence' with much more freedom than would otherwise have been possible. Again and again, Latin American states have tried to appeal to the UN to by-pass the inter-American system, and it is instructive to see in what a variety of ways their efforts have been frustrated.

In 1954 Guatemala was invaded from Honduras by a force of 'exiles' supported by the Nicaraguan air force. The government of President Arbenz appealed first to the OAS and secondly to the Security Council, accusing Honduras and Nicaragua of aggression. A resolution before the Security Council, sponsored by the United States and the Latin American members of the Council and calling for the issue to be referred to the OAS, was vetoed by the Soviet Union. Instead a simple resolution calling for a cease-fire was adopted. A subsequent second request from Guatemala for a meeting of the Security Council was blocked by the United States, and soon afterwards the Guatemalan government fell. On this second occasion, though Brazil supported the United States position, two major allies of the United States, Britain and France, abstained from voting (UK *State Papers*, Cmd 9277). Subsequently, as noted above, it became clear that although Honduras and Nicaragua were named in the original appeal, the body of 'exiles' was in fact a clandestine force organised and sponsored by the United States (Schlesinger and Kinzer 1982), whose Ambassador, Henry Cabot Lodge, was at the time of the incident serving as President of the Security Council. The United States had therefore successfully used the argument that this was a regional issue to avoid any discussion and this caused considerable concern among the Latin American delegations, the Uruguayan delegate pointing out to the General Assembly that: 'The legal protection offered by both systems should be combined, never substituted for one another' (Connell-Smith 1966, p. 236).

In 1960, after the OAS had imposed sanctions on the Trujillo dictatorship in the Dominican Republic, the Soviet Union presented a resolution in the Security Council to authorise the move under Article 53 of the UN Charter. The resolution, which would have given the Council a precedent to control regional enforcement action, was defeated without the United States having to use its veto, when the Soviet Union abstained on the adoption of the American text.

When in 1961 the United States launched the ill-fated Bay of Pigs expedition against Cuba, Cuba appealed to the Security Council, accusing the United States and other regional states of aggression. The Security Council failed to act, but the invasion speedily proved to be a failure. The following year, 1962, President Kennedy announced his 'quarantine' of the waters around Cuba before informing the OAS. Ironically when in 1962 the United States and Cuba agreed that UN monitors should supervise the withdrawal of Soviet missiles from Cuban soil, the Cuban government refused to admit them.

The inability of both the United Nations and the OAS to handle disputes between an individual Latin American state and the United States, as one of the world superpowers, was now quite clear, and was to be shown even more clearly in 1964. In January riots erupted in the Canal Zone when some US students foolishly raised the US flag over their school, a provocative gesture that was to lead to loss of life. Panama then complained to both the UN Security Council and to the OAS of US aggression. The US did not oppose consideration of Panama's charges by the Security Council, but when Panama agreed that they could be handled by the Inter-American Peace Committee no further discussion took place in New York, though the question remained on the agenda of the Security Council.

In 1965 the OAS was, as we have seen in Chapter Six, quickly enlisted on the evening of 28 April by the administration of President Lyndon Johnson to support and give validity to the unilateral US intervention in the Dominican Republic that had already begun. At the same time the Security Council was informed. However since the intervention came some four days after the outbreak of civil war in the Republic, as time went on there was increasing concern at the number of US troops that were being poured into the island and impatience at the slowness with which the OAS appeared to be acting to restore peace. On 1 May, therefore, the Soviet Union called for an urgent meeting of the Security Council. When it met, two days later, the Soviet delegate submitted a draft resolution condemning US intervention and demanding the immediate withdrawal of US forces. Though the US was able to block the adoption of this resolution (which it could in any case have vetoed) France, another of the permanent members, was critical of its actions. The Latin American group was divided. Bolivia, where President Paz Estenssoro had been overthrown in a right-wing military coup in November 1964, now supported the US. The delegate of the elected collegial government of Uruguay, on the other hand, was emphatic that the intervention was in contravention of the Charter of the OAS. Consequently, he argued, it was for the Security Council, not the OAS, to take charge of the situation (Connell-Smith 1966, p. 338). Though legally correct, this position was unrealistic, and in the event no further action followed.

In 1973 Panama, following its call the previous year for the 'return' of the Panama Canal, appealed to the Security Council over its dispute with the United States. A meeting took place in Panama itself but though a resolution favourable to Panama's position gained widespread support, it was vetoed by the United States – the first occasion since 1945 that the US veto had been used. Despite this, within a year the Tack-Kissinger Agreement of 1974 was signed establishing principles, including the elimination of the concept of perpetuity, which were was to form the basis for the bilateral agreement between the two countries and the Panama Canal Treaties of 1977 (Weeks and Gunson 1991, p. 37).

When in early 1984 naval forces sponsored by the United States struck at port facilities at Puerto Sandino, El Bluff and Corinto, and laid mines which damaged four vessels, one a Soviet-registered freighter, the Nicaraguan Government appealed to the Security Council. On 5 April the United States vetoed a very general resolution criticising the mining of the ports. It was clear from this that no further action could be expected from the United Nations, and hence, as discussed above in Chapter Five, Nicaragua took its case to the International Court of Justice (World Court), which ruled in its favour.

The United States failed in its view to secure satisfaction of its grievances against Panama from the OAS in 1989. Consistent with its traditional position that such disputes were exclusively the concern of the inter-American system, it did not then refer the case to the United Nations Security Council, as, if the actions complained of really constituted a breach of the peace, it was obliged under the Charter to do. When the Security Council did debate the matter in August 1989 the US argued that General Noriega's government had so flagrantly violated the norms of international conduct that its overthrow was justified, but obtained little support.

However after the invasion in December 1989 Nicaragua moved a resolution before the Security Council, strongly critical of the US action in invading the premises of the Nicaraguan Embassy for an hour and a half in the course of the occupation. The resolution achieved widespread support and would certainly have carried had it not been vetoed by the US Government on the grounds that it had already formally apologised for the serious breach of diplomatic immunity.

Regional organisation and external disputes

The record in disputes between the American states and countries outside the hemisphere has been conditioned by two factors: the attitude of the United States and the extent to which the dispute could be handled within the inter-American system.

From 1953 onwards, both in the UN and elsewhere, the United States government tried to extend the meaning of the term aggression to cover irregular warfare or even subversion, and by 1993 the term had been stretched so far that it was being used to defend a unilateral air strike on Baghdad in retaliation for an alleged plot to assassinate ex-President Bush two months earlier. However throughout this period it has been generally accepted as a basic principle of customary international law that even in response to an armed attack, any response must be *timely* and *proportionate*.

In 1962, when the United States revealed to the Security Council the Soviet decision to emplace intermediate range ballistic missiles (IRBMs) in Cuba, it did not rely exclusively or even primarily on the UN for support. President Kennedy's government simultaneously requested a Special Meeting of Consultation of Foreign Ministers of the OAS. The United States resolution before the meeting invoked Articles Six and Eight of the Rio Pact, branding Cuba, not the Soviet Union, as an aggressor, and authorising member nations (including the United States) to take all necessary steps, including the use of force, to remove the threat to peace. Though a number of votes hung in the balance until the last moment, the vote, when it came, was unanimous in favour of the US position (Morrison 1965, pp. 242–8).

In 1973, following the ill-judged decision of the then British government to hold military exercises in its dependency, Belize, there followed a strong protest from Guatemala. In view of their claim to Belize, the Guatemalans regarded the exercises as an attempt by the British government to put undue pressure upon them and tried to convince the Security Council to see matters in that light. However

Belize received strong support from independent Commonwealth states in the area and the Security Council failed to act on the request.

In 1982, on the other hand, it was Britain who complained to the Security Council about the Argentine attack on the Falkland Islands (Islas Malvinas), and was successful in obtaining the strongly worded Resolution 502 calling for the immediate withdrawal of Argentine troops. The views of the OAS (see Chapter Six) were disregarded. It was striking that members of the Security Council specifically rejected the Argentine argument that their seizure of the islands was an act of belated decolonisation. Only Panama voted against Resolution 502. Guyana, Jordan, Togo, Uganda and Zaire accepted Argentina's claim to the islands but opposed the use of force, and voted for the Resolution. Kenya went further in the meeting of 24 May 1982, rejecting Argentina's anti-colonial credentials and describing the claim as 'a pure territorial claim against the United Kingdom based on history, in total disregard of the people who now live on the Falkland Islands' (Claude in Coll & Arend 1985, p. 126).

However, once the war had started there was growing concern among those who had supported Resolution 502, and at the beginning of June 1982, Spain and Panama proposed a resolution in the Security Council calling for an immediate ceasefire. Despite the protests of Tom Enders and Ambassador Jeane Kirkpatrick, Secretary of State Haig directed the US delegation to cast their vote with Britain against the proposal, thus joining in vetoing it. Five minutes later, to general surprise, she called for the floor to say that she had now been directed to abstain, and that though rules forbade a change of vote that was what she wished the other delegates to understand (Gustafson 1988, pp. 136–7). A month later Haig himself was dismissed.

Peacekeeping operations

Not surprisingly, Latin American forces have been keen to take part in UN peace-keeping operations, and contingents have regularly formed a significant part of the various UN formations created for this purpose.

Their active involvement began with the Korean War (1950–53) when, acting in the name of the United Nations, President Truman of the United States sent US forces to resist an invasion of South Korea from communist North Korea. Subsequently both Colombia and Cuba sent troops in support of what, in the absence of the Soviet Union from the Security Council, was immediately recognised as an official UN operation. Most other Latin American states gave aid (not Chile, Dominican Republic, Guatemala, Haiti and Honduras, however), since like all UN peace-keeping operations it had to be funded separately from the normal contributions of member states.

After the Suez Crisis (1956) Brazil and Colombia were among the ten countries who supplied in total 6,000 troops for the United Nations Expeditionary Force (UNEF) set up to replace the allied forces as they withdrew from the disputed area (James 1990, p. 210). Offers of assistance from Chile, Ecuador and Paraguay were not taken up.

Argentina and Brazil supplied forces for United Nations forces in the Congo (Leopoldville), now Zaire. Thirty-nine states in all contributed to the United Nations Organization in the Congo (ONUC). Some three and a half thousand troops were sent to maintain order after chaos had ensued on independence, and were reinforced after the most powerful province, Katanga, had tried to secede. By mid-1961 their numbers had risen to a peak of some twenty thousand, but after the capitulation of 'President' Tshombe, they were as rapidly run down and the force was withdrawn in 1964.

In May 1967 UNEF (later known as UNEF I) was withdrawn by Secretary-General U Thant at the request of President Sadat of Egypt (Rikhye 1980). The Six Day War that followed, however, was to prove a disaster for Egypt and for its allies, Jordan and Syria, and led to renewed deployment of UN forces. Chile was one of the six states chosen to contribute forces to the new United Nations Emergency Force (UNEF II), which was deployed in the Sinai Peninsula, while Peru contributed an infantry batallion to the United Nations Observer Force (UNDOF) on the Golan Heights, but withdrew it in 1975 (Pelcovits 1984, p. 3; James 1990, pp. 309, 330). After the peace treaty between Egypt and Israel in 1979, UNEF II was withdrawn. Colombia was one of three nations which agreed to contribute an infantry batallion to the Multinational Force and Observers (MFO) set up under a protocol of August 1981 to supervise the Israeli withdrawal, while Uruguay contributed specialised units to this non-UN organisation (Pelcovits 1984, p. 7; James 1990, pp. 124–5).

In 1972 India refused to recognise the continuing existence of UNMOGIP, the observer force set up in 1949 to monitor the truce line between India and Pakistan after the stalemate in their war over Kashmir. However in 1989 among the thirty-five observers still stationed there were some from both Chile and Uruguay (James 1990, pp. 158–61)

Venezuela pledged support for United Nations Forces in Cyprus (UNFICYP), the force set up in 1975 to patrol the 'green line' between Turkish-occupied northern Cyprus and what was left of the Republic of Cyprus in the south, after a ceasefire had been obtained (James 1990, p. 226). Their offer of troops was not taken up, and until June 1993, when the Canadians gave notice that they were withdrawing their contingent, no Latin American forces served in Cyprus. This would have left no forces other than those supplied by Britain in the island had the government of Argentina not agreed to replace them. In September seventy-three Argentine soldiers took up positions at the western end of the 'green line' separating Greeks and Turks, with some three hundred to follow (*Guardian*, 30 September 1993).

The fact is that, since the end of the Cold War, demands on the UN for peacekeeping are showing an alarming tendency to exceed the available resources. In 1990, in what was to prove to be the run-up to the Gulf War, the Argentine Government under President Menem sent two ships to aid in the UN blockade of Iraq. They later gave active support for the Gulf War, serving alongside British vessels of the Armilla Patrol, and although criticism at home was muted, there was evident concern about the high cost of such operations. In the event, the costs of the Gulf War were largely borne by Saudi Arabia. However with UN forces deployed in more locations than ever before, and many countries, including both the United States and Russia, in arrears on their regular contributions, there must be serious concern about how this essential role is to be maintained.

The law of the sea

One area in which Latin American states have had a major impact on world politics, which has had very important implications, both positive and negative, for the global environment, has been the law of the sea.

In the colonial period, Spain regarded the Caribbean as a closed sea, within which it had exclusive right of navigation and exploitation. This view was disputed by other European powers, and with the power of Spain in decline it was their view that prevailed. It was generally accepted that states had a right to sovereignty over as much of the sea as they could command from shore batteries, a distance then fixed at three miles. Beyond that all states had a right of freedom of navigation.

Interestingly enough, in the light of later developments, it was the United States that first called the validity of the three-mile limit into question. The US Anti-Smuggling Act of 1935 gave the President power to proclaim a seaward zone out to 62 miles in the vicinity of a suspected smuggler. In 1939 the US government established the 200-mile 'hemispheric safety belt', a measure that was accepted by the other states of the region and indeed extended to 300 miles by the Declaration of Panama (see Chapter Six). But President Truman's unilateral declaration in 1945 claiming jurisdiction over the 'natural resources of the sub-soil and sea bed of the continental shelf beneath the high seas but contiguous to the coasts of the United States' was accompanied on the same day by a similar Fisheries Proclamation and was soon followed by Mexico (October 1945) and Argentina (October 1946).

In 1947, however, Chile, in June, and Peru, in August, formally claimed sovereignty over a maritime zone extending outwards to the unprecedented distance of 200 nautical miles, based on the approximate range of land-based whalers. At that time the US had no fishing interests in the area, but nevertheless objected to the move on the grounds that they had not been taken into account. The Latin American response was hostile. Costa Rica, El Salvador, Honduras and in 1951 Ecuador all adopted the new formula. In August 1952 Ecuador joined Peru and Chile in a joint declaration affirming their right to do so on the specific ground that the zone included the narrow but economically rich Humboldt current. The Draft Convention they produced, approved by the Inter-American Juridical Committee, also extended sovereignty over the sea bed.

It was not long before US boats fishing off these coasts came into conflict with the local authorities, for after a resolution on the two-hundred-mile limit had been successfully blocked at the Tenth Inter-American Conference, the US Congress passed the Fisherman's Protective Act of 1954, by which the US Treasury assumed responsibility for any fines they might incur and Aristotle Onassis dispatched a whaling fleet to Peru to challenge the limit. Not only was it stopped and fined, but the Peruvian navy for the first time started to stop US tuna fishers as well. In 1955 a formal conference in Santiago between representatives of the three South American states and the US failed to reach a conclusion. A US proposal that the matter be referred to the World Court was rejected (Loring 1972, pp. 57 ff.)

In the meantime other states had begun to follow the South American example and to claim 200 mile maritime zones. Growing concern among the maritime powers led in time to the first UN Conference on the Law of the Sea, held at Geneva in 1958, which defined key terms. But neither it, nor a second UN Conference held in 1960, succeeded in resolving the real issues involved.

There was a sharp division of opinion between the three original states and Brazil, which had followed their example and claimed a 200-mile zone, and the Central American and Caribbean states, including Colombia, Mexico and Venezuela, which for reasons of close proximity to other states found themselves unable to claim similar zones, without embroiling themselves in potentially serious conflicts. However the net effect of the failure to agree was to leave Chile, Peru and Ecuador in a stronger position than before. In the year to May 1963 Ecuadorian authorities seized and fined some twelve US boats. Then on 11 July the government was overthrown by a military coup. Contrary to its stated policy of not recognising military coups, the Kennedy administration not only recognised but concluded a 'secret' agreement with the new military junta, by which the US fishermen were able to fish in the disputed zone without fear of seizure.

When news leaked out of the agreement in June 1965 it helped bring down the junta. In October 1966 the US implicitly conceded its moral position by unilaterally extending its fishery jurisdiction from 3 to 12 miles, an action not authorised by the 1958 Convention on the Territorial Sea and Contiguous Zone (Loring 1972, p. 76). The following month Ecuador formally claimed a 200-mile 'territorial sea', and the new Argentine military government claimed sovereignty over a 200-mile zone in December. By the time nine Latin American governments signed the Declaration of Montevideo on the Law of the Sea in 1970, Panama, Uruguay and Brazil had all established a 200-mile 'territorial sea' and eleven states in all had claimed a 200-mile limit: Chile, Peru, Costa Rica, El Salvador, Honduras, Ecuador, Nicaragua, Argentina, Panama, Uruguay and Brazil. The gradual extension of claims in each case towards a full claim of a 'territorial sea', ironically, strengthened the argument of the United States for what has been termed 'the doctrine of creeping jurisdiction'. The US Defense Department feared that this could result in time in the partition of the Caribbean and the Mediterranean, the effective annexation by neighbouring states of an area equal in size to the Atlantic and the effective end of the freedom of navigation of all of the world's straits.

Hence what had begun as a relatively minor regional dispute, specific to a small group of countries, had escalated into a global question with serious implications for the rest of the world. This did not make it any easier to settle. The Third UN Conference, which met for the first time in New York in 1973, continued to meet over a period of several years, slowly developing a working consensus that separated the issue of sovereignty from that of patrimony. It was felt nations had a right to sovereignty over a 12-mile territorial sea, though ships could and should have the right of innocent passage through it. In addition they should have the right to exploit the resources of a 200-mile economic zone (including the 12-mile territorial sea).

However when a Law of the Sea Convention was eventually drawn up, the United States, under Ronald Reagan, refused to sign it, as did the government of the United Kingdom. The effective result of this was to leave the waters of the continental shelf open to predatory fishing by modern factory vessels of any nation – a victory for no one, least of all the fish.

Appropriately enough, one of the first victims of the failure to agree was Britain, represented in this case by the government of the Falkland Islands. The Falklanders themselves had no fishing vessels, and the Argentines were unable to fish within the Protection Zone around the islands for security reasons. However, Soviet, Bulgarian, Japanese and many other nations' fishing fleets fished within the zone quite freely, until Britain took the unilateral decision to introduce a licensing system to conserve fish stocks. There were immediate objections from Argentina, despite the obvious indirect advantage to its government of conserving the resources to which they laid claim. However when it appeared that the system was working quite effectively and thus generating a significant revenue for the government of the Islands, the Argentine Government changed tack and, in an entirely businesslike way, offered licences to fish within mainland coastal waters at a lower price, thus effectively undercutting the islanders. Whether these moves were best calculated to encourage the islanders to accept future Argentine rule was of course another matter.

Arms control

Both the strength and the weaknesses of the Latin American states are most clearly shown in their record on arms control agreements. On conventional arms the record is very sparse. An early agreement between Peru and Colombia in 1829 to reduce troops on their common frontier was not followed up. In 1858 Costa Rica and Nicaragua agreed to demilitarise a zone bordering Lake Nicaragua and the San Juan River. But a comprehensive disarmament treaty signed by the five Central American states in 1923 had no means of enforcement and so was ineffective. It expired without renewal in 1943 (Husbands 1979, p. 209).

Chile and Argentina agreed to demilitarise the Straits of Magellan in 1881 and a mutual reduction of naval armaments, that formed part of their agreement in 1902 to settle the question of their territorial boundaries by arbitration, led to a satisfactory and effective reduction of tension between the two protagonists, though the agreement itself broke down in face of a naval build-up in Brazil. Between 1906 and 1908 they were not successful in resolving their overlapping claims to sectors of Antarctica centring on the Palmer Peninsula (Graham Land), which not only overlapped with each other but also with the sector claimed by the United Kingdom (Mericq 1987).

The first treaty since the Second World War to contain explicit clauses enjoining demilitarisation was the Antarctic Treaty of 1959, which came into effect in 1962. Initially, the outlook for the treaty looked unpromising. Argentina and Chile had incorporated their claims into the zone covered by the Rio Pact of 1947, and by the Donoso-La Rosa Declaration of March 1948 announced their intention jointly to defend their demands by legal means (Beck 1990, p. 103). Both sides had then taken a variety of steps to occupy their chosen sectors. Despite this, in 1959 the seven states which claimed sovereignty in the region, together with the two superpowers and six other states which had by that stage actively explored the continent, agreed to 'freeze' their claims for a period of at least thirty years and to demilitarise the area south of the Sixtieth Parallel.

The treaty, which came into effect in 1962, prohibits in general 'any measures of a military nature, such as the establishment of military bases and fortifications, the carrying out of military manoeuvres as well as the testing of any types of weapons', though it does allow military personnel and equipment to be deployed in the region for scientific or other peaceful purposes (Beck 1986). Undoubtedly this represents a potentially serious loophole in the treaty as it stands, but full rights of mutual entry and inspection accorded by it have been used and no breaches have as yet been reported.

The treaty further specifically prohibits the testing of nuclear weapons or the disposal of nuclear waste, reflecting the special concerns that led to the agreement in the first place. However during the 1980s increasing attention came to be given to two very different but related problems: on the one hand, a new interest in the possibility of prospecting for oil or other minerals in the area, and on the other the increasing pollution of the Antarctic environment both by the presence of so many people and by the long-range contamination of the atmosphere, the so-called 'ozone hole'.

The Treaty of Tlatelolco

While the Antarctic Treaty was still awaiting ratification, Brazil proposed in 1961 that the whole of Latin America be made a nuclear-free zone. Though Cuba supported the draft resolution, it insisted that it should also cover US territory in the Caribbean, and in the end the matter did not come to a vote.

After the Cuban Missile Crisis of October 1962, the Brazilian proposal received fresh impetus. The strong support for the US position shown by Latin American governments was, after all, partly a matter of simple self-interest. If missiles from Cuba could strike Seattle, Oregon, they could alternatively be launched successfully at almost all the major Latin American capitals. A joint declaration by the Presidents of Bolivia, Brazil, Chile, Ecuador and Mexico, expressing their willingness to sign a denuclearisation treaty received the support of the UN General Assembly on 27 November 1963.

After the military assumption of power in Brazil in 1964, Mexico took steps to keep the initiative alive, and a drafting conference was held in Mexico City in November 1965. The formal signing of the Treaty for the Prohibition of Nuclear Weapons in Latin America was held at the Mexican Foreign Ministry in the Tlatelolco district of Mexico City on 14 February 1967; hence the Treaty is usually known for short as the Treaty of Tlatelolco. With the support of the UN, the Treaty came into force on 22 April 1968.

The Treaty of Tlatelolco designates the whole of Latin America and its surrounding territorial waters as a zone within which 'the testing, use, manufacture, production or acquisition' of nuclear weapons' is prohibited, as is the 'receipt, storage, installation, deployment and any form of possession of any nuclear weapons, directly or indirectly'. However the 'transport' of nuclear weapons through the zone is not banned, nor is the use of nuclear power for propulsion purposes; either prohibition would, of course, have made the Treaty unacceptable to the United States, which might then have decided to try to block it.

Cuba has refused to sign the treaty. Argentina signed it but failed to ratify it. Argentina and Chile both signed and ratified it but stated that the treaty did not apply to them until all other eligible states had ratified it. The 1970s military governments of both Argentina and Brazil then went ahead with nuclear programmes designed to achieve a full nuclear fuel cycle independently of outside safeguards, and did so in each case in conjunction with a programme of rocket development to provide a suitable delivery vehicle capable of carrying nuclear weapons. These programmes only came to an end with the collapse of military government and the bankruptcy of the countries involved (Leventhal and Tanzer 1992). Hence even within Latin America the Treaty cannot be said to have been an unqualified success.

Two additional protocols cover states outside the hemisphere. Protocol I invites states with dependent territories within the region to adhere to the provisions of the Treaty. The Netherlands and the United Kingdom have both signed and ratified it; France and the United States have not. Protocol II invites the nuclear states to respect the non-nuclear status of Latin America and not to use or threaten to use nuclear weapons against any signatory state. The People's Republic of China, France, the United Kingdom and the United States have all signed and ratified it. The former Soviet Union refused to sign it, but its successor state, Russia, has done so.

It is not known whether any nuclear state has intentionally violated the provisions of Protocol II by transiting weapons through the designated area with a view to their 'deployment'. Given the geography of the region it is hard to see how the United States can have maintained a submarine launched missile capability without doing so more or less regularly. Since the zone designated by the Tlatelolco Treaty is contiguous with that designated by the Antarctic Treaty, common sense suggests that most if not all of the nuclear powers have had to violate one or other at some time, if their submarines were to be able to get round Cape Horn. As for US vessels in the Caribbean, it is obviously relevant that the United States has refused to sign Protocol I, since if nuclear weapons are stationed in US dependencies they have to be received, stored and installed.

Press reports at the time of the Falklands War suggested that, in the rush to get the Task Force ready, British warships had set sail for the South Atlantic still carrying at least part of their regular NATO complement of nuclear depth charges. Though it appears that this was so, it was not intentional. A Royal Fleet Auxilliary was sent to collect the devices at Ascension Island and consequently none were taken into the South Atlantic. Apparently circumstantial tales about radioactive penguins being washed up on Argentine shores, however, continue to attract some credence, despite this (Freedman in Danchev 1992, pp. 171–2). Throughout the conflict Britain did not at any time threaten to use nuclear weapons against Argentina, let alone actually use them. (The use of nuclear propulsion is not banned by the Treaty of Tlatelolco.) It is noteworthy, however, that, on the other hand, the possession of nuclear weapons by Britain did not deter the Argentine Government from launching its attack in the first place, which suggests that at the least their deterrent value has been much exaggerated (Calvert 1982, p. 158).

The Non-Proliferation Treaty (NPT)

Concern at the rapid spread of nuclear weapons led the two major nuclear states and the United Kingdom to take steps to inhibit their spread (proliferation). In 1967–68, with the aid of the first three nuclear states, a group of non-nuclear states drafted the Treaty on the Non-Proliferation of Nuclear Weapons, commonly called the Non-Proliferation Treaty (NPT).

Curious as it now seems, many of the non-nuclear states regarded the possession of nuclear weapons as a blessing of which they were being unjustly deprived. They were therefore able to negotiate concessions from the nuclear powers in return for their signatures, the most important of which is that they would be granted access to (peaceful) nuclear technologies on a non-discriminatory basis but under safeguards. These safeguards were to be monitored by a new UN agency, the International Atomic Energy Agency (IAEA), based in Vienna, and the working of the treaty would be reviewed in a review conference to be held every five years after the treaty entered into force on 5 March 1970 until 1995, when a general extension conference would be held to determine whether and on what terms the NPT system would continue.

All the Latin American states except Cuba have signed the NPT. By the time the treaty was in draft, the military government that had seized power in Brazil in 1964 had determined to embark on a nuclear programme. It did not take part in formulating the treaty and refused to ratify it. In response, Argentina, too, refused to ratify the treaty, though both states, and Cuba, sent observers to the first review conference in Geneva in May 1975. Meanwhile there had begun a gradual but nevertheless significant series of moves on both sides towards acquiring nuclear weapons capability. Reprocessing began in Argentina on a laboratory scale as early as 1969, and was followed by the construction of a gaseous diffusion enrichment facility at Pilcaniyeu, outside IAEA safeguards. With feedstock supplied in 1981 by China, the plant started to operate in 1983. Brazil is believed to have operated a laboratory-scale plant from 1983 to 1987, when President Sarney announced plans to build an unsafeguarded gas centrifuge enrichment facility at Aramar. In the meanwhile under a 1975 agreement with West Germany Brazil acquired the basic engineering knowledge to build its own plant. Both sides also took significant steps towards the construction of a ballistic missile (Redick 1990).

Since the return of democracy to the region Argentina and Brazil have both had to cut sharply back on their nuclear ambitions for financial reasons, though a report published in April 1991 by the Carnegie Endowment for Peace claimed that they had been able to circumvent international restrictions on their programmes. At the First Ibero-American Summit at Guadalajara, Mexico, in July 1991, they signed a bilateral treaty renouncing the use of their domestic technology for the manufacture of nuclear weapons. Though neither country had yet agreed to ratify the NPT, Presidents Collor and Menem signed a further agreement at Vienna in December 1991, opening all nuclear installations to reciprocal inspection under the auspices of the IAEA, which was widely felt to have the same effect. In 1992 the Argentine Congress finally ratified the NPT, but suspended its effect until Brazil did likewise, which it has not yet done. President Menem promised in December 1993 to ratify the NPT by 1995 whether or not Brazil did the same. Both countries are now ratifying the Tlatelolco Treaty, and Cuba has announced its intention to do so once Argentina, Brazil and Chile are full members. However, until both also adhere to the NPT there will in effect be no way in which third parties can ensure that they do not break their obligations under that treaty by mutual agreement (see also Redick 1994).

Latin American nuclear diplomacy, however, has not been confined to South America. Mexico has long been opposed to the US policy of continuing nuclear testing and at the fourth review conference of the NPT in Geneva in August–September 1991, presided over by the Peruvian Ambassador, Sr Oswaldo de Rivero (Simpson and Howlett 1990), consensus on a final declaration, which had been achieved at the third review conference in 1985 only by an elaborate fudge, was blocked as a result. In 1993 President Clinton announced a voluntary US moratorium on further nuclear testing and invited other nations to follow suit. However with the further horizontal proliferation of nuclear weapons since 1991 as a result of the disintegration of the former Soviet Union, the outlook for the 1995 Extension Conference was not altogether encouraging.

The Non-Aligned Movement (NAM)

As its name suggests, the Non-Aligned Movement arose out of disenchantment with the Cold War. The principles of non-alignment and peaceful co-existence were first expressed in Latin America, by Juan Domingo Perón of Argentina, who spoke of a 'Third Position'. However, it was the Bandung Conference of 1955 which gave currency to the term 'non-alignment', and the Non-Aligned Movement as such was not put on an institutional basis until 1961, when representatives of 25 nations attended the first formal Non-Aligned Summit Meeting in Belgrade in 1961. Since that time the movement has gone from strength to strength, as the progress of decolonisation brought it a constant flow of new members, and by 1988 it had 101 members.

At the Belgrade meeting, whose main protagonists were Nehru of India, Sukarno of Indonesia, Nasser of Egypt and Tito of Yugoslavia, the African and Asian states invited Cuba to take part. As they had not been consulted, other Latin American countries did not participate actively, though Bolivia, Brazil and Ecuador did send observers. The meeting issued a strong declaration in favour of independence for colonial states and the right of self-determination – a theme echoed by Cuba ('Free Territory of the Americas') in the Second Declaration of Havana in 1962 (Government of Cuba 1962).

Since 1962, when Bolivia, Brazil and Mexico, along with Cuba, were represented at ministerial level at the Cairo Economic Conference, a variable number of Latin American states have taken part in the movement's activities. Some, like Argentina, have joined, only to withdraw again when they felt that non-alignment was in itself a confession of second-class status. Others have gone beyond mere participation and tried to use their membership to assert a wider international role, independent of the United States. Their position has however been made much more difficult by Cuban ambiguity about what was meant by non-alignment and its definite refusal to renounce the advocacy of revolution (Domínguez 1989). At the Sixth Summit Meeting of the Non-Aligned Movement at Havana in 1979, President Castro, acting as host, over-estimated his position badly when he called on other members to recognise the Soviet Union as the true friend of the non-aligned; the Soviet invasion of Afghanistan, however, speedily demolished whatever moral pretensions it might have had, and the attempt ended in failure.

No other Latin American country has been successful in asserting leadership over the movement for more than a brief period. Peru under the left-wing military government of General Velasco Alvarado (1968–75) was perhaps the most successful. His reform programme was widely admired, and Lima was chosen as the scene of the ministerial meeting of 1971 and of the Fifth Summit in 1975. Though he had opened the Summit, however, General Velasco, who had been in failing health for some months, was deposed by a military coup led by his Prime Minister, General Morales Bermúdez, during the course of the week, and it was he who, to the bemusement of delegates, presided over the closing ceremony.

In the meanwhile first President Salvador Allende of Chile (1970–73) and then President Luis Echeverria Alvarez of Mexico

(1970–76) had taken an active role in non-aligned politics. However Allende was deposed in 1973 and Mexico was seen as much too close to the United States to provide a convincing role model, though Echeverria himself did subsequently get three votes for the job of Secretary-General of the United Nations.

The military government of Argentina between 1976 and 1981 initially used its membership of the Non-Aligned Movement to gain support for its military policy in the South Atlantic. However with the seizure of power by General Galtieri in December 1981, Argentina offered to withdraw from the NAM to strengthen its credentials with the US (Dabat and Lorenzano 1984, p. 93), which had secured agreement in September to the employment of Argentine instructors to stiffen the resistance of Salvadorean forces to the guerrilla challenge with which they were currently faced. Despite this, when war broke out, the Movement recognised Argentine sovereignty over the islands, condemned Britain and censured the United States. But consistent with its principles, its members refused to endorse Argentina's action in using military force. Shortly after the war both Colombia and Venezuela decided to join the NAM. At the meeting in India in March 1983 General Bignone, who had been nominated by the armed forces as interim president of Argentina to engineer the transition back to democracy, declared his opposition to both militarism and outside interference in Central America (Dabat and Lorenzano 1984, p. 151).

Castro himself recovered quickly from his *faux pas*. His farewell speech at the New Delhi Summit in 1983 was devoted entirely to the global economic crisis, which he blamed on the world capitalist system. By so doing, he both caught the mood of the hour and brought himself back into line with the rest of Latin America. Again, however, the passage of time showed up the central ambiguity of his position. While calling on other nations, particularly in Latin America, not to pay their debts, Cuba was invariably punctilious about meeting its own obligations, justifying this with the tendentious argument that since those which had lent to it had defied US pressure in order to do so, they were entitled to have their money back. It never seems to have occurred to him that the money that the others had borrowed was not the property of the banks or institutions that had lent it, but of millions of ordinary citizens, either directly or through savings and pensions funds.

Conclusion

Latin American states benefited from their long isolation from the rest of the world. However much they may have resented it, they have been protected from two world wars, to say nothing of the conflicts that have afflicted the Middle East or South-East Asia. At the same time, though their individual direct influence has been slight and/or intermittent, their collective influence has been considerable.

The main limitation upon their power to influence events has been the need to consult the interests of the United States. Where they have been in conflict with the United States, it is the latter that has prevailed, though it is not altogether clear why this should be the case. Ironically the emergence of the Latin American states into full participation in post-war multilateral diplomacy has coincided with the multiplication of states and, with the end of the Cold War, the general downgrading of the structures on which they have relied for influence. Cuba however remains – for the time being, at least – an example of what, at a cost, a small nation can do to assert itself (Jordan 1993).

Chapter Eight

The future of Latin American international relations

The new world order

The future environment of international politics in Latin America will, first and foremost, be conditioned by the nature of what President Bush called 'the new world order'. Though the nature of this new world order is as yet far from clear, and in some ways less clear than it initially appeared, the circumstances in which the phrase was coined does have some relevance.

Following what by general consensus was the dirtiest presidential election campaign in the United States for 148 years, President Bush included in his Inaugural Address in January 1989 a passage which was either obliquely repentant or amazingly cynical, or both: 'America is never wholly herself unless she is engaged in high moral principle. We as a people have such a purpose. It is to make kinder the face of the nation and gentler the face of the world.'

Within the first year of the Bush presidency, the Berlin Wall came down and the Warsaw Pact had disintegrated. With the secession of the Baltic States the prospect loomed of the almost unthinkable, the actual disintegration of the Soviet Union itself. In his address to Congress on 11 September 1990 Bush first gave a name to the new world order that these startling events could leave the United States free to create:

> Out of these troubled times, our fifth objective – a new world order – can emerge; a new era – freer from the threat of terror, stronger in the pursuit of justice, and more secure in the quest for peace, an era in which the nations of the world, East and West, North and South, can prosper and live in harmony.
>
> A hundred generations have searched for this elusive path to peace, while a thousand wars have raged across the span of human endeavor. Today a new world is struggling to be born, a world quite different

from the one we have known, a world where the rule of law supplants
the rule of the jungle, a world in which nations recognise the shared
responsibility for freedom and justice, a world where the strong
respect the rights of the weak.

(*Congressional Quarterly Weekly Report*)

The ultimate origin of the phrase 'the new world order' is almost
certainly the Great Seal of the United States. This bears the motto:
'*novus ordo saeculorum*', which is usually translated as 'a new order
of the ages' but could be freely rendered as 'a new world order'. Since
it is also the motto of Yale University, it is more likely that that was
the immediate source for Bush, who is a graduate of Yale.

As was noted in Chapter One, the distinction between the Old
World and the New is intrinsic to US thought on international
relations, and lies at the root of both Washington's Farewell
Address, 1797, and the Monroe Doctrine, 1823. The 'new world
order' is very specifically an order based on the New World, and this
had obvious implications for the rest of the Americas.

As Bush went on to say in his Address to Congress, 'America and
the world' must:

1 defend common vital interests;
2 support the rule of law; and
3 stand up to aggression.

But the US must provide the leadership. Other commentators have
identified not three but four points which seem to make up the Bush
view of the world:

1 peaceful settlement of disputes;
2 solidarity against aggression;
3 reduced and controlled arsenals;
4 just treatment of all peoples.

These can be summarised as four 'Ds': *detente, democracy,
deterrence, and diplomacy*

Latin America in the new world order

How these are to be interpreted depends on one's assessment of the
probable nature of the world after the Cold War. There are three
main scenarios. The interesting thing is that each has its origins in

United States relations with Latin America, and each was first put into practice within the hemisphere before being applied in the global context. The US experience of Latin America has shaped its outlook on the world almost throughout its history, and it may be expected to continue to do so in the future (Desch 1993). Indeed, with the ending of the Cold War, a withdrawal to the hemispheric arena is a distinct possibility.

1   The first possibility is a return to the principle of collective security, the basis of the 'proper' functioning of the world system based on the United Nations. This was the vision both of Woodrow Wilson and, in his last months, of Franklin D. Roosevelt, and may be termed the Wilsonian view.

2   The second is that the US, as the only remaining superpower, will be 'forced' to act as the 'policeman' not just of the Western hemisphere but of the world. This was the policy most clearly expressed by Theodore Roosevelt in the Roosevelt Corollary, and expanded to global proportions by Dwight D. Eisenhower, John F. Kennedy and Ronald Reagan. It could be called the Rooseveltian view.

3   The third view envisages the further relative decline of the United States into the early years of the twenty-first century and perhaps beyond. The US is suffering from 'imperial overstretch' already, and it may be that there are (or will be soon) no remaining superpowers. Hence the world will be anarchical and dangerous. There are early hints of this in Richard M. Nixon's policy of 'benign neglect' of Latin America and Jimmy Carter's efforts to build a new relationship with the other American states. Latterly, however, it has been made much more explicit by the historian Paul Kennedy and the 'declinist school', so it may be termed the declinist view.

As yet it is difficult to discern clear lines of policy in the new Clinton administration towards Latin America. The main area of engagement thus far is the economic. In his campaign Clinton was notably cool towards NAFTA, and now that he is President he has to reckon with a substantial number of members of his own party in Congress whose enthusiasm for free trade is entirely quenched by the prospect of millions of American jobs being lost in competition with low-wage, low-cost Mexican production. With an election due for President Salinas's successor in July 1994, Mexico's continued enthusiasm for the project cannot be taken for granted. Salinas sees access to the rich US market as the only force powerful enough to accelerate Mexico's economic growth into self-sustainability. Others in Mexico see it as a betrayal of Mexican national pride. However the Mexican economy is already so closely linked to that of the United States that any realistic appraisal suggests that Mexico already enjoys very little real autonomy in its economic decisions.

The decision of far-off Chile to apply for association with NAFTA is undoubtedly a pointer to the likely future incorporation of the smaller Central American states into the new North American trading bloc, should it come into existence. Chile, having been excluded from the Andean Pact, has not so far chosen to join any other trading bloc, and on the assumption that the Uruguay Round will eventually be concluded successfully and the new GATT come into effect, a hemispheric trading bloc could seem like a feasible outcome.

However it is difficult to see the traditional regional pattern dissolving so quickly. The alternative strategy thus far has been demonstrated by the four countries of the Southern Cone which are engaged in constructing a regional trading block of their own, Mercosur. Despite the crisis in the capitalist economies of Europe, there is general agreement that capitalism is now the only game in town, and there, as elsewhere, rapid steps are being taken to open up their economies and carry out extensive programmes of privatisation. Whatever the rhetoric, the United States is now once more the unquestioned exemplar of economic progress, though for Latin Americans Japan and other states of the Pacific Rim exert a certain fascination. For this reason we could add a fifth feature to the new world order: *development.* However the Bush administration showed itself curiously reluctant to accept any responsibility for promoting development, where that would have involved the spending of money. One very conspicuous exception was the case of Mexico, where the administration was uniquely prepared to give the backing of the US Treasury to Salinas's measures for financial stabilisation. It was a particular irony that under Bush's successor, one of the major factors endangering the successful passage of NAFTA through the US Congress was the impact of Mexico's unchecked economic development on the environment of the frontier zone shared by the two countries.

The new interventionism

Before considering the role of enviroment and development in Latin America, some consideration of the role of power politics in the new world order seems timely. Here Bush's intervention in Panama is particularly significant, since it was the first, and so far the only one, to take place in the region since the 1920s which owed little or nothing to the Cold War. The electoral victory of the opposition in Nicaragua in 1990 seems to have been as unexpected to Washington as it clearly was to the Sandinistas, and it is a major irony that in it the communists were to be found among the fourteen parties supporting the opposition front and not the Sandinistas. However the success of the coalition enabled the US administration to claim a cheap victory for democracy without having had to take any significant risks.

Since then the Cold War itself has come to an end. With the disintegration of the last great European empire, new zones of instability have appeared and the need for UN peacekeeping operations has been rapidly outstripping the capacity of the UN system to fund them. As the sole remaining superpower, the United States is going to be essential to all such operations. However, as with the OAS, it is not going to want to seem to act unilaterally, without support, and in consequence, with the advantage of remoteness, the Latin American states are likely to be increasingly seen as an important source of peacekeeping personnel, and are in fact contributing to existing UN operations in various parts of the world.

This might impose limits on the propensity to intervene. In any case, in this respect as in others, things might be different under the new administration. However one thing that is clear about Clinton is that he is a realist. The Clinton administration inherited Bush's last-minute decision to send US troops to Somalia to assist in the passage of relief supplies. Under Clinton the decision has already turned sour, and the plan now is for increased numbers, a return to the original objectives and a fixed time for withdrawal. With this chastening experience, it is hardly likely that the Clinton administration will wish to take any more direct role in peacekeeping outside the hemisphere, and it is probably significant that the only troops to be sent to the former Yugoslavia have been sent to Macedonia, where so far, fortunately, they have nothing to do. In response to critics of his policy towards Bosnia, Clinton has specifically blamed Britain for its opposition to intervention as the reason why the

United States has not been able to take a more activist role.

On the other hand, with the US intervention in Panama still fresh in the mind, and the United States unchallenged within the hemisphere, President Clinton has been finding it increasingly difficult to explain why he is not doing more about Haiti.

Haiti, the first of the Latin American states to gain its independence, and the only country actively to offer support to Simón Bolívar, has yet to attain democracy itself. At its first resasonably free election in 1991, the electorate chose as its new President a priest of the poor, Fr Aristide, whose entire background made him an object of great suspicion to the mulatto elite. Within four months he had been deposed by a military coup, with the result that effective power fell into the hands of the commander of the army, General Raoul Cédras.

Faced with this crisis, member states of the OAS were as usual torn between their opposition to intervention in any form and their desire to uphold democracy – the more so since the autogolpe in Peru had weakened hemispheric unity on the latter issue already. After unsuccessful visits by the Secretary General and by a special delegation had failed, it became abundantly clear that the Haitian armed forces had no intention of yielding to pressure. Hence, in an interesting breach with a long-established tradition, the United Nations found itself involved for the first time in trying to mediate an inter-American dispute. In the circumstances, the efforts of the OAS mediator, Dante Caputo, the former Argentine Minister of Foreign Affairs, to secure the peaceful restoration of the democratically elected government of Fr Aristide, were hardly likely to be successful, and in fact they were not. What was not anticipated, however, was that the Haitians would allow the comedy to reach the point at which US observers, acting on behalf of the UN, landed to take up their positions, before rousing a crowd to drive them out, to the open humiliation of the United States.

Though Haiti is in some senses a special case, there can be no doubt that armed intervention there, coming so soon after US action in Panama, would mark a very serious breach of the principle of non-intervention which it would be virtually impossible for the OAS – or any other agency – to counteract. For the moment, and despite pressure from Cuban exiles within the US, there is as yet no sign of possible intervention there. However there has been a public statement that contingency plans are being drawn up to deal with the

possible collapse of civil government in Cuba, and that suggests that
the chance of some kind of action cannot be ruled out of court.

Environment and development

There is as yet no very strong environmental lobby in most Latin
American countries. Costa Rica, where 'eco-tourism' is seen as one
of the few possible ways of seeking new income, is a small but
important exception. In common with other states in the Third
World, however, Costa Rica attaches a higher priority to development than to the protection of the environment. The effect of this,
paradoxically, is to make environmental politics in Latin America as
much a matter of international as of domestic politics, because the
advanced industrialised countries of the North are seen as seeking to
use the environmental issue to hold up development in the South.
The Earth Summit (the United Nations Conference on Environment
and Development) became possible when agreement was reached
that both issues – environment and development – would figure
together on the agenda (Thomas 1992).

At Rio de Janeiro in June 1992, Brazil were the hosts and Latin
American heads of state played a notably active role. Even in this
company the most striking public relations success was secured by
President Fidel Castro of Cuba. Although looking in some respects a
figure from the past in a strange and very old-fashioned Soviet-style
uniform, and this in a gathering where uniforms were conspicuous
by their absence (President Babangida of Nigeria having arrived too
late to deliver his speech on behalf of the Organization of African
Unity), he gripped delegates' attention with a speech of striking
brevity. Taking only 7 of his allotted 15 minutes, he used the time to
punch home two simple messages: that it was the advanced capitalist
countries that were responsible for damaging the environment, and
that it was for them to pay to put it right.

Even President Bush of the United States, who had arrived in the
hall a few minutes before, joined in the unusually heavy applause.
No doubt he had not been listening, or in fact understood what the
speech was about. President Endara of Panama prudently did not
attend, and Bush's ill-timed decision to stop over in Panama on his
way to the conference to meet Endara led to violent rioting which
blanketed the headlines on his arrival. The problem, of course, was

the continued misery of the Panamanian population, few of whom had benefited from the many promises made at the time of the 1989 intervention. Having announced on the eve of the Conference that the United States would not sign the Biodiversity Convention, Bush was not likely in any case to be popular with the majority of delegates.

Yet Castro's own policies had throughout his career been based on the same economic strategies for which he was now criticising the advanced industrialised countries. After the initial failure in the 1960s of his strategy for heavy industry, he had returned Cuba to monoculture, relying on increased productivity in sugar to balance the books. Fortunately for him, he had been able in addition to capitalise on Cuba's strategic location to obtain a constant and very substantial subsidy from the Soviet Union, both in terms of guaranteed sugar prices and in the supply of oil over and above Cuba's needs, which could be and was sold for dollars on the world market. When he came to Rio, therefore, he had left behind him in Cuba an economy devastated by the collapse of the Soviet Union, whose only hope for survival, let alone recovery, seemed to lie in the rediscovery, of all things, of dollar tourism.

On the other hand, the insatiable demand of the advanced industrialised countries for oil enabled Saudi Arabia to secure the deletion of all reference to conservation measures from either the Declaration of Rio or the major product of the Conference, Agenda 21. Other oil-producing countries accordingly were spared the embarrassment of publicly declaring their opposition.

The central problem of UNCED was on a global scale the issue of the conflict of interests between political elites and the masses of their own countries, in Latin America as elsewhere. The massive security presence mounted to 'protect' the delegates did not disguise the serious economic and political difficulties of Brazil itself. President Collor had prepared a statement of his own 'social-liberal' beliefs, and the Brazilian government its own report, *The challenge of sustainable development*, as its contribution to the worldwide debate (Governo do Brasil 1992c, 1992a). However, on 24 May, on the eve of the conference, Collor had been accused of corruption by his own brother, Pedro. Within three months he was facing impeachment by a Congress dominated by his political opponents, and by the end of the year he had capitulated, and had been replaced by his Vice-President, Itamar Franco.

Brazil remained politely defiant about its right to manage its own resources. Since 1980 a massive integrated programme of development, the Carajás programme, had been under way covering a designated area of some 900,000 kilometres^2 or about a quarter of Brazilian Amazonia (Hall 1991). In face of external criticism, Collor's predecessor, José Sarney, who had been responsible for bringing UNCED to Rio (but was not invited to take part), had gone so far as to assert the absolute right of Brazil to destroy its own natural resources if it wished. By 1992 a gentler spirit prevailed, and Brazil was eager to show delegates how much it was doing to protect the environment. Sadly, the destruction of the Amazon rainforest at the hands of would-be settlers continued. Led by the Prime Minister of Malaysia, Dr Mahathir, Brazil and other states with substantial tropical forest holdings resisted Northern pressure for a Forestry Convention, suspecting that the advanced industrialised countries merely wanted to use the tropical forests as 'carbon sinks' so that they would not have to check their own utilisation of fossil fuels. Ironically, declining industrial production in Europe, and more efficient use of fuels by the advanced industrialised states, had already reduced the pressure to do so, although the problem of acid rain remained.

Meanwhile the *garimpieros* (gold prospectors) invaded Indian lands, carrying with them disease and other problems, and endangering the survival of the indigenous populations. In this case both federal and state governments proved either helpless or unwilling to intervene. Some ten thousand prospectors, in addition, had crossed the frontier into Guyana, giving a new international dimension to the destruction of the rain forest (*The Guardian*, 1 November 1991). The long-term prospects for a check to global warming were not encouraging.

However, that major engine of the world weather system we call the Amazon Basin had already demonstrated its global significance in other ways. As is well known, for a quarter century since the 1960s, originally under the inspiration of military developmentalism, government policy had been to promote large-scale invasion of and settlement in the region. In addition, there was increasingly clear evidence of the climatic impact of deforestation in the coastal forest, the Mata Atlántica, only some 2 per cent of which still remained by 1992. For the first time in recorded history there was frost in Paraná state in 1963 which devastated the coffee plantations of the region. Since then frost has become a regular occurrence, leading to large-scale diversification out of coffee, notably into soy beans. Other effects of the later invasion of Amazonia included increased run-off, loss of the thin laterite soils and the silting of rivers. There is also reason to believe that it has contributed to the prolonged drought in the north east which set in from 1977.

It is likely that deforestation in Brazil has also had an impact on neighbouring states, though similar deforestation has more recently been taking place at the hands of Brazilian settlers in Eastern Paraguay. The Province of Buenos Aires was severely flooded by prolonged cloudbursts in April 1987. Within two years, however, there were electricity blackouts in the capital because of shortage of water in the Río Uruguay which supplies the hydro-electric plant at Salto Grande just to the north of Concordia on the Uruguay River, built under an Argentine-Uruguayan agreement signed on 30 December 1946.

Rivalry between Brazil and Argentina for the exploitation of the hydro-electric potential of the Paraguay-Paraná river system was effectively resolved in favour of Brazil, which had the advantage of being upstream. Currently the largest dam in the world is Itaipú, which straddles the River Paraná on the frontier between Brazil and Paraguay and contains some 12.6 million cubic metres of concrete and cost $18.3 billion. It stands on the site of what used to be one of the highest waterfalls in the world, the Salto de Guairá (in Portuguese, Sete Quedas). The site had apparently been regarded as Paraguayan territory ever since the demarcation of the frontier in 1874. But in May 1964, after a series of claims, the Brazilian government sent troops into the disputed area and established de facto control in the region (Nickson 1982; Latin American Bureau 1980, pp. 46ff.). Seeing no alternative, the government of General Gustavo Stroessner eventually acceded to Brazilian pressure and in 1973 signed the Treaty of Itaipú, authorising the joint project. The project, which created the largest human construction on the face of the planet, was completed in May 1991 (*Financial Times*, 7 May 1991). The Treaty of Itaipú provides that each government receive half the energy generated by the eighteen turbines. Any that cannot be consumed must then be offered to the other country at a preferential rate. The intention of this provision was that Paraguay, which is a relatively small country with few natural resources, would profit from the resale of electrical energy, and Brazil would benefit from massive supplies to the port cities of its southern states of Santa Caterina and Rio Grande do Sul. However, Brazil's energy tariffs are very low. Hence, of the $45–50 per MWh paid, Itaipú receives only $18.75 and even then the payments are far in arrears. Debt service consequently eats up some 80 per cent of the net revenues and Paraguay, which uses only 1.8 per cent of the electricity generated, receives much less than it feels it should. Recently, therefore, the Paraguayan government has been seeking a revision of the 1973 treaty to allow it to sell some or all of its surplus to Argentina instead.

Lower down the canyon of the Paraná River at Ituzaingó, on the frontier between Argentina and Paraguay, Argentina has long planned to build a much larger dam, Yaciretá-Apipé, comparable in scale with Itaipú. An agreement to build it, signed jointly by Presidents Juan Domingo Perón and Stroessner in 1973, envisaged 20 turbines generating a total of 2,760MW. Unlike Itaipú, which was privately financed, the project received much of its loans, totalling some $4 billion, from the World Bank and the Inter-American Development Bank. However, continually interrupted in its early stages by civil war and economic crisis in Argentina, the dam is well behind schedule and still only two-thirds complete (*The Economist*, 10 August 1991).

For human beings, however, power generation is a secondary consideration and the first target of good resource management must be the provision of good-quality, potable water. The Americas are one of the two major regions of the world where there has actually been a decline in the rate of rural water supply connections in the last decade (MacDonald and Kay 1988, p. 86). The international ramifications of this situation were dramatically highlighted by the 1991 cholera epidemic originating in Peru, the first in Latin America since the 1880s.

In early January 1991, when the initial infection came ashore at Chimbote from a ship newly arrived from Asia, the outbreak might have been contained at source. Instead it spread down the coast, carried mainly by contaminated marine fish and shellfish, locally consumed raw. Once the infection had entered the food chain, it spread rapidly, carried by travellers to other settlements (including Lima itself), where in turn the deadly combination of inadequate water supplies (40 per cent of the inhabitants of Lima lack access to clean water) and no satisfactory sanitation accelerated its dispersal.

The authorities' response was to try to conceal the extent of the problem until they had lost control of the situation. President Fujimori of Peru even appeared on nationwide television personally and ate raw fish to assure the public that it was safe to eat, following which his Minister of Health, Carlos Vidal Layseca, resigned.

By 22 April, when a meeting of regional health ministers convened in Sucre to concert measures to combat the epidemic, it had already spread to four neighbouring states: Colombia, Ecuador, Bolivia and Chile. Over 1,200 had died and some 160,000 had been infected. The same month the infection crossed the continental divide to become established in the headwaters of the Amazon (*The Guardian*, 20 April 1991). Thereafter it was only a matter of time before the epidemic spread downstream to Manaus and Belém in Brazil. By the end of the year, the director of a hospital in Belém said that thirty people had arrived with symptoms on one boat, of which a passenger said: 'There was no hygiene. Drinking water came from a large pot without a lid and the glasses weren't washed' (*The Guardian*, 19 December 1991).

Meanwhile, in June 1991, the epidemic had spread to southern Mexico (*Keesing's*: 38286), probably carried by drug-smugglers travelling on a light aircraft from Colombia. By the end of the year an estimated 16,000 people had died in all affected states. Ironically, in view of the excessive concern of the Peruvians for their export trade, that trade had long since collapsed, costing the country some $400 million in 1991 alone (*The Guardian*, 3 January 1992). At the beginning of 1992 the first cases of cholera were reported in the Province of Salta in Argentina. A total of 62,000 cases were reported from the region in the first two months of the year alone, and regional health ministers estimated the cost of clearing up insanitary conditions in the five Andean countries alone at $350 million (*The Guardian*, 14 March 1992).

The cholera epidemic is, however, only the most striking evidence that environmental questions are set to assume increasing importance in regional politics, both domestic and international. However the 'factored' decision-making characteristic of loose bureaucratic systems presents formidable difficulties, precisely because of the wide ramifications of environmental issues. With their brief fixed terms, Latin American presidents have, indeed, traditionally welcomed the sort of massive public works projects which could be completed and opened before they went out of office. Complex programmes of land and water management, being very difficult to administer and cutting across vested interests, were particularly unappealing. Industrial growth has been so highly regarded that governments have been prepared to disregard any question of safety or toxicity in case it hinders investment. Pollution continues to be ignored, to be dumped or channelled into rivers (as with the gold prospectors' mercury in Brazil) or into the sea, and in due course this too will have to be included in the long agenda of questions that will have to be resolved by international negotiation.

The end of history?

In the confusion of 1989 and after a curious paper by a State Department analyst, Francis Fukuyama, attracted considerable attention both at home and abroad, *The end of history* argued that with the fall of communism in Eastern Europe history, at least in a Hegelian sense, had come to an end. That is to say, with democracy unchallenged, no major intellectual questions remained to be answered or indeed asked (Fukuyama 1992).

Democracy had, it was clear, secured a substantial victory, and the change might even be described without exaggeration as a revolution (Rustow 1990). The thesis that democracy was unchallenged, could even be accepted in principle, although there remained a significant number of authoritarian regimes in existence, one of which, China, commanded the allegiance of one-quarter of the world's rapidly growing population. However it was not at all clear that the same was true of liberal democracy's alter ego, capitalism. The fact that communism was quite out of fashion did not mean – on the analogy of earlier movements such as liberalism, conservatism or anarchism – that it might not again return to favour, though no doubt in a significantly modified form. Even more importantly, it certainly did not mean that at a stroke all political leaders had been converted to a belief in the virtues of the sort of free-market, unregulated capitalism associated with the United States.

As Brazil's Minister of External Relations put it in a speech in London in January 1993:

> in the 80's (sic), the prevailing economic model, based on import-substitution, faded away as we felt the need for thorough, balanced and firmly progressive openness to the world economy and inter-

national flows of capital and technology. The country is undergoing a careful process of privatization. The role played by the Government is under review, in an effort to find a balance between an overwhelming State presence in the economy and the improvident dismantling of the whole State structure and capabilities.

(Cardoso 1993)

The long duration of the Cold War had, it was clear, enabled people to forget that before it had existed, states had disputed, quarrelled and warred with one another, that they had continued to do so throughout it, and were likely to continue to do so in the future. Certainly the Cold War had imposed order, of a sort, and up to a point. But only from a European standpoint could it be described as a period of peace (Gaddis 1987), and then only if one was to disregard (for example) the eleven wars fought by the United Kingdom between 1947 and 1982. Latin America, as we have seen, belatedly was drawn into the conflict, with the active collaboration of its political elites. Interpreting its politics in the light of known paradigms (Shafer 1988), successive governments in the United States took a variety of counter-measures to what they saw as the threat of communism. In the process, US hegemony over the Caribbean basin system was not only consolidated by the incorporation of the territories that had formerly been part of rival European empires, but extended, directly and indirectly, to that of South America.

But the structures that had enabled this to happen, and to which Latin American states had themselves contributed, were intended for a more equal world order. Hence it was just as possible that with the polarising effect of the superpower conflict removed, these structures might now come for the first time to be used for their intended purpose.

Bibliography

Alberdi, Juan Bautista (1980), *Bases y puntos de partida para la organización política de la República Argentina*, Buenos Aires, Editorial Plus Ultra.

Alexander, Robert J. (1973), *Aprismo: the ideas and doctrines of Víctor Raúl Haya de la Torre*, Kent, OH, Kent State University Press.

Allison, Graham T. (1971), *Essence of decision: explaining the Cuban Missile Crisis*, Boston, Little Brown.

Alvarez Natale, Hugo E. (1984), *Beagle: de brujos y fantasmas a la decisión final*, Buenos Aires, Ediciones Politeia.

Ambursley, Fitzroy, and Dunkerley, James (1984), *Grenada – whose freedom?*, London, Latin American Bureau.

Anell, Lars, and Nygren, Birgitta (1980), *The developing countries and the world economic order*, London, Methuen.

Anglade, Christian and Fortín, Carlos (1985), *The state and capital accumulation in Latin America*, London, Macmillan.

Aquinas, Thomas (1959), *Aquinas selected political writings*, ed. and intro. A. P. d'Entreves, tr. J. G. Dawson, Oxford, Blackwell.

Arias Plan, The (1987), *International Legal Materials*, 26, 5, September, 1164–74.

Atkins, G. Pope (1977), *Latin America in the international political system*, New York, Free Press.

Atkins, G. Pope (1989), *Latin America in the international political system*, 2nd edition, revised, Boulder, CO, Westview Press.

Bailey, Norman A., ed. (1966), *Latin America: politics, economics, and hemispheric security*, New York, Praeger.

Balfour, Sebastian (1990), *Castro*, London, Longman.

Baran, Paul A. (1957), *The political economy of growth*, New York, Monthly Review Press.

Barros, Alexandre de S. C. (1984), 'The formulation and inplementation of Brazilian foreign policy: Itamaraty and the new actors' in Heraldo Muñoz and Joseph S. Tulchin, eds (1984), *Latin American nations in world politics*, Boulder, CO, Westview Press, 30–44.

Barry, T. B., Wood, B. and Preusch, D. (1984), *The other side of paradise: foreign control in the Caribbean*, New York, Grove.

Bath, C. Richard, and James, D. D. (1976), 'Dependence analysis of Latin America: some criticisms, some suggestions', *Latin American Research Review*, 11, 3, 3–54.

Beck, Peter J. (1986), *The international politics of Antarctica*, London, Croom Helm.

Beck, Peter (1988), *The Falkland Islands as an international problem*, London, Routledge.

Beck, Peter J. (1990), 'International relations in Antarctica: Argentina, Chile and the Great Powers', in Michael A. Morris, ed., *Great power relations in Argentina, Chile and Antarctica*, Basingstoke, Hants, Macmillan, 101–30.

Best, Edward (1987), *US policy and regional security in Central America*, Aldershot, Hants, Gower for the International Institute of Strategic Studies.

Bethell, Leslie, and Roxborough, Ian, eds (1992), *Latin America between the Second World War and the Cold War, 1944–1948*, Cambridge, Cambridge University Press.

Bilateral Commission on the Future of United States–Mexican Relations (1989), *The challenge of interdependence: Mexico and the United States*, Lanham, MD, University Press of America.

Black, Jan Knippers (1977), *United States penetration of Brazil*, Philadelphia, PA, University of Pennsylvania Press.

Black, Jan Knippers (1986), *The Dominican Republic: politics and development in an unsovereign state*, Boston, MA, Allen & Unwin.

Bonilla, Frank, and Girling, Robert, eds (1973), *The structures of dependency*, Stanford, CA, Institute of Political Studies.

Booth, D., and Sorj, B. (1983), *Military reformism and social classes: the Peruvian experience, 1968–80*, New York, St Martin's Press.

Borchard, E. M. (1930), 'Calvo and Drago Doctrines', in *Encyclopedia of the Social Sciences*, New York, The Macmillan Co., 3, 153–6.

Brasil: AIAA/Sopral (1992), *Ethanol: energy source for a sustainable society*, Rio de Janeiro, n.p.

Brasil, Governo do (1992a), *The challenge of sustainable development: the Brazilian report for the United Nations Conference on Environment and Development*, Brasília, Press Secretariat of the Presidency of the Republic.

Brasil, Governo do (1992b), *Ethanol: Brazil's cleaner renewable fuel*, Brasília, n.p.

Brasil, Governo do (1992c), *President Fernando Collor: agenda for consensus: a social-liberal proposal*, Brasília, Press Secretariat of the Presidency of the Republic.

Bull, Hedley (1977), *The anarchical society*, London, Macmillan.

Burns, E. Bradford (1966), *The unwritten alliance: Rio-Branco and Brazilian-American relations*, New York, Columbia University Press.

Cable, Vincent (1969), 'The "Football War" and the Central American Common Market', *International Affairs*, 45, 4, October, 658–71.

Calvert, Peter (1971), 'The last occasion on which Britain used coercion to settle a dispute with a non-colonial territory in the Caribbean: Guatemala and the Powers, 1909–1913', *Inter-American Economic Affairs*, 25, 3, 57–75.

Calvert, Peter (1982), *The Falklands Crisis: the rights and the wrongs*, London, Frances Pinter.

Calvert, Peter (1983), *Boundary disputes in Latin America*, London, The Institute for the Study of Conflict.

Calvert, Peter (1986), *The foreign policy of new states*, Brighton, Sussex, Wheatsheaf.

Calvert, Peter, ed. (1988a), *The Central American security system: North/South or East/West?* Cambridge, Cambridge University Press.

Calvert, Peter (1988b), 'US decision-making and Central America: the Reagan Administration', in Peter Shearman and Phil Williams, eds, *The superpowers, Central America and the Middle East*, London, Brassey's Defence Publishers, 3–18.

Calvert, Peter and Calvert, Susan (1990), *Latin America in the twentieth century*, Basingstoke, Hants, Macmillan.

Calvert, Peter, and Forbes, Ian (1988), 'Security: the issues', in Peter Calvert, ed., *The Central American security system: North/South or East/West?* Cambridge, Cambridge University Press, 3–17.

Calvert, Peter, and Milbank, Susan (1987), *The ebb and flow of military government in South America*, London, Institute for the Study of Conflict (Conflict Studies no. 198).

Calvert, Susan, and Calvert, Peter (1989), *Argentina: political culture and instability*, Basingstoke, Hants, Macmillan.

Camp, Roderick A. (1984), *The making of a government: political leaders in modern Mexico*, Tucson, AR, University of Arizona Press.

Canovan, Margaret (1981), *Populism*, London, Junction Books.

Caporaso, James A. (1978), 'Dependence, dependency, and power in the global system: a structural and behavioral analysis', *International Organization*, 32, 1, 13–43.

Cardoso, Fernando Henrique (1972), 'Dependency and development in Latin America', *New Left Review*, 74, 83–95.

Cardoso, Fernando Henrique (1973), 'Associated-dependent development: theoretical and practical implications', in Alfred Stepan, ed., *Authoritarian Brazil*, New Haven, CT, Yale University Press.

Cardoso, Fernando Henrique (1993), *Brazil and European integration*, London, Brazilian Embassy.

Cardoso, Fernando Henrique, and Faletto, Enzo (1979), *Dependency and development in Latin America*, Berkeley, CA, University of California Press.

Cardoso, O. R., Kirschbaum, R., and van der Kooy, E. (1983), *Malvinas: la trama secreta*, Buenos Aires, Editorial Planeta.

Carey, James C. (1964), *Peru and the United States 1900–1962*, Notre Dame, Indiana, University of Notre Dame Press.

Charlton, Michael, ed. (1989), *The little platoon: diplomacy and the Falklands dispute*, Oxford, Blackwell.

Chilcote, Ronald H. (1974), 'A critical synthesis of the dependency literature', *Latin American Perspectives*, 1, 1, 4–29.

Chilcote, Ronald H. (1978), 'A question of dependency', *Latin American Research Review*, 12, 2, 55–68.

Chilcote, Ronald H., and Edelstein, Joel C., eds (1974), *Latin America: the struggle with dependency and beyond*, Cambridge, MA, Schenkman.

Child, Jack (1985), *Geopolitics and conflict in South America: quarrels among neighbors*, New York, Praeger.

Child, Jack, ed. (1986), *Conflict in Central America: approaches to peace and security*, London, C. Hurst for the International Peace Academy.

Clapham, Christopher, and Philip, George, eds (1985), *The political dilemmas of military regimes*, London, Croom Helm.

Clarke, Michael, and White, Brian (1989), *Understanding foreign policy: the foreign policy systems approach*, Aldershot, Hants, Edward Elgar.

Claude, I. L. (1964), 'The OAS, the UN, and the United States', *International Conciliation*, 547, March, 1–67.

Claude, Inis L. (1985), 'UN efforts at settlement of the Falkland Islands Crisis', in Alberto R. Coll and Anthony C. Arend, eds, *The Falklands War: lessons for strategy, diplomacy and international law*, London, Allen & Unwin, 118–31.

Clissold, Stephen, ed. (1970), *Soviet relations with Latin America 1918–68: a documentary survey*, London, Oxford University Press for Royal Institute of International Affairs.

Coll, Alberto R., and Arend, Anthony C., eds (1985), *The Falklands War: lessons for strategy, diplomacy and international law*, London, Allen & Unwin.

Collier, Ruth Berins, and Collier, David (1991), *Shaping the political arena: critical junctures, the labor movement, and regime dynamics in Latin America*, Princeton, NJ, Princeton University Press.

Conil Paz, Alberto A., and Ferrari, Gustavo E. (1966), *Argentina's foreign policy 1930–1962*, tr. John J. Kennedy, Notre Dame, Indiana, University of Notre Dame Press.

Connell-Smith, Gordon (1966), *The Inter-American system*, London, Oxford University Press for Royal Institute of International Affairs.

Conniff, Michael L., ed. (1982), *Latin Amerian populism in comparative perspective*, Albuquerque, NM, University of New Mexico Press.

Conoboy, P. J. (1976), 'Money and politics in Chile, 1878–1925', unpublished Ph.D. dissertation, University of Southampton.

Crabtree, John (1987), *The great tin crash: Bolivia and the world tin market*, London, Latin American Bureau.

Cuba, Government of (1962), *Declarations of Havana*, Peking, Foreign Languages Press.

Cumberland, Charles Curtis (1968), *Mexico, the struggle for modernity*, New York, Oxford University Press.

Da Cunha, Euclydes (1944), *Rebellion in the backlands (Os Sertões)*, tr. Samuel Putnam, Chicago, University of Chicago Press, Phoenix Books.

Dabat, Alejandro, and Lorenzano, Luis (1984), *Argentina: the Malvinas and the end of military rule*, tr. Ralph Johnstone, London, Verso.

Danchev, Alex, ed. (1992), *International perspectives on the Falklands conflict*, London, Macmillan.

Davidson, Scott (1987), *Grenada: a study in politics and the limits of international law*, Aldershot, Avebury.

Debray, Régis (1965), 'Latin America: the long march', *New Left Review*, 33, September–October, 17.

Dennis, W. J. (1967), *Tacna and Arica*, New York, Archon Books.

Desch, Michael C. (1993), *When the Third World matters: Latin America and United States grand strategy*, Baltimore, MD, Johns Hopkins University Press.

Di Palma, Giuseppe, and Whitehead, Laurence, eds (1986), *The Central American impasse*, London, Croom Helm with the Friedrich Naumann Foundation.

Di Tella, Guido, and Rodríguez Braun, Carlos, eds (1990), *Argentina, 1946–83: the economic ministers speak*, Basingstoke, Hants, Macmillan in association with St Antony's College, Oxford.

Di Tella, Torcuato (1965), 'Populism and reform in Latin America', in Claudio Véliz, ed., *Obstacles to change in Latin America*, London, Oxford University Press, 48–51.

Diedrich, Bernard (1982), *Somoza and the legacy of US involvement in Central America*, London, Junction Books.

Dix, Robert (1985), 'Populism: authoritarian and democratic', *Latin American Research Review*, 20, 2, 29–52.

Domínguez, Jorge I., ed. (1982), *Cuba: internal and international affairs*, Beverly Hills, CA, Sage Publications.

Domínguez, Jorge I. (1989), *To make a world safe for revolution: Cuba's foreign policy*, Cambridge, MA, Harvard University Press.

Domínguez, Jorge I., and Lindau, Juan (1984), 'The primacy of politics: comparing the foreign policies of Cuba and Mexico', *International Political Science Review*, 5, 75–101.

Dos Santos, Theotonio (1969), 'The crisis of development theory and the problem of dependence in Latin America', in Henry Bernstein, ed., *Under-*

development and development: the Third World today, Harmondsworth, Middx, Penguin, 1973, 55–60.

Dos Santos, Theotonio (1970), 'The structure of dependence', *American Economic Review,* 60, May, 291–336.

Downes, Richard (1992), 'Autos over rails: how US business supplanted the British in Brazil, 1910–28', *Journal of Latin American Studies,* 24, 3, October, 551–84.

Dozer, Donald M. (1962), *Latin America, an interpretive history,* New York, McGraw-Hill.

Dunkerley, James (1980), *Bolivia: coup d'etat,* London, Latin American Bureau.

Dunkerley, James (1984), *Rebellion in the veins: political struggle in Bolivia 1952–82,* London, Verso.

Dunkerley, James (1985), *The long war: dictatorship and revolution in El Salvador,* 2nd edn, London, Verso.

Durán, Esperanza (1985), *European Interests in Latin America,* London, Royal Institute of International Affairs.

Durham, William H. (1979), *Scarcity and survival in Central America: ecological origins of the Soccer War,* Stanford, CA, Stanford University Press.

Einaudi, Luigi (1972), 'US relations with the Peruvian military', in Daniel A. Sharp, ed. (1972), *US foreign policy and Peru,* Austin, TX, University of Texas Press for the Institute of Latin American Studies.

Espejo, Luis Guillermo (1981), 'Neutral but not indifferent: Colombian foreign policy since 1900', unpublished Ph.D. dissertation, University of Southampton.

Etchepareborda, Roberto (1978), *Historia de las relaciones internationales argentinas,* Buenos Aires, Editorial Pleamar.

Farer, Tom J., ed. (1979), *The future of the inter-American system,* New York, Praeger.

Feinberg, Richard E. (1983), *The intemperate zone: the Third World challenge to US foreign policy,* New York, W. W. Norton.

Ferguson, James (1990a), *Far from paradise: an introduction to Caribbean development,* London, Latin American Bureau.

Ferguson, James (1990b), *Grenada: revolution in reverse,* London, Latin American Bureau.

Ferguson, James, and Pearce, Jenny, eds (1988), *The Thatcher years: Britain and Latin America,* London, Latin American Bureau.

Finer, S. E. (1975), *The man on horseback,* 2nd revd edition, Harmondsworth, Middx, Penguin.

Fluharty, Vernon L. (1957), *Dance of the millions: military rule and social revolution in Colombia, 1930–1956,* Pittsburgh, PA, University of Pittsburgh Press.

Francis, Michael J. (1977), *The limits of hegemony: United States relations with Argentina and Chile during World War II*, Notre Dame, Indiana, University of Notre Dame Press.

Frank, André Gunder (1966), 'The development of underdevelopment', *Monthly Review*, 18, 4, 17–31.

Frank, André Gunder (1967), *Capitalism and underdevelopment in Latin America*, Harmondsworth, Middx, Penguin.

Frank, André Gunder (1969), *Lumpenbourgeoisie: lumpendevelopment, dependence, class, and politics in Latin America*, New York, Monthly Review Press.

Frank, André Gunder (1970), *Latin America: underdevelopment or revolution*, New York, Monthly Review Press.

Frank, André Gunder (1974), 'Dependence is dead, long live dependence and the class struggle: a reply to critiques', *Latin American Perspectives*, 1, 1, 87–106.

Fukuyama, Francis (1989), 'The end of history?', *The National Interest*, Summer, 3–18.

Fukuyama, Francis (1992), *The end of history and the last man*, London, Hamish Hamilton.

Furtado, Celso (1970), *Economic development of Latin America: a survey from colonial times to the Cuban Revolution*, Cambridge, Cambridge University Pres.

Gaddis, John Lewis (1987), *The long peace: enquiries into the history of the Cold War*, Oxford, Oxford University Press.

Galeano, Eduardo (1973), *Open veins of Latin America: five centuries of the pillage of a continent*, New York, Monthly Review Press.

Gauhar, Altaf, ed. (1985), *Regional integration: the Latin America experience*, London, Third World Foundation for Social and Economic Studies.

Giddens, Anthony (1990), *The consequences of modernity*, Cambridge, Polity Press.

Gleijeses, Piero (1978), *The Dominican crisis: the 1965 Constitutionalist revolt and American intervention*, Baltimore, MD, Johns Hopkins University Press.

Gleijeses, Piero (1992), 'The limits of sympathy: the United States and the independence of Spanish America', *Journal of Latin American Studies*, 24, 3, 481–506.

Golbery do Couto e Silva, General (1947), *Geopolítica do Brasil*, Rio de Janeiro: Libraria José Olimpio Editora.

Gonzalez, Mike (1990), *Nicaragua: what went wrong?* London, Bookmarks Publications.

González Prada, Manuel (1985), *Horas de lucha* in *Obras*, prólogo y notas par Luis Alberto Sánchez, Lima, Cope.

Goodman, David, and Redclift, Michael, eds (1991), *Environment and development in Latin America: the politics of sustainability*, Manchester, Manchester University Press.

Gordon-Ashworth, Fiona (1978), 'International and national commodity control, 1930 to 1945; sugar and the Brazilian case', unpublished Ph.D. dissertation, University of Southampton.

Gordon-Ashworth, Fiona (1984), *International commodity control: a contemporary history and appraisal*, London, Croom Helm.

Gott, Richard (1970), *Guerrilla movements in Latin America*, London, Nelson.

Grabendorff, Wolf, and Roett, Riordan, eds (1985), *Latin America, Western Europe and the US; reevaluating the Atlantic Triangle*, New York, Praeger with Hoover Institution Press, Stanford University, Stanford, CA.

Grotius, Hugo (1964), *Hugo Grotius: De jure belli ac pacis libri tres*, tr. F. W. Kelsey, London, Wildy & Sons.

Guevara, Ernesto Che (1967), *Guerrilla warfare*, New York, Monthly Review Press.

Guglialmelli, Juan Enrique (1980), *El conflicto del Beagle*, Buenos Aires, El Cid Editor.

Gustafson, Lowell S. (1988), *The sovereignty dispute over the Falkland (Malvinas) Islands*, New York, Oxford University Press.

Hall, Anthony L. (1991), *Developing Amazonia: deforestation and social conflict in Brazil's Carajás programme*, Manchester, Manchester University Press.

Haya de la Torre, Víctor Raúl (1935), *A donde va indoamérica?* Santiago de Chile, Editorial Ercilla.

Haya de la Torre, Víctor Raúl (1946), *Y después de la Guerra, que?* Lima, Editorial PTCM.

Hicks, John D. (1961), *The populist revolt*, Lincoln, NB, University of Nebraska Press.

Husbands, Jo L. (1979), 'Nuclear proliferation and the Inter-American System', in Tom J. Farer, ed. (1979), *The future of the inter-American system*, New York, Praeger, 204–31.

Ianni, Otavio (1968), *Crisis in Brazil*, New York, Columbia University Press.

Ianni, Otavio (1975a), *A formaçao do estado populista na América Latina*, Rio de Janeiro, Civilizaçao Brasiliera.

Ianni, Otavio (1975b), *La formación del estado populista in América Latina*, Mexico, Ediciones Era.

Immerman, Richard H. (1982), *The CIA in Guatemala: the foreign policy of intervention*, Austin, TX, University of Texas Press.

International Court of Justice (1986), *Military and paramilitary activities in and against Nicaragua (Nicaragua vs United States of America), Judgment of the Court*, International Court of Justice, Communiqué 86/8 of 27 June 1986.

Ionescu, Ghita, and and Gellner, Ernest, eds (1969), *Populism: its meaning and national characteristics*, New York, The Macmillan Co.

Jackson, Geoffrey (1973), *People's prison*, London, Faber.

Jaeger Calderón, A. R. (1988), 'Multilateral corporations and government relations: the oil industry in Ecuador, 1972–1979', unpublished Ph.D. dissertation, University of London.

Jaguaribe, Helio (1967), *Problems do desenvolvimiento Latino-Americano*, Rio de Janeiro, Ed. Civilização Brasiliera.

James, Alan (1990), *Peacekeeping in international politics*, London, Macmillan for International Institute of Strategic Studies.

Jaworski C., Helan (1984), 'Peru: the military government's foreign policy in its two phases (1968–1980)', in Heraldo Muñoz and Joseph S. Tulchin, eds, *Latin American nations in world politics*, Boulder, CO, Westview Press, 200–17.

Jennings, R. Y. (1962), *The acquisition of territory in international law*, Manchester, Manchester University Press.

Jennings, R. Y. (1972), 'The Argentina–Chile boundary dispute, a case study' in Humphrey Waldock *et al.*, *International disputes, the legal aspects*, London, Europa for the David Davies Institute of International Relations.

Jessel, David (1983), *Heart of the Matter*, on Chile, BBC Television, February 1983.

Johnson, Haynes (1965), *The Bay of Pigs: the invasion of Cuba by Brigade 2506*, London, Hutchinson.

Johnson, John J. (1964), *The military and society in Latin America*, Stanford, CA, Stanford University Press.

Jordan, David C. (1993), *Revolutionary Cuba and the end of the Cold War*, Lanham, MD, University Press of America.

Jorden, William J. (1984), *Panama Odyssey* (1984), Austin, TX, University of Texas Press.

Kantor, Harry (1953), *The ideology and program of the Peruvian Aprista movement*, Berkeley, CA, University of California Press.

Kempe, Frederick (1990), *Divorcing the dictator: America's bungled affair with Noriega*, New York, G.P. Putnam's Sons.

Keohane, Robert O., and Nye, Joseph S. (1973), *Transnational relations and world politics*, Cambridge, MA, Harvard University Press.

Keohane, Robert O., and Nye, Joseph S. (1977), *Power and interdependence: world politics in transition*, Boston, Little Brown and Co.

Kirkpatrick, Jeane (1982), *Dictatorships and double standards*, New York, Simon & Schuster.

Kitching, G. (1982), *Development and underdevelopment in historical perspective: populism, nationalism and industrialization*, London, Methuen.

Lanús, Juan Archibaldo (1984), *De Chapúltepec al Beagle: política exterior argentina, 1945–1980*, Buenos Aires, EMECÉ Editores.

Lapper, Richard (1985), *Honduras: state for sale*, London, Latin American

Bureau.

Latin American Bureau (1978), *Panama and the Canal Treaty*, London, Latin American Bureau.

Latin American Bureau (1980), *Paraguay: power game*, London, Latin American Bureau.

Leventhal, Paul L., and Tanzer, Sharon, eds (1992), *Averting a Latin American nuclear arms race: new prospects and challenges for Argentine-Brazilian co-operation*, London, Macmillan.

Leys, Colin (1983), 'Underdevelopment and dependency: critical notes', in Leter Limqueco and Bruce McFarlane, eds, *Neo-Marxist theories of development*, London, Croom Helm, 29–47.

Lieuwen, Edwin (1961a), *Arms and politics in Latin America*, New York, Praeger.

Lieuwen, Edwin (1961b), *Venezuela*, London, Oxford University Press for Royal Institute of International Affairs.

Lieuwen, Edwin (1964), *Generals versus Presidents*, London, Pall Mall Press.

Light, Margot, and Groom, A. J. R., eds (1985), *International relations: a handbook of current theory*, London, Pinter.

Lins, Alvaro (1965), *Rio-Branco (O Barão de Rio-Branco)*, São Paulo, Editorial Nacional.

Loring, David C. (1972), 'The fisheries dispute', in Daniel A. Sharp, ed., *US foreign policy and Peru*, Austin, TX, University of Texas Press for the Institute of Latin American Studies.

Love, Joseph L. (1990), 'The origins of dependency analysis', *Journal of Latin American Studies*, 22, 143–68.

Loveman, Brian, and Davies, Thomas M., eds (1978), *The politics of anti-politics: the military in Latin America*, Lincoln, NB, University of Nebraska Press.

Lozoya, Jorge, and Estevez, Jaime, eds (1980), *Latin America and the new international economic order*, Oxford, Pergamon Press.

McCann, Frank D., Jr. (1973), *The Brazilian-American Alliance, 1937–1945*, Princeton, NJ, Princeton University Press.

McCullough, David (1977), *The path between the seas*, New York, Simon & Schuster.

MacDonald, A. T. and Kay, D. (1988), *Water resources: issues and strategies*, London, Longman.

McGrew, Anthony G., Lewis, Paul G. *et al.* (1992), *Global politics: globalisation and the nation-state*, Cambridge, Polity Press.

Madero, Francisco Indalecio (1911), *La sucesión presidencial en 1910*, 3rd edition, Mexico, Librería de la Vda. de Ch. Bouret.

Manley, Michael (1979), *The politics of affirmation*, London, Third World Foundation, Third World Foundation Monograph 1.

Mariátegui, José Carlos (1955), *Siete ensayos de interpretación de la realidad peruana*, Santiago de Chile, Ed. Universitaria.

Martínez Cantú, M. A. (1992), 'The politics of the debt crisis in Mexico (1982–1988)', Ph.D. dissertation, University of Leeds.

Martínez de Hoz, José Alfredo (1990), in Guido di Tella and Carlos Rodríguez Brown, eds, *Argentina, 1946–83: the economic ministers speak*, Basingstoke, Hants, Macmillan in association with St Antony's College, Oxford, 151–80.

Martz, John D. (1984), 'Venezuelan foreign policy and the role of political parties', in Heraldo Muñoz and Joseph S. Tulchin, eds, *Latin American nations in world politics*, Boulder, CO, Westview Press, 133–49.

Martz, John D., ed. (1988), *United States policy in Latin America: a quarter century of crisis and challenge, 1961–1986*, Lincoln, NB, University of Nebraska Press.

Martz, John D., and Schoultz, Lars, eds (1980), *Latin America, the United States, and the inter-American system*, Boulder, CO, Westview.

Mecham, J. Lloyd (1965), *A survey of United States–Latin American relations*, Boston, Houghton Mifflin.

Menchú, Rigoberta (1984), *I. . .Rigoberta Menchú, an Indian woman in Guatemala*, tr. Ann Wright, ed. and intro. Elisabeth Burgos-Debray, London, Verso.

Mercier Vega, Luis (1969), *Guerrillas in Latin America: the techniques of the counter-state*, London, Pall Mall Press.

Mericq, Luis H. (1987), *Antarctica: Chile's claim*, Washington, DC, National Defense University, Fort Lesley J. McNair.

Mesa-Lago, Carmelo (1981), *The economy of socialist Cuba: a two-decade appraisal*, Albuquerque, NM, University of New Mexico Press.

Migdal, J. S. (1988), *Strong societies and weak states: state-society relations and state capabilities in the Third World*, Princeton, NJ, Princeton University Press.

Milenky, Edward S. (1978), *Argentina's foreign policies*, Boulder, CO, Westview Press.

Millán, Victor (1983), 'Controlling conflict in the Caribbean Basin: national approaches', in Michael A. Morris and Victor Millán, eds, *Controlling Latin American conflictrs: ten approaches*, Boulder, CO, Westview Press.

Millet, Allan Read (1968), *The politics of intervention: the military occupation of Cuba 1906–1909*, Columbus, OH, Ohio State University Press.

Molina Enríquez, Andrés (1909), *Los grandes problemas nacionales*, Mexico: Imprenta de A. Carranza e hijos.

Morris, Michael A., ed. (1990), *Great power relations in Argentina, Chile and Antarctica*, Basingstoke, Hants, Macmillan.

Morris, Michael A., and Millán, Victor, eds (1983), *Controlling Latin American conflicts: ten approaches*, Boulder, CO, Westview Press.

Morrison, de Lesseps S. (1965), *Latin American mission: an adventure in hemisphere diplomacy*, ed. and intro. Gerold Frank, New York, Simon &

Schuster.

Morse, Edward L. (1969), 'The politics of interdependence', *International Organization*, 23, 311–26.

Morse, Edward L. (1970), 'The transformation of foreign policies: modernization, interdependence, and externalization', *World Politics*, 22, 371–92.

Muñoz, Heraldo and Tulchin, Joseph S., eds (1984), *Latin American nations in world politics*, Boulder, CO, Westview Press.

Munro, Dana Gardner (1964), *Intervention and dollar diplomacy in the Caribbean, 1900–1921*, Princeton, NJ, Princeton University Press.

Munro, Dana Gardner (1974), *The United States and the Caribbean Republics, 1921–1933* Princeton, NJ, Princeton University Press.

Needler, Martin C. (1966), 'Political development and military intervention in Latin America', *American Political Science Review*, 60, 616–26.

Needler, Martin C. (1975), 'Military motivations in the seizure of power', *Latin American Research Review*, 10, 63–77

Nickson, R. A. (1982), 'The Itaipú hydro-electric project; the Paraguayan perspective', *Bulletin of Latin American Research*, 2, 1, 1–20.

Nunn, Frederick M. (1992), *The time of the generals: Latin America professional militarism in world perspective*, Lincoln, NB, University of Nebraska Press.

O'Brien, Philip J. (1973), 'Dependency: the new nationalism?', *Latin American Review of Books*, 1, 35–41.

O'Brien, Philip J. (1975), 'A critique of Latin American theories of dependency', in I. Oxaal, T. Barnett, and D. Booth, eds, *Beyond the sociology of development: economy and society in Latin America and Africa*, London, Routledge, 7–27.

O'Brien, Philip, and Cammack, Paul, eds (1985), *Generals in retreat: the crisis of military rule in Latin America*, Manchester, Manchester University Press.

O'Donnell, Guillermo (1988), *Bureaucratic authoritarianism: Argentina, 1966–1973, in comparative perspective*, Berkeley, CA, University of California Press.

O'Shaughnessy, Hugh (1984), *Grenada: revolution, invasion and aftermath*, London, Sphere Books with *The Observer*.

Oppenheimer, Martin (1970), *Urban guerrilla*, Harmondsworth, Middx, Penguin.

Oxaal, I., Barnett, T., and Booth, D., eds (1975), *Beyond the sociology of development, economy and society in Latin America and Africa*, London, Routledge.

Painter, James (1987), *Guatemala: false hope, false freedom: the rich, the poor and the Christian Democrats*, London, Catholic Institute for International Relations and Latin American Bureau.

Parker, Franklin C. (1964), *The Central American Republics*, London,

Oxford University Press for Royal Institute of International Affairs.

Parkinson, Fred (1974a), *Latin America, the Cold War and the world powers 1945–1973*, Beverly Hills, CA, Sage.

Parkinson, Fred (1974b), 'Latin American foreign policies in the era of detente', *International Affairs*, 50, 439–50.

Pastor, Robert A. (1987), *Condemned to repetition: the United States and Nicaragua*, Princeton, NJ, Princeton University Press.

Patman, Robert G. (1990), *The Soviet Union in the Horn of Africa: the diplomacy of intervention and disengagement*, Cambridge, Cambridge University Press.

Payne, A. J. (1980), *The politics of the Caribbean community 1961–79: regional integration among new states*, Manchester, Manchester University Press.

Payne, A. J. (1989), *Politics in Jamaica*, London, Christopher Hurst.

Payne, Anthony, and Sutton, Paul, eds (1984), *Dependency under challenge: the political economy of the Commonwealth Caribbean*, Manchester, Manchester University Press.

Payne, Anthony, and Sutton, Paul, eds (1993), *Modern Caribbean politics*, Baltimore, MD, Johns Hopkins University Press.

Pearce, Jenny (1981), *Under the eagle*, London, Latin American Bureau.

Pearce, Jenny, ed. (1982), *The European challenge: Europe's new role in Latin America*, London, Latin American Bureau.

Pelcovits, Nathan A. (1984), *Peacekeeping on Arab–Israeli fronts; lessons from the Sinai and Lebanon*, Boulder, CO, Westview Press for the Foreign Policy Institute, School of Advanced International Studies, Johns Hopkins University.

Perkins, Dexter (1960), *A history of the Monroe Doctrine*, London, Longman.

Philip, George (1982), *Oil and politics in Latin America: nationalist movements and state companies*, Cambridge, Cambridge University Press.

Philip, George (1984), 'Military-authoritarianism in South America: Brazil, Chile, Uruguay and Argentina', *Political Studies*, 32, 1–20.

Philip, George (1985), *The military and South American politics*, London, Croom Helm.

Philip, George (1992), *The presidency in Mexican politics*, Basingstoke, Macmillan in association with St Antony's College, Oxford.

Pike, Frederick B. (1992), *The United States and Latin America; myths and stereotypes of civilization and nature*, Austin, TX, University of Texas Press.

Pinochet Ugarte, Augusto (1968), *Geopolítica: diferentes étapas para el estudio geopolítica de los estados*, Santiago de Chile, Ejército, Estado Mayor General.

Plant, Roger (1978), *Guatemala: unnatural diaster*, London, Latin American Bureau.

Poppino, Rollie (1968), *Brazil, the land and the people*, New York, Oxford University Press.

Prebisch, Raúl (1950), *Economic development of Latin America and its principal problems*, New York, United Nations Department of Economic Affairs, ECLA document E/CN 12/89/Rev.1.

Pugh, Michael (1994), 'The historical record and the relevance of force thresholds', in Michael Pugh, ed., *Maritime security and naval peacekeeping*, Manchester, Manchester University Press.

Quirk, Robert E. (1964), *An affair of honor: Woodrow Wilson and the occupation of Vera Cruz*, New York, McGraw Hill.

Rabe, Stephen G. (1988), *Eisenhower and Latin America: the foreign policy of anticommunism*, Chapel Hill, NC, University of North Carolina Press.

Rachum, Ilan (1993), 'Intellectuals and the emergence of the Latin American political right, 1917–1936', *European Review of Latin American and Caribbean Studies*, 54, June, 95–110.

Ray, David (1973), 'The dependency model of Latin America underdevelopment: three basic fallacies', *Journal of Inter-American Studies and World Affairs*, 15, 1, 4–20.

Redick, John R. (1990), *Argentina and Brazil: an evolving nuclear relationship*, Southampton, Centre for International Policy Studies for Programme for Promoting Nuclear Non-Proliferation.

Redick, John R. (1994), 'Argentina–Brazil nuclear non-proliferation initiatives', *Programme for Promoting Nuclear Non-Proliferation Issue Review*, 3, January, 1–4.

Reidy, Joseph W. (1964), 'Latin America and the Atlantic Triangle', *Orbis*, 8, 1, 52–65.

Rikhye, Indar Jit (1980), *The Sinai blunder: withdrawal of the United Nations Emergency Force leading to the Six Day War of June 1967*, London, Frank Cass.

Rippy, J. F. (1937), 'The initiation of the customs receivership in the Dominican Republic', *Hispanic American Historical Review*, 17, 4, 419.

Rodó, José Enrique (1967), *Ariel*, ed. and intro. Gordon Brotherston, Cambridge, Cambridge University Press.

Rojas, Isaac F., and Medrano, Arturo L. (1978), *Argentina en el Atlántico, Chile en el Pacífico*, Buenos Aires, Nemont Ediciones.

Ronfeldt, David (1983), *Geopolitics, security and US strategy in the Caribbean Basin*, Santa Monica, CA, Rand Corporation.

Rosenau, James N. (1972), 'Adaptive polities in an interdependent world', *Orbis*, 16, 1–45.

Roxborough, Ian (1979), *Theories of underdevelopment*, London, Macmillan.

Rustow, Dankwart A. (1990), 'Democracy: a global revolution', *Foreign Affairs*, 69, 4, fall.

Sampson, Anthony (1980), *The Seven Sisters: the great oil companies and the world they made*, London, Coronet.

Sarmiento, Domingo Faustino (1961), *Life in the Argentine Republic in the days of the tyrants (Facundo)*, New York, Collier Books.

Schilling, Paulo (1978), *El expansionismo brasileño*, Mexico, El Cid Editor.

Schlesinger, Stephen, and Kinzer, Stephen (1982), *Bitter fruit: the untold story of the American coup in Guatemala*, London, Sinclair Browne.

Schoultz, Lars (1987), *National security and United States policy towards Latin America*, Princeton, NJ, Princeton University Press.

Scranton, Margaret E. (1991), *The Noriega years: US–Panamanian relations, 1981–1990*, Boulder, CO, Lynne Rienner.

Searle, Chris (1983), *Grenada: the struggle against destabilisation*, London, Writers and Readers.

Selcher, Wayne A. (1984), 'Recent strategic developments in South America's Southern Cone', in Heraldo Muñoz and Joseph S. Tulchin, eds, *Latin American nations in world politics*, Boulder, CO, Westview Press, 101–18.

Shafer, D. Michael (1988), *Deadly paradigms: the failure of US counter-insurgency policy*, Princeton, NJ, Princeton University Press.

Sharp, Daniel A., ed. (1972), *US foreign policy and Peru*, Austin, TX, University of Texas Press for the Institute of Latin American Studies.

Shearman, Peter (1987), *The Soviet Union and Cuba*, London, Routledge for the Royal Institute of International Affairs.

Shearman, Peter, and Williams, Phil, eds (1988), *The superpowers, Central America and the Middle East*, London, Brassey's Defence Publishers.

Sigmund, Paul E. (1993), *The United States and democracy in Chile*, Baltimore, MD, Johns Hopkins for Twentieth Century Fund.

Simpson, John and Howlett, Darryl (1990), *The need for a strong Nuclear Non-Proliferation Treaty: issues at the Fourth NPT Review Conference*, Southampton, Centre for International Policy Studies for Programme for Promoting Nuclear Non-Proliferation.

Skocpol, Theda (1977), 'Wallerstein's world capitalist system: a theoretical critique', *American Journal of Sociology*, 82, 1075–90.

Slarke, D. J. (1985), 'Mexico and the Great Depression', unpublished Ph.D. dissertation, University of Southampton.

Smith, Tony (1978), 'The underdevelopment of development literature, the case of dependency theory', *World Politics*, 31, 2, 247–88.

Stepan, Alfred (1971), *The military in politics: changing patterns in Brazil*, Princeton, NJ, Princeton University Press for The Rand Corporation.

Stepan, Alfred, ed. (1973), *Authoritarian Brazil*, New Haven, CT, Yale University Press.

Stepan, Alfred (1978), *The state and society: Peru in comparative perspective*, Princeton, NJ, Princeton University Press.

Stepan, Alfred (1988), *Rethinking military politics: Brazil and the Southern Cone*, Princeton, NJ, Princeton University Press.

Stone, Samuel (1992), *The heritage of the conquistadors: ruling classes in Central America from the conquest to the Sandinistas*, Lincoln, NE, University of Nebraska Press.

Stubbs, Jean (1989), *Cuba: the test of time*, London, Latin American Bureau.

Sunkel, Osvaldo (1969), 'National development policy and external dependence in Latin America', *Journal of Development Studies*, 6, 1, 23–48.

Sunkel, Osvaldo, and Paz, Pedro (1970), *El subdesarrollo latinoamericano y la teoría de desarrollo*, Mexico, Siglo Vientiuno.

Sutton, Paul (1988), 'The Caribbean as an arena for strategic and resource rivalry', in Peter Calvert, ed., *The Central American security system: North/South or East/West?*, Cambridge, Cambridge University Press, 18–44.

Sutton, Paul (1991), *Europe and the Caribbean*, London, Macmillan Caribbean.

Thomas, Caroline (1985), *New states, sovereignty and intervention*, Aldershot, Hants, Gower.

Thomas, Caroline (1987), *In search of security: the Third World in international relations*, Brighton, Sussex, Wheatsheaf.

Thomas, Caroline (1992), *The environment in international relations*, London, Royal Institute of International Affairs.

Thompson, R. (1987), *Green gold: bananas and dependency in the Eastern Caribbean*, London, Latin American Bureau.

Thorndike, Tony (1985), *Grenada: politics, economics and society*, London, Frances Pinter.

Thorp, Rosemary, and Whitehead, Laurence, eds (1987), *Latin American Debt and the Adjustment Crisis*, Basingstoke, Hants, Macmillan.

Tiwathia, Vijay (1987), *The Grenada War: anatomy of a low-intensity conflict*, New Delhi, Lancer International.

Tuchman, Barbara W. (1959), *The Zimmermann Telegram*, London, Constable.

United Kingdom, Government State Papers, 1953–54, 33, Cmd 9277, Guatemala No. 1 (1954), *Report on events leading up to and arising out of the change of regime in Guatemala, 1954*, London, Her Majesty's Stationery Office.

United States. Department of State (1977), *Intervention of international communism in Guatemala*, London, Greenwood Press.

Vacs, Aldo César (1984), *Discreet partners, Argentina and the USSR since 1917* (trs. Michael Joyce), Pittsburgh, PA, University of Pittsburgh Press.

Vagts, Alfred (1959), *A history of militarism, civil and military*, London, Hollis and Carter.

Vanucci, Albert P. (1986), 'The influence of Latin American governments on the shaping of United States foreign policy: the case of US–Argentine relations, 1943–1948', *Journal of Latin American Studies*, 18, 2, 355–82.

Vasconcelos, José (1958), *Ulises criollo*, Mexico, Editorial Jus.

Vincent, R. J., ed. (1986), *Foreign policy and human rights: issues and responses*, Cambridge, Cambridge University Press in association with the Royal Institute of International Affairs.

Walker, Thomas W., ed. (1987), *Reagan versus the Sandinistas; the undeclared war on Nicaragua*, Boulder, CO, Westview.

Wallerstein, Immanuel (1974), *The modern world system*, New York, Academic Press.

Waltz, Kenneth N. (1959), *Man, the state, and war*, New York, Columbia University Press.

Weeks, John, and Gunson, Phil (1991), *Panama: made in the USA*, London, Latin American Bureau.

Whitaker, Arthur P. (1951), 'The Americas in the Atlantic Triangle', in Arthur P. Whitaker, *Ensayos sobre la historia del Nuevo Mundo*, Mexico, reprinted in Lewis Hanke, ed., *Do the Americas have a common history?*, New York, Knopf, 1964, 141–64.

Whitaker, Arthur P. (1954), *The western hemisphere idea: its rise and decline*, Ithaca, NY, Cornell University Press.

Wiles, Peter (1969), 'A syndrome, not a doctrine: some elementary theses on populism', in Ghita Ionescu and Ernest Gellner, eds, *Populism: its meaning and national characteristics*, New York, The Macmillan Co.

Wilhelmy, Manfred (1984), 'Politics, bureaucracy and foreign policy in Chile', in Heraldo Muñoz and Joseph S. Tulchin, eds, *Latin American nations in world politics*, Boulder, CO, Westview Press, 45–62.

Wood, Bryce (1961), *The making of the Good Neighbor policy*, New York, Columbia University Press.

Wood, Bryce (1966), *The United States and Latin America wars, 1932–1942*, New York, Columbia University Press.

Wood, Bryce (1985), *The dismantling of the Good Neighbor policy*, Austin, TX, University of Texas Press.

Woodward, Ralph Lee, Jr (1976), *Central America: a nation divided*, New York, Oxford University Press.

World Bank, The (1990), *World development report 1990*, New York, Oxford University Press.

World Bank, The (1992), *Global environment facility: a selection of projects from the first three tranches*, Washington, DC, The World Bank, GEF Working Papers Series, no. 2, June 1992.

World Bank, The (1993), *Environment and development in Latin America and the Caribbean: the role of the World Bank*, Washington, DC, The World Bank.

Wynia, Gary A. (1978), *The politics of Latin American development*, Cambridge, Cambridge University Press.

Zimbalist, Andrew (1989), 'The failure of intervention in Panama: humiliation in the back yard', *Third World Quarterly*, 11, 1–28.

Zimbalist, Andrew and Weeks, John (1991), *Panama at the crossroads: economic development and political change in the twentieth century*, Berkeley, CA, University of California Press.

Index